Whisperin;
Writings from

Jesus lived in India
Holger Kearston

Whispering Deodars
Writings from Shimla Hills

Edited by
Minakshi Chaudhry

Rupa & Co

Published by 2009
Rupa . Co
7/16, Ansari Road, Daryaganj,
New Delhi 110 002

Sales Centres:

Allahabad Bangalooru Chandigarh Chennai
Hyderabad Jaipur Kathmandu
Kolkata Mumbai

Typeset by
Mindways Design
1410 Chiranjiv Tower
43 Nehru Place
New Delhi 110 019

Printed in India by
Rekha Printers Pvt Ltd.
A-102/1, Okhla Industrial Area, Phase-II,
New Delhi-110 020

'By all the life that fizzes in
The everlasting Hills,
If you love me as I love you
What pair so happy as we two?'

An *Old Song* by RUDYARD KIPLING

Contents

Preface

Isn't it overwhelming to know that a 'mere halting ground' with 'a few miserable cultivators' huts' in 1817 when the Scot brothers, Patrick and James Gerard reached here on 30 August, went on to become the summer capital of the British Raj in 1864?

The story of the rise of 'Simla, a middling sized village where a faquir is stationed to give water to the visitors' and the surrounding hills into prominence defies logic but that is the way history weaves its magic. Even then let us give some flight to our fancies and ponder over some silly questions as historians would call these.

What if the Gerard brothers has taken a different route and never reached this *hill abode*? What if the Gurkhas had not subjugated the hill states with the ruthlessness with which they did? What if the hill chiefs had not invited the British to deliver them from the tyrannies of the Gurkhas? What if the desire to locate a viable route to Tibet had taken a different turn? What if Captain Charles Pratt Kennedy had chosen a different place to build his house? What if...?

But the deal was clinched in favour of these hills. There are very few hill stations in India which have such a rich historical past, strategic location, salubrious climate and plentitude of architectural splendor.

For me the heart of Shimla town is warm and delightful with the freshness and effervescence of a child, laughter echoing all around. It is the cockpit of Shimla hills.

Life in Shimla hills has a rhythm of its own. It dances to its soft and laid back melody of poignant lyrics symbolising the beauty of nature and its relationship with man made things.

This anthology is not just a collection of articles but a tale flowing through time and space...a story that beats with the hearts of people relating their experiences.

One main reason for the British to have taken fancy for Shimla hills was the climate and environment. Cooler temperatures compared to burning and humid summer months in the plains of India, mist filled monsoons and snowy winters reminded them of *home*. Clean mountain air, deep glens, thick conifers, all combined to create the magic of the English weather and made them nostalgic about their homeland.

For them, these hills were a place to rest, relax and enjoy the fun, frolic and festivities. Though for Indians it was a different story altogether who had to brave '*the three and half month long monsoon, its hard to digest mineral water, the panting uphill and break neck down walks, since most Indians could not afford either horse or Rickshaw.*' A place which was *home* to the British but was a symbol of exploitative imperial government for the Indians, as Mahatma Gandhi described, '*the distance equal to the height of 500 floors separates the empire from us...*'

At the centre of it all was Shimla town that was for the British, and still is, for the multitude of Indian and foreign travellers who throng to it in all seasons, the ideal retreat. The reasons can be many...to escape to the natural air-conditioner in the summers; to walk hand in hand on meandering footpaths in the forests where tall deodars whisper tales of love; to enjoy incessant downpour with hot tea and *pakoras*; to build a snowman with kidney beans for eyes, broomsticks for hands and charcoal piece for nose; to be with the nature and hear the sound of silence....

The articles in this volume are written by some of the best known writers. They capture and portray this flowing story which will make you feel the pulse of the hills...time flows with these contributions yet it stands still...back and forth...present and past...past and future...the train of thought is as thrilling as the journey from the plains to the hills; be it in the toy train or on the winding, curvy road presenting the panorama of rolling hills. The festivities of the rulers and the plight of the locals; the natives and their master; the rulers and the ruled—all find expression here. From the prominence as the summer capital to the orphan like post independence status and then another life as the capital of Himachal Pradesh, the authors capture every nuance of life in these hills.

On the one hand, the anthology assembles the vital and momentous moments and the pieces of life away from the prominent and mainstream happenings, on the other and then performs the difficult task of gauging the present along with the past.

Primarily based on contributors' personal experiences, the anthology has been supplemented with historical and literary accounts. It is a collective effort for which a variety of inputs were added. I have attempted to bring together in a single volume a characteristic group of people who have a link, an association with the period covered in the present collection. I chose a wide variety of topics designed to appeal to all despite the indefatigable effort in unearthing little known or quite forgotten tales. It may not be a really perfect collection as I would have liked to make it but has any anthology pleased its maker and then every critic, every reader?

It would be natural for every reader to get maddened by the omission and inclusion of specific topics but these are the kind of complaints that no anthologist can escape, Moreover, the first limitation was that of space. I have tried to offer substance of the finest quality in optimum quantity.

SIMLA changed officially to SHIMLA in the beginning of the 1980s but I have retained both spellings as used by the contributors who chose to spell the town as per their own familiarity.

Reflections on Himachal Pradesh, My Adopted Home

His Holiness the Dalai Lama

I first came to live in Himachal Pradesh in 1960 when the territory that would comprise the state was still part of Punjab. Therefore, I have had the privilege of witnessing the state's birth and watching it grow up, as it were. I arrived here after spending my first year in India in Mussoorie. To begin with two things struck me. One was a welcome sense of free and empty space compared to the more crowded Mussoorie. The other was a certain dismay at its isolation. I wasn't entirely happy at the prospect of being unable to communicate easily with the rest of the world. In those days, telephone facilities were almost non-existent, in contrast to today when Himachal Pradesh is one of the better connected parts of the country and the roads were not very good. Indeed, building roads in hilly regions was one of opportunities to work offered to able bodied Tibetan refugees in those early days.

In due course, the relative isolation and uncrowded tranquillity we found here served me well, because in those early years life was quiet here and I was able to resume my studies and do some meditation

I remember that first arrival quite clearly. Following an overnight train journey, we reached Pathankot in the morning and began the drive to Dharamsala. We passed through some of the most beautiful countryside in India, the lush green fields dotted with trees and colourful wild flowers. After about an hour I was cheered to catch a first glimpse of the clear white peaks of the Dhauladhar range towering in the distance, straight ahead of us.

My new home, Swarg Ashram, formerly Highcroft House and residence of the divisional commissioner in the days of the British Raj, was a house, set in woodland and surrounded by a compound of outbuildings. It was quite late when we arrived so I was not able to see much, but the following morning, when I woke, the first thing I heard was the distinctive call of a bird which I later discovered is peculiar to this place. 'Kara-chok, Kara-chok,' it seemed to say. I looked out of the window to see where it was, but could not find it. Instead, my eyes were greeted by a view of magnificent mountains.

On the whole, my experience of Himachali life has been quite happy. I have had the privilege of regarding the green hills of Himachal Pradesh as my adopted home for more than half my life, nearly fifty years. It is a delightful place to be; the air is clean and full of birdsong, and the climate is pleasant. What's more, the people are friendly, straightforward and welcoming.

In the years I have spent here I have been regularly reminded that India is perhaps the one country whose civilisation and culture have survived intact from their first beginnings. This is not a just a matter of the ancient monuments that we come across here and there, but also a certain gentleness in the people we meet and observe living nearby. Because India and her people have, from ancient times, cherished a rich and sophisticated philosophy of non-violence at the core of their hearts, it has developed into a kind of natural reflex. What's more, friendship between India and Tibet is also not something new. Bonds of love and understanding between our two nations are centuries old, because of course Tibet's Buddhist tradition comes from India.

Himachal Pradesh and Tibet have always been neighbours and we share a common border even today. In fact, a thousand years ago, Western Tibet and its adjoining regions, including Spiti, which is now part of upper Himachal Pradesh, came under the sway of the Kings of Gu-ge. One of them, Lha Lama Yeshe Öd, is remembered to this day for his contribution to the revival of Buddhism throughout Tibet and the Himalayas that would prove crucial to its later development. One of the twenty-one able young men he sent to India to study and translate Buddhist scriptures from Sanskrit survived to fulfil that aim. Rinchen Zangpo not only translated many Indian texts that are revered and in use today, but also established temples and monasteries as centres of education and invited craftsmen and artists to decorate them. The temples at Tabo and Lhalung, with their exquisite statues and paintings of Buddhas and meditational deities, are wonderful surviving examples of his achievements.

With its deep blue skies, stark hills reaching up to glistening white peaks and rolling down to green fields along the river banks, the Spiti landscape has much in common with my homeland, Tibet. Due to the annual snowmelt, the water here is cool and clear, and generally the air is clean and unpolluted. With a shared religious and cultural background the people of these regions until quite recently have followed a similar, unhurried way of life. Over the last twenty years I have visited Spiti several times myself and have often been struck by the lingering charm of a region that although slowly changing with the arrival of development, has remained much the same for hundreds of years. Living conditions may be hard, but the inhabitants are robust, resilient and good hearted.

Because of the difficulties its terrain places on transport, the Himalayan region as a whole has been much slower to change than other places. The people who live here are much more governed by the seasons than elsewhere. They place a much lower premium on time than the inhabitants of our teeming modern cities. And, while it is Tibetans who I know best, I have observed that the majority of the Himalayan people, among who I include our Himachalis, are similarly mild-mannered, easily contented, satisfied with whatever conditions are available and resilient in the face of hardship. The rigours of both the climate and the environment contribute to this, but another significant factor is the spiritual culture that has flourished in the Himalayas for thousands of years. Teachings on love, kindness and tolerance, an emphasis on compassion and the conduct of non-violence, and the idea that all things are relative, pervade the hearts and minds of people throughout the Himalayas as a source of inner peace.

For centuries, life has gone on in the Himalayan region, quietly and relatively undisturbed. During the long winters, for example, travel, farming and outdoor activities are restricted. Skilled artisans have the time and leisure to carve wood, to paint, to weave, to create ornamental metalwork and stone sculpture without pressure or haste. This patient unhurried approach is reflected in the architecture throughout the region. Traditional buildings are strong and sturdy, constructed in a practical way from natural materials, often decorated with careful attention to detail. They are also well suited to their environment. This may be why building techniques have changed so little down the centuries. These qualities, to some extent, reflect the character of the people of the region.

We live in times of far-reaching change and I am very wary of simply idealising old ways of living, because there is much that is commendable in the modern world. With significant populations of nomadic shepherds among the Gaddis, for example, as well as state of the art hydroelectric installations, Himachal Pradesh is a place where modern development is thriving amidst traditional patterns of living. However, the clear challenge that faces us, whether we feel part of the developed or developing world, is to discover how we can enjoy the same degree of harmony and tranquillity that we find in traditional communities, while benefiting fully from modern material developments. It is important that we improve standards of living, broaden educational opportunities, raise levels of health and ease modes of transport. But as we progress from one way of life to another, there is a risk of abandoning what is tried and tested, what appears to be old, merely to have something modern instead. It would be a great shame if in the process, we were to lose our sense of positive values.

As I have already mentioned, Himachal Pradesh is my second home and I will always remain grateful to the people of Himachal Pradesh for the warm hospitality and friendliness with which they have received us all during our stay here. I hope too that they will feel that we Tibetans have also made some small contribution towards local development. Himachal is fast emerging as one of the country's major tourist attractions. I have no doubt that this will lead to further development in the coming years, not only attracting more tourists, but also bringing increased benefit to the people who live here.

Summer Connection

Khushwant Singh

Himachal has been my summer home since my childhood. With some justification I describe myself as half-Himachali, half-Dilliwala-Punjabi. However, my Himachal abodes were restricted to Shimla, Mashobra and, for the last thirty years, Kasauli. I explored the neighbouring hills and valleys as much as I could on foot. I walked down to the banks of the Sutlej to the sulphur hot water springs Tatta Pani (thirty-six miles). I walked from Shimla to Narkanda and back on the Hindustan-Tibet Road (seventy-two miles) almost non-stop on two full moonlit nights and a day. Till a few years ago, I used to go from Kasauli to Kalka to catch trains to Delhi on foot. I saw quite a lot of wildlife: leopards, wild cats, mouse-deer, porcupines, jackals, foxes, snakes and a vast variety of birds. I wanted to know more about the flora and fauna, about the village folk and their customs. Almost every book I picked up on Himachal in second-hand bookstores in England, Canada and the USA had been written by an Englishman. Many things escaped their attention. For instance, I came across huts near streams with channels diverting water into a trough with taps which sent a steady trickle of water on shaved heads of men who lay fast asleep on the floor. I never discovered what it was all about. You don't see them any more. I was also told that an annual *mela* took place in Sipi village below Mashobra, where girls were sold by auction. I went to the *mela* twice. I saw many pretty Himachali lasses, fair-skinned, doe-eyed and with sharp features. I would have liked to buy a few. There were none for sale. When and why did the legend begin?

There is still much to be explored and written about Himachal.

◆

Travelling by train across the Indo-Gangetic plains after the summer monsoon has spent itself is a refreshing experience. What a couple of months ago was a khaki, dusty flat land now has different shades of green as far as the eye can see. Haryana looks what its name denotes, a green land—*hara bharaa*—green as green could be. On both sides of the rail track there are long stretches of water hyacinth or green scum. Water buffaloes wallow in the water with only their heads above it. When they get out to munch grass, snow-white cattle egrets follow them to pick up insects disturbed by them. To supplement their diet, some brood besides ponds to catch unwary frogs. The scene remains much the same till you reach the foothills of the Shivaliks. Then there are thick jungles of lantana, mesquite (keekar) covered with yellow blossoms and ever-in-bloom ipomoea with purple flowers and thorny cactus. The Shatabdi Express reaches its terminal at Kalka. The Kalka station has the longest platform I have encountered. And unlike other stations where there are stray dogs scampering around for food, Kalka has goats. They are familiar with the coming and going of trains. They jump down from one platform to the rail tracks and leap up to the other side just as an incoming train pulls up.

The hills are also greener and appear more afforested. Stream beds which are dry most of the year have water gushing over rocks and boulders. There are not many flowers to be seen along the roadside but it does not seem to matter: for the eyes, green is the most soothing colour. All along the route the fragrance of farm fresh challis or *bhuttas*, roasted on charcoal amber, are being guzzled by men and women. A freshly roasted corn-on-the cob smeared with salt, pepper and lemon-juice is a feast for kings.

I wish there were fewer trucks and buses on the road. They belch smoke, their engines make a lot of noise as they grind their way uphill, their horns pierce one's eardrums and they slow down other motorised traffic. A journey which should take no more than forty minutes takes one and a half hours.

◆

There was a time when the very mention of Kasauli raised peoples' eyebrows: 'Kyoon, paagal kuttey nay kaata hai' (why, have you been bitten by a mad dog?) was the knee-jerk verbal reaction. It was much the same if you said you were going to Agra or Ranchi. People asked you with a smile: 'Are you all right in the head?' Agra was known for its paagal khaana (lunatic asylum):, Ranchi for its hospital for people suffering from mental problems. Likewise, Kasauli got a bad name because of its Pasteur Institute which treated people bitten by mad dogs. The Pasteur Institute became the Central Research Institute (CRI). Even locals, who do not know what the letters stand for, know it as 'see-are-eye'.

In May 2005, the CRI celebrated its hundredth birthday. The word 'celebrated' should be put in inverted commas as there was no visible signs of celebrations of any kind—nor did the media give it much coverage besides a stingy disclosure of corruption in its functioning. There was a *preeti bhojan*. Perhaps, the present director, Usha Soren Singh cut a birthday cake in her office and sent a slice each to her senior colleagues. No cake would be large enough to go round the entire staff of 800 men and women: doctors, nurses to peons and bottle-washers.

Actually the story of the CRI goes back more than a hundred years. The Pasteur Institute was set up in 1900 under the directorship of Major David Semple. Kasauli was chosen for its salubrious climate and pine-scented air. It was initially an army-based institution to prepare vaccines and sera against diseases which most afflicted the British. On 3 May 1905, it was designated a research institute and

Dr Semple elevated in rank and knighted, became Lt. Colonel Sir David Semple and its first director. To his credit go the production of anti-snake bite serums and vaccines for the prevention of typhoid, malaria and kalaazar.

My family connection with the CRI began (and ended) during the tenure of Sir J. Taylor who became director in 1932. My father got the contract for building additional laboratories, offices, and classrooms required for research, production of sera and vaccines and teaching facilities. He rented a house for his staff on an offshoot of the lower Mall, where I spent two summer vacations. A tenuous connection was re-established after Independence when Lt. Colonel M.L. Ahuja took over as the first Indian head of the CRI. And a much closer one when Dr A.K. Thomas who had been with the institute since 1948 took over from Dr J.B. Srivastav as director in 1965. Thomas, or Tommy as we knew him, lived in Sanawar School, where his wife Lila was teaching. Instead of moving into the spacious director's bungalow, he continued to stay in Sanawar. Every morning, rain, snow or sunshine, he strode downhill to Garkhal village and two miles uphill to Kasauli with his Alsatian following closely on his heels. Tommy was passionately attached to his dog. It stayed with its master in office and walked back with him to Sanawar in the evening. We got on very well and soon our two families were meeting occasionally for dinner either in Sanawar or Kasauli. I was hoping they would settle down in Kasauli. They preferred to be among their own people, Syrian Christians, and have made their home in Ooty. We keep in touch.

My only contact with the CRI now is the youthful Dr Santosh Kutty, his wife Lila who teaches in the local convent and their son Varun. Santosh drops in at times to check my wayward blood-pressure, Lila sends me cooked fish, which appears in the market once a week. And Varun comes to borrow books: Kasauli has no library and he is a voracious reader.

I have two grouses against the CRI. Next to the IAF which destroyed Kasauli's picnic spot, Ladies Grove, at the base of Monkey

Point, the CRI has the ugliest building atop Kasauli's prominent ridge. The exterior is a multi-storeyed edifice of garish pink colour. If I had my way I would send for its architect and confiscate his licence. Or make him redesign and rebuild it at his cost. The second grouse is more serious. Like other institutes in the country, there is not much research done in Kasauli's CRI. They merely replicate research done abroad and reproduce it in quantities required. It has not been able to evolve research culture. I can add a third shortcoming. For years, it has been plagued with trade unionism and indiscipline. At times that spills out in the open when workers assemble at the gate close to the *bazaar* and shout slogans. Their only audiences are monkeys and langoors. When people's main obsession is extracting more money and benefits for themselves, their minds become unfit to produce anything worthwhile. However, it maintains its stocks of horses, sheep, white mice, guinea pigs and poultry to produce sera and vaccines for those bitten by mad dogs, snakes or afflicted by a variety of diseases. If Maneka Gandhi ever becomes the health minister (Heaven forbid) even this activity may be closed down.

◆

I cannot understand people who complain about being bored with life. They moan 'nothing to do, nowhere to go, no one to talk to. There is nothing worse than being alone'. I tell them, 'I like being alone but never feel lonely'. There is so much to read, write and see. I never seem to get enough of the world without people. What I find boring is humans, chiefly those who complain of being bored. I put up with them for a few minutes and then politely ask them to depart as I have more interesting things to do—by which I mean to be left alone. I don't think they mind my being blunt; if they do, I don't care. I will be the master of my time not they.

I have so many dates to keep: I come out in the garden at 6 a.m. A Himalayan barbet perches itself on the top of a fir tree and begins to wail. It is a bit of a ventriloquist: its calls sound as if they are from a long distance, whereas it is only a few yards away from me. Another barbet somewhere far down in the valley responds. Wailing and counter-wailing goes on for almost five minutes. Barbets depart, koels take over. They are followed by crows, white-cheeked bulbuls, mynahs, Simla tits and a whole variety of tiny birds my aged eyes fail to identify. If you have eyes to see and ears to hear, there is not a dull moment in any garden. If there are no birds, lie back, gaze at the sky and watch the clouds float by overhead. Why are some going from north to south and others from south to north? Evidently at different levels, winds move in different directions. Why do clouds assume different shapes and colours? Why are some dark, moisture-laden and bring rain, while others are like fluffs of dry cotton and simply float about?

In the afternoons, particularly over weekends, people drop in uninvited. It is odd that over the years I find total strangers more interesting than those known to me. So go the days. I spend the last hour of the day wrapped in a shawl against the evening chill and swarms of mosquitoes. I watch the sun disentangle itself from the branches of pine trees and go down over the hill. With twilight a strange calm descends on me.

I turn in, switch on the lights and pour myself a whisky. Then I order the greatest musicians in the world to entertain me. They come cheap. Bach, Beethoven, Mozart, Bismillah Khan, Ravi Shankar, Mehdi Hassan, Farida Khanum, Nusrat Fateh Ali Khan, Abida Parveen, Lata Mangeshkar, Asha Bhosle, Darshan Singh Ragi, Singh Bandhu—name them. I order them to sing or play at the press of a button. You can't enjoy music or drink in company. To savour its fulness, you have to take scotch alone, feel it going down your throat and warm your entrails. I get slightly tipsy, a bit of *suroor* and float at eye-level as I walk to the dinner table and then to bed. Boredom? I do not have the time to get bored when I am all by myself.

◆

People like to return to the scenes of their childhood days if for no other reason than to see how much of what they remember is correct and see if there were some old people still around who could recall their parents and grandparents. Once a British cantonment with a school and a large hospital, Kasauli had quite a few English boys and girls who were born or went to school there. So there is always a trickle of English visitors every year whose sole aim is to visit homes they once lived in and go round the cemeteries, including those in neighbouring cantonments in Sabathu and Dagshai, to see if any names or tombstones ring a bell of the past.

This April we had two English couples who return to India every two or three years to visit scenes of their childhood, which includes Kasauli. One couple I had known for many years and had them stay with me in my home in Delhi. They are Giles and Lisanne Radice. When we first met, Giles was a Labour Party Member of Parliament and into writing books on contemporary British political history. Prime Minister Tony Blair put him in the House of Lords.

Now, he spends three days of the week in London to attend to his parliamentary duties and the remaining four with his wife in their country home in Lincolnshire. Lady Lisanne Radice is also his writing partner and edits books for a publishing house.

Giles' father and grandfather were in the ICS and amongst the Brits who supported India's freedom movement. I suggested to him that he do a book on Englishmen and women who supported India's demand for Independence. The Indian National Congress was set up by an Englishman, A.O. Hume; Annie Besant (Irish) was president of the INC, B.G. Horniman and C.F. Andrews were ardent supporters of Gandhiji. Madeleine Slade (Mira Bai) was a close disciple.

Spratt and Ben Bradley were imprisoned in the Meerut Conspiracy Case. There were dozens of others in India and England who agitated for India's freedom. Giles seemed to be taken up by the idea. 'I get good reviews for the books I write,' he said ruefully, 'but they don't earn me much royalties.' I replied, 'I get panned by most critics but manage to make to the bestsellers list. You do one on Brit supporters of Gandhi and I bet it will make the top of bestsellers in both countries.'

The other couple was David and Gina Alexander. David was in the Army (Sappers) during the Second World War. He also spent some time in Kasauli and other Indian cantonments. He speaks Hindustani fluently and makes it a point to come back to India every four years to refresh his memories of the days of his youth as a soldier and keep up his Hindustani.

It is to Brits like the Radices and Alexanders to extend their hands of friendships to the Indians; I know there are thousands of Indians who will grasp them eagerly to start a new chapter in Indo-British person-to-person relationships.

◆

If you happen to be in the Simla (sorry Shimla) hills and love reading poetry, you can't do better than read Rudyard Kipling, who spent a few summers there. Kipling is a much maligned and under-rated poet. Maligned because of his outspoken praise of his countrymen as the paradigm of colonialism. The British brag that they never boast; so Kipling did the boasting for them and they were ever grateful to him for doing so on their behalf. He was under-rated as a mere rhymester who rigidly followed the rules of rhyming and metre. This is a grossly unjust assessment of his calibre as a poet. In addition, long before any Indian writing in English had started using Hindustani words, Kipling was doing so without restraint. In his poem 'The Heathen' (he spelt it like the cockney eathen), he wrote:

> All along o'dirtiness, all along O'mess
> All along O'doin things rather more-or-less
> All along of abhy naheen, kal, hazar ho
> Mind you keep your rifle an yourself Jus so.

At the time Kipling went to Shimla there was neither railway nor *pukka* road; people travelled along a *kutcha* track from Kalka to

Sabathu, Solan and Tara Devi on *tongas*, horseback or palanquins. Kipling captured the scene beautifully:

> So long as neath the Kalka hills
> The tonga-horn shall ring,
> So long as down to Solan dip
> The hard-held ponies swing,
> So long as Tara Devi sees
> The lights of Simla town
> So long as pleasure calls us up,
> or duty drives us down,
> If you love me as I love you,
> What pair so happy as we too?

◆

In Kasauli there is an old British cemetery dating back to the 1840s when the English built a line of cantonments on the Shivalik ranges to billet troops in the event of a war which seemed imminent against the Sikh kingdom. This cemetery is a good way down the hill from the military hospital, and few people bother to visit it. In my younger days, I went there thrice to see which was the oldest grave. I could not find it as many marble tombstones had been stolen and the inscriptions on others had become illegible. Even in broad daylight pine and yew trees cast eerie shadows; the place looked haunted. However, I found one epitaph on a grave which I found to be a good example of the sort of macabre honour only the British have. I memorised the lines:

> Halt stranger, do not go by,
> As you are now, so once was I;
> Prepare therefore to follow me,
> As I am, so will you be.

Later I discovered this epitaph was by no means unique: it had been used elsewhere and is found in many quotations books.

Kasauli has been my summer home for well over half a century; I know its denizens, including a succession of Brigade commanders, as the cliché goes, like the back of my hand.

◆

Never again will I go to my summer home in Kasauli by road: the last journey was a torture. Besides the never-ending construction of overbridges in Panipat, Karnal and Ambala, the main highway was in sad state of disrepair. I used to pray that there would be no hold-ups going through the narrow bazaars of Pinjore and Kalka: my prayers were answered as there were none.

But there was a twenty-mile traffic gridlock extending from Panchkula near Chandigarh to Pinjore. Thousands of cars, buses, trucks, tractors, motor cycles, scooters stood still for over an hour and a half with no one knowing the reason why.

A journey which took me between five and six hours door-to-door from Sujan Singh Park, New Delhi, to Raj Villa, Kasauli, took more than eight hours. You can guess what that kind of ordeal can do to a ninety-four-year old *buddha*. I swore this is the last time I will undertake this journey.

That night I slept for almost nine hours: Complete silence and clean air have soporofic qualities. I was woken up by the sunlight streaming in through my window opening out to the east. 'Get up lazy bones!' it seemed to say. 'See how the mountains are lit up, autumn flowers in bloom and hear birds in full-throated song.'

I dragged myself to sit out in the garden and soak in the sun. The first thing my eyes fell on is the havoc caused by the monsoons. The approach road I had re-tarmaced only two years ago was a shamble of loose pebbles. A huge pine tree near the entrance of my villa had come down crushing the rickshaw shed, including the rickshaw, under its massive trunk and blocked the approach. It had been cut to clear the way, and the wood stacked away.

In a cantonment, trees, including those growing in private compounds, belong to the cantonment. At many places the corrugated tin roof had sprung leaks. It was a long litany of woes I have to hear this time of the year. Last May there were swarms of white butterflies swirling round the garden. This time there was not one to be seen. Birds were there—crows, whistling thrushes, bulbuls, mynahs, blackbirds and woodpeckers. I could not hear their calls: I had become deafer than I was four months ago.

Owning a second home in the hills is a status symbol, which bores a big hole in one's pocket. Nevertheless, homes which were bought for paltry sums of under Rs 30,000 barely twenty years ago are today selling for over two crore rupees. Most of the year they remain unlived in. Nevertheless, people continue to buy old ones and build new ones.

Recently, a home barely fifty yards along the same hillside as mine was bought and renovated by retired Brigadier Wazir Singh Chaudhary, who lives half the year in Panchkula playing golf, half the year in Kasauli playing bridge. He is, as the saying goes, happy as a lark.

The family dropped in to introduce themselves. Their names are very easy to memorise: the wife's name was Gursharan Kaur, the daughter's Sonia. He had no regrets buying a second home in Kasauli. After a hefty Patiala peg, he fished out a piece of paper from his trouser pocket. He had never written poetry in his life till he was hospitalised with a heart ailment and put in intensive care unit. Then the muse burst open.

He asked for a piece of paper and a pen. He scribbled an ode in Urdu in praise of Kasauli: 'Its soft, misty, mornings, its gentle breezes fragrant with pine-scented air, its hillsides bedecked with a variety of wild flowers and the singing of birds from dawn to dusk.' I was moved.

How could I ever forget what Kasauli has given me in the eighty years that I have been coming up, to spend a few weeks of the summer and autumn, in the little cantonment township? It is I who have become an old, crotchety grumbler. Thank you Kasauli!

Down Memory Lane: Snippets, Aroma and Flavours of Bygone Years

RAKESH KANWAR

Early English explorers and first mention of Simla

British officers working with the East India Company ventured in the Himalayan region occasionally for reasons that were mainly personal. Thomas Coryat visited Nagarkot (Kangra) and Jawalamukhi in AD 1615 but it took nearly two hundred years before the political ambitions of the British turned to the Himalayas. They started exploring the Himalayan region in the early nineteenth century. One of the early explorers was W.S. Webb, an army officer, who went from Haridwar to Gangotri in 1807 traversing the region along the Ganges.

In April 1809, the British, worried about Napoleon's ambition and his romping over Europe, negotiated a treaty with Maharaja Ranjit Singh of Punjab. This treaty extended their influence up to the Satluj and led to active exploration of the Punjab Himalayas. William Moorcroft, a veterinary surgeon was the pioneer. Passionate to engage in wool trade with Tibet, he along with Hearsay, disguised as *sadhus*—Mayapuri and Harigiri respectively—entered the Hundes province of Tibet after crossing Niti Pass in 1812. From 1820 to 1825, Moorcroft trekked extensively in the Punjab Himalayas.

James Baillie Frazer was the first European traveller who trekked through the hills and valleys of the present-day Himachal after the Anglo-Gurkha war. In 1815, he came to Nahan with the British army and then traversed through Sirmour, Jubbal, Rohru, Narkanda, Kumarsain and Bushahr areas. On his return, he entered Uttranchal after crossing Pabbar river.

Trade with Tibet was one motivation to explore trans-Satluj sector. In 1814, Colonel Ochterlony, in charge of the army in this sector, got excited over the information that an elephant given in dowry had been sent from Nahan to Bushahr. This meant existence of a proper track up to Rampur, capital of Bushahr State, on the banks of the Satluj, popular as the half-way stage en route from Tibet and Ladakh where traders from the plains met the sellers from Tibet, Ladakh and Yarkand.

Simla lay on this trade route but the first definite mention of this 'mere halting ground—a name given to a few miserable cultivator's huts' dates back to 30 August 1817 when two Scot brothers, Patrick and James Gerard recorded in their diary that they stopped at 'Simla, a middling sized village where a fakir is stationed to give water to travelers.' They were surveying and mapping the newly subjugated hill States.

Another important traveller was Captain Alexander Gerard who started from Subathu in June 1821 and for three months travelled along Pabbar river and entered Sangla valley of Kinnaur district and then explored the interiors of Kinnaur including the remote villages of Nako, Namgia, Leo and Shipki on the Tibetan border. On the return journey, Gerard travelled south the along Satluj to Rampur Bushahr and ended his travel at Kotgarh after visiting Dalash, across the Satluj in Kullu and gave a dramatic description of the unique and traditional Bhunda festival.

In August 1847, Thomas Thomson and Captain Henry Stracy and Major Cunningham of the Bengal Engineers started from Shimla and followed the present day Hindustan-Tibet road to reach Kinnaur via Nichar and Wangtu. Thereafter, they entered Spiti valley and went west crossing the cold desert of Spiti and Lahaul to end their journey in Ladakh on the banks of Indus river.

The beginning and the rise

Though Simla, the small, non-descript hill hamlet was brought into limelight by the British, the hill states that comprise the present- day Shimla were in existence since long. Bushahr state is said to have been founded by *Pradhumna*, son of Lord Krishna. In effect, the people and the rulers of small hills states were living in remote seclusion from the excitement of Indian political scene till the Gurkhas of Nepal commanded by Amar Singh Thapa took control of and plundered the the hill states of Himachal in the early nineteenth century. After suffering defeat at the hands of the Sikhs in the battle of Kangra, they consolidated their position by attacking small hills states of Shimla Hills.

The British felt.threatened by the growing power of Gurkhas as they controlled the important trade routes to Tibet and Central Asia. In November 1814, the British declared war on Gurkhas. On the war, Charles Metcalfe, resident at Delhi and later governor-general of Canada, wrote:

> We have met an enemy who shows decidedly greater bravery and greater steadiness than our troops possess...In some instances our troops, European and Native, have been repulsed by inferior numbers with sticks and stones. In others our troops have been charged by the enemy sword in hand and driven for miles like a flock of sheep.

The British under Major General Sir David Ochterlony, combined the forces with the hill chiefs and fought the Gurkhas who surrendered in 1815. On their defeat the Gurkhas signed the 'Treaty of Sanjauli' ceding strategic forts of Subathu, Kotgarh, Ramgarh and Sandoch to the East India Company.

After the Anglo-Gorkha War, the common border of British domain and Punjab became very sensitive. In 1845, when the Sikhs invaded the British territory by crossing the Satluj, the rulers of many hill States sided with the British. However, after the first Anglo-Sikh War was over, the British did not restore the hill territory vacated by Sikhs to the hill rulers.

Slowly and gradually, Simla started to spread over seven nearby hills and connecting ridges: Jakhu hill (2,454m), Prospect hill (2,176m), Observatory hill (2,149m), Elysium hill (2,256m), and Summer hill (2,103m). Different stories about the origin of the name Simla go round: it was derived from Shyamala, (blue house) referring to the house built by a fakir on Jakhu hill with blue slates; it takes its name from Shamla, one of the names of Goddess Kali.

In 1819, the then assistant political agent of hill states, Lt. Ross set up the first British residence, a mere wooden thatched cottage. His successor Lt. Charles Patt Kennedy erected the first *pucca* house in 1822—'Kennedy House'. For fourteen years, till he retired in 1835, Kennedy made Simla virtually his 'royal estate', and was associated with and responsible for much of the town's growth.

The thickly wooded Shimla ridge with its forests and wildlife—hyena, bear, leopard, barking deer and jackal—became a hunting ground for British officers. The tide started to turn in Simla's favour when Amherst, the governor general chose it for a summer trip in 1827. He arrived with his entourage and 1,700 coolies in attendance.

The earliest Simla houses were built preferably near springs on flat pieces of land and there was shortage of accommodation from the beginning. Captain Mundy, aide-de-camp to the Commander-in-Chief Lord Combermere, thanked his luck when he got to occupy an attic below a wooden roof, where he could stand upright only in the centre. He writes that hundreds of mountain labourers and coolies were employed for cutting timber, laying blocks of stone and erecting buildings in 1828. Captain Mundy's journal ends with the prophetic words:

> I cannot doubt that Simla will rise in importance every year,
> as it becomes better known. Its delightful climate is sure to

recommend it for invalids; and its beautiful scenery, healthful temperature, and, above all *procol negotiis* relaxation which they will there enjoy, will induce the Governors-General and Commanders-in-Chief to resort there, during the hot months, in their official tours through the upper provinces.

It is interesting that there were 'illegal occupants' and 'encroachers' even then. There is a case of one Major Spiller who pitched his tents on a plot for two seasons, from April 1829 to September 1830, and then claimed the right to construct a house there. Kennedy's refusal saying that the site was for the office and establishment of the military department was replied with defiance, 'a fact known to every person in Simlah, is that the ground in question has been occupied by my tents and my servants ever since I have been on this location.' His succeeded but was later accused of encroaching on additional land.

By 1830, a township of thirty British-owned houses had come up which was then acquired by the East India Company from Maharaja of Patiala and other hill chiefs. Simla started to grow both in size and importance to become the summer capital of the British Empire in 1864...and the rest, as they say, is history.

Hilly sanitarium

One reason that the British took fancy for Simla was the climate. The cool breeze, the conifers and the gurgling springs not only gave the much needed escape from the scorching Indian plains but also made them nostalgic about home. Sir William Lloyd (6 May 1821) was ecstatic when he wrote:

> The mountain air seemed to have instilled ether into my veins, for I felt as if I could have bounded headlong down into the deepest glens, or spring nimbly up their abrupt sides with a daring ease...It was not, however, the effect of the prospects, for they were unlike those among the Welsh hills,

but it was because I recognized a great number of trees and flowers common there; such as the fir, the oak, the apricot, the pear, the cherry, together with wild roses, raspberries, thistles, dandelion, nettles, daisies, and many others. There was, too, an indescribable something in the breeze, which brought back a comparative similarity of feeling. I shall never forget this day.

Simla caught their imagination: 'whatever the ailing, low fever, high fever, "brandy pawney" fever, malaria, caught in the chase of tigers in the Terai, or dysentery imbibed on the banks of the Ganga, there was only one cure, the hills, and the chief hill station was Simla.'

But there were some who scoffed at this over-zealousness. Sir John Kaye, one time political secretary to the India Office said, 'This pleasant hill sanitarium has been the cradle of more political insanity than any place within the limits of Hindustan.' It is not surprising that there were some who talked disparagingly about 'the idiots on the hill'. Simla, however, continued to gain popularity even though it was seen what Victor Jacquemont, a twenty-nine-year-old Frenchman termed as 'the resort of the rich, the idle and the invalid'.

British society

For the British, Simla meant gaiety, fun, frolic and festivity. Balls at Viceregal Lodge and at the residences of lieutenant-governor and commander-in-chief were the main annual events. Then there were more than half a dozen plays by Amateur Dramatic Club, tennis, dinners and evening parties. Annandale was the venue of weekly gymkhanas on Saturdays; rifle shooting, polo, cricket and football were other events there.

That was not all. Garden parties; concerts; picnics; excursions of eight to ten days to woods and forests of Hatu; hunting trips; rides in and around Simla; three-day racing events in May and October and occasional bazaar for charitable purposes filled the days.

In his book *Raj: A Scrapbook of British India (1877-1947)*, author Charles Allen writes that Simla 'was one of the few places in India where the British could relax among their own kind and throw off some of the inhibitions that kept them in check while down in the plains.' He describes the events that were organised at the 'Moonlight Gymkhana' held at Annandale in 1924, with surgeon and ambulance in attendance:

Sabine Stakes: All ladies are penned up quite 'tight' in a Hurdle pen. Men will be mounted at the far end of the Polo Ground. Names of the Ladies will be drawn from a hat. Each man will gallop to the pen, dismount, struggle into the pen, seize his Lady, drag her out, and both will proceed on foot hand-in-hand, round an obstacle course to the winning post. No talking allowed until the pen is empty.

Ballooning: Pairs will start in line, each pair with an air balloon. Balloon must be hit into the air and not carried till the second line is reached, where each pair will find a fire balloon on the ground. First fire balloon to go up wins.

Laureate Stakes: Pairs will be given a quarter of an hour to make up a Limerick on a given subject. The subject will be given at the time.

The Nightie Hustle: Partners start mounted at opposite ends of bending course. Men go and meet their partners with lighted candle, light partner's candle and return together with both candles lighted.

The Geisha's Return: Ladies, at intervals, at one end of the ground, each with an unlighted Japanese lantern. Men draw for partners, taking their lady's horse with them, proceed from the far end of the ground to the ladies, where they search for partners; light the lantern and return together to the winning-post. Trotting will not be exceeded either way—Ladies only allowed to reply 'yes' or 'no' to inquiries.

The Fairies' Delight: Pairs will start with two matches in a box, and trot to the middle of the ground; light a page of the 'Times', wait until it has burnt out, trot to a table, dismount, light a firework, and run past the Winning-Post with the firework alight.

The Viceregal Lodge

Another highlight of the Gymkhana was Treasure Hunt.

Simla was 'enormously romantic' for the British. Iris Portal who lived here as a teenager wrote, 'the warm starlit nights and bright, huge moon, those towering hills and mountains stretching away, silence and strange exotic smells...very often coming home from dances the current boyfriend used to walk by the side of the rickshaw, murmuring sweet nothings and holding hands over the side of the hood, nothing much more than that, but it was very romantic. Everything was intensely romantic and a lot of people were lonely.'

In addition, Simla reminded the British of home. In her book *Imperial Shimla: Political Culture of the Raj*, Pamela Kanwar writes, 'When Simla was a hill village and had one thatched cottage, a traveller, after he had breathlessly climbed the ascent from Sairi to Boileauganj for a view of Jakhu hill, recounted that he would remember the journey 'for it reminded me of home, the days of my boyhood, my mother and the happiest of varied recollections.'

Emily Eden, sister of Lord Auckland, the governor-general found the clear air of Simla 'English and exhilarating'. For her, the thick white fog of the monsoons had a 'smell of London, only without the taste of smoked pea soup, which is more germane to a London fog.'

Lord Princep had found 'everything so English' about Simla in 1877 and by the 1930s Simla had acquired complete English flavour. Malcom Muggeridge, later editor of *Punch* observed in 1930s that Simla was 'an authentic English production; designed by Sahibs for Sahibs without reference to any other consideration—not even Maharajas.'

The summer crowd at Simla comprised mainly officers and officials, military and civilian, who came here on postings or on leave. Most considered themselves as 'exiles' in India and Simla for them was a means to be nostalgic about England.

Having a reputation for gaiety the Simla atmosphere was that of an oversized English club. The affluent, the fashionable and the high-ranking officers of the East India Company made it a status symbol and the wives, families and maidens made it popular. While

Captain Mundy counted sixteen women in 1828, Lockwood Kipling, Rudyard's father remarked in 1885, 'Simla is full of pretty girls and has a strong light brigade of sportive matrons of all ages. I never go near a dance, but I hear the nicest possible girls sit out in rows.'

Simla had its 'Grass Widows', these 'lively, attractive and with a talent for mild and respectable flirting' unattached ladies came here to spend a 'season' while their husbands baked in the hot summer of Indian plains. Young women who sailed out from England, usually chaperoned, in search of husbands were known as the 'Fishing Fleet'. Not all were lucky as some were destined to become 'Returned Empties'.

Though, to use the words of Mrs Lee, a British lady living at that time, 'a jumble of houses of every imaginable semi-suburban British kind perched on the top of a ridge' greeted the first-time visitor to Simla, yet almost everyone felt 'a sort of English feeling about them. The smell was English, the houses were furnished in a much more English kind of way and there were fires in the evening.' No wonder Jacquemont encountered 'the most friendly and lively of the rich idlers and imaginary invalids' here at Simla.

Rickshaw

The rickshaw was an essential part of Simla life. Though many Englishmen detested it, there was no escape from the rickshaw. On their visit to Simla, Mahatma Gandhi and Jawaharlal Nehru were also vociferous in decrying their use.

Till 1869, the Mall was a narrow hill path, suitable only to pedestrians. Edward J. Buck writes in his book *Simla: Past and Present* that 'it was so narrow at places that only two horses could go abreast, and this not without some danger to the riders, as in early days ponies were generally unruly, squeling beasts, always ready to kick or bite, and very different from the well trained animals which are now ridden in Simla'.

Ian Stephens who lived in Simla during those days remembered later, 'the annual move to Simla was romantic but rather horrifying.

I felt the same repugnance to traveling around Shimla in a rickshaw. Eventually one got accustomed to it, but never quite used to it. I always made a point of paying my rickshaw men very well which somehow satisfied my conscience—and thereby had the pleasure of a very fast rickshaw team to get me quickly to dances'.

Edwin Montagu (of Montagu-Chelmsford reforms) found the rickshaw in Simla as a 'most distasteful' form of conveyance and added: 'one would never allow a pony to take one up hill, and to make men do it, puffing and panting seems to me quite horrible...the scenery is, however, magnificent, and it is so jolly to see daffodils, lilac, wisteria, pansies, banksia roses, but, oh, the rickshaws, I hate them more and more.'

It is said that the first rickshaw brought to Simla belonged to Rev J. Fordyce, a chaplain of St. Marks's Church—though Sir Louis Dane claimed that he had introduced the rickshaw from Japan in about 1880. Though rickshaw was preceded by horses, jhampans and dandies, it went on to become part of Simla folklore more than any other mode of conveyance.

A satirist wrote a witty song 'The Origin of Simla Rickshaws' that was published in Liddlell's *Simla Weekly* on 12 August 1933:

The Ancestor of Rickshaws; Had a curious pedigree;
And whenever old C. saw It; He went red, as red could be,
For the Dame who sat within it; Dressed in Bugle beads and silk,
Did not condescend to flatter; Old stagers of his ilk.
The hood of that first rickshaw; Was square, and trimmed with fringe,
Such as dangled from the mantelpiece; In many a Berlin tinge
During the early Eighties; When Mrs Reverend J.
Invented our first rickshaw; For Simla during May,
Old C. declared it was "a cross; 'Twixt Bath-chair and a hearse"

But others said they thought it might be something even
worse!
The wheels had once belonged, 't was said,
To a perambulator; The cushioned seats appeared to be
With neither form nor data.
I still could draw from memory; That quaint historic chair,
Which as a child I never did; Because I didn't dare!

Viceroys, ladies and lords

Emily Eden who lived in India from March 1836 to March 1842 has
left a vivid account of her stay here. She reached Simla in April and
liked the place saying:

> Well, it really is worth all the trouble—such a beautiful
> place and our house, that everybody has been abusing, only
> wanting all the good furniture and carpets we have brought,
> to be quite perfection. Views only too lovely; deep valleys
> on the drawing-room side to the west, and the snowy range
> on the dining room side, where my room also is. Our sitting
> rooms are small, but that is all the better in this climate,
> and the two principal rooms are very fine. The climate! No
> wonder I could not live down below. We never were allowed
> a scrap of air to breathe—now I come back to the air again
> I remember all about it. It is a cool sort of stuff, refreshing,
> sweet, and apparently pleasant to the lungs. We have firs in
> every direction, and beautiful walks like English shrubberies
> cut on all sides of the hills. Good, I see this is to be the
> best part of India.

Sir John Lawrence agreed to become viceroy on the condition that
Simla be made the summer headquarters of the Government of India.
He explained strategic advantages of such a decision to Charles Wood,
the secretary of state thus:

This place, of all hill stations seems to me the best for the Supreme Government. Here you are with one foot, I may say, in the Punjab, and another in the North-West Provinces. Here you are among a docile population, and yet near enough to influence Oude. Around you, in a word, are all the warlike races of India, all those on whose character and power our hold in India, exclusive of our own countrymen, depends. No doubt there is the danger of being cut off from the seat of Government. Still, on the other hand, railways will lessen the danger.

Thus, it was Sir John Lawrence, who was instrumental in making Simla the summer capital of the British Empire in India and in April 1864, accompanied by his council, he started the first summer move to Simla from Calcutta.

Everything about Simla amused Lady Dufferin, wife of Lord Dufferin, who got the Viceregal Logde built. She recorded in her diary on 15 July 1887:

D. (Dufferin) took Hermie and me, all over the house (under construction Viceregal Lodge) in the afternoon. We climbed up the most terrible places, and stood on single planks over yawning chasms. The workpeople are very amusing to look at, especially the young ladies in necklaces, bracelets, earrings, tight cotton trousers, turbans with long veils hanging down their backs, and a large earthenware basin of mortar on their heads. They walk about with the carriage of empresses, and seem as much at ease on top of the roof as on the ground-floor; most picturesque masons they are. The house will really be beautiful, and the views all around magnificent. I saw the plains distinctly from my boudoir window, and I am glad to have that open view, as I shall not then feel so buried in the hills.

Lady Curzon (wife of Lord Curzon, the viceroy and the governor-general of India from 1889 to 1905) recorded her impression about Simla in these words:

The first view of Simla amused me so—the houses slipping off the hills and clinging like barnacles to the hill-tops and then our house! I kept trying not to be disappointed. A Minneapolis millionaire would revel in it, and we shall love it and make up our minds not to be fastidious...a look out of the window makes up for all and I can live on views for five years.

But Lord Curzon had a different view, he remarked to Sir Walter Roper-Lawrence: 'How I hate the place.' He disapproved of the annual migration to Simla.

Gradually, however, the government's move to Simla became the accepted practice and construction of Railway line from Calcutta to Delhi and then to Ambala in 1869; construction of Cart road from Kalka to Shimla through Dharampur and Solan eased the travails of journey to Simla. In 1874, a bullock cart service for goods and a tonga service for mail and passengers came into general use. In 1874, a traveller calculated that the viceroy with his staff, the members of his Council, and secretaries to government could be at Ambala in about twelve hours after leaving Simla. Fifty hours by rail would get them to Calcutta and sixty to Bombay. The Ambala-Kalka rail link was extended in 1891; twelve years later the first passenger train arrived at Simla on 9 November 1903.

George Aberigh-Mackay who bestowed Simla with names such as 'Mount Olympus' and 'Abode of the Little Tin Gods' wrote a verse:

On the hills like gods together, careless of Mankind
For they lie beside their boxes and Gazettes are hurled
Far below them in the valleys, and the clouds are lightly curled
Round their golden houses, girdled with the gleaming world.

Britishers, Indians and Natives

Contemporary British accounts and newspaper articles by the Englishmen generally avoided mentioning about the natives; they focus on the 'red-tape tempered with picnics and adultery'. The dominant attitude of the British towards Indians and Indian things was that of 'contempt' and they 'despised' social interaction with them.

The deputy commissioner proposed to remove Indian shops from the Ridge and the Mall in 1861: 'My idea is to give Simlah as much an European tone as possible...I look forward to the gradual removal of the Bazar at Simlah which is at present occupied by natives and to substitute European traders in their stead, in improved buildings.'

The municipal authorities of Simla were peeved at the messy and crowded Lower Bazaar where Indians lived in cramped and shabby tenements. The Annual Report of the Simla Municipality of 1877-78 recorded: 'If you want to improve Simla knock down the bazaar. The removal of the whole bazaar at a very moderate estimate for compensation would cost sixteen lakhs of rupees.' The municipality was, however, concerned about the rehabilitation of the natives at a suitable location as they were 'essential to the existence of Simla.'

If the Lower Bazaar was the place where natives cramped together, the Mall was seen as exclusive domain of the white men. The Mall was out of bounds for sweepers, coolies, mule leaders and workmen every evening between four and seven. Any violation was considered to be a sacrilege, a gross aberration. A letter in *The Pioneer* complained (1883):

> The good old rule which forbade the presence of coolies and porters, and loafers generally (as distinguished from promenaders), upon the Mall between the hours of four and seven of the afternoon has lately fallen utterly and miserably into abeyance. In former days, up to the present season that is to say, the one road of Simla was vigilantly kept clear during these hours by the police, and the gangs of labourers and hill men relegated to the cart road below.

Victor Jacquemont remarked on this English attitude with the characteristic French sarcasm, 'They esteem themselves too highly, they despise the coloured races too much to be flattened by their homage.'

The Indian residents in Simla most of whom moved here with the government from Bengal and plains, oscillated between 'awe at the privilege of staying in Simla' and 'repugnance at the sense of inferiority'. For Indians it was not gaiety and festivities; they had to brave 'the three-and-a-half month long monsoon, it's hard to digest mineral water, the panting-uphill, and breakneck-down walks, since most Indians could afford neither horse nor rickshaw.' And Imperial Simla's two months of 'healthy' and 'salubrious' climate were followed by cold and wet Simla weather which Indians were left to face as the caravans moved downhill at the end of summer sojourn.

In fact, more interesting than what the foreign rulers thought about natives is what the locals thought of them.

William Howard Russell, a London *Times* correspondent, got the following answer when he asked an Indian what he thought of British behaviour in 1858:

> Does the Sahib see those monkeys? They are playing very pleasantly. But the Sahib cannot say why they play, nor what they are going to do next. Well, then, our poor people look upon you very much as they would on those monkeys, but that they know you are very fierce and strong, and would be angry if you were laughed at. They are afraid to laugh. But they do regard you as some great powerful creatures sent to plague them, of whose motives and actions they can comprehend nothing whatever.

One occasion when European Simla came in contact with the natives was the annual Sipi fair held near Mashobra. But here too the description echoes the moral high ground taken by the British. In 1882, a newspaper report commented that a newcomer to Simla is told that: 'the real business of the day is purchase of wives, and a part of the hillside is pointed out to him where the youth and beauty of the surrounding country is closely packed together, decorated with nose-rings and bright chudders, and showing willingness to respond to critical inspection with smiles of the most winning frankness.' The typical pahari woman was 'as a rule, extremely good-looking, and a born flirt; she has a pleasant gay manner, and can always see a joke; people who wish to chaff her discover an adept at repartee.'

A contributor to *Chambers Journal (1872)* commented on the fair: 'Look at those gaily dressed, fair and pretty women. They come from the valleys immediately under the snowy range, to buy nose rings and bangles which their souls love. Although some of them have two or three husbands they are good and happy women, and have pleasant homes among those giant mountains of the Himalaya and beyond Satluj.'

The extent to which the British showed their high-headedness towards Indians can be gauged from this incident. In 1919, Jawaharlal Nehru and his wife Kamla underwent a humiliating experience. Nehru was at Simla as a member of Annie Besant's Home Rule League and was staying in the same hotel where an Afghan delegation was put up. A British magistrate told Nehru that his presence was not desired in Simla. He was asked to give an undertaking that he would not contact the Afghans who had come to discuss a peace treaty. Nehru was not even aware that there was an Afghan delegation, and deeply hurt he refused to give any such pledge. The magistrate then said, 'In that case, we give you four hours to leave Simla, or we escort you out.'

Simla in literature

Rudyard Kipling, the Nobel laureate, created a larger-than-life Simla. His fictional creations—the police men, officers, administrators and antique dealers—were seen as 'real' characters and the British visitors coming here decades later, hoped to encounter them.

Describing Simla's life 'in a nutshell' as 'strenuous work and strenuous play' Kipling wrote the following verse:

By docket, billet-duox and file, By mountain, cliff and fir,
By fan and sword and office-box, By corset, plume and spur,
By riot, revel, waltz and war, By women, work and bills,
By all the life that fizzes in, The everlasting hills.

His sister, Mrs Flemming, portrayed Simla's social scene in her novel, A Pinchbeck Goddess. Simla has been portrayed by several writers like M.M. Kaye, Penelope Chetwode, J.G. Farrell, Ruskin Bond, Mohan Rakesh and Nirmal Verma in their books. Gurudev Rabindranath Tagore stayed in Simla for some time and wrote his verses.

Simla's tryst with destiny: treaties, agreements and momentous decisions

Famous for the Simla Conference held in 1945 where the boundaries between India and Pakistan were finally demarcated and the Shimla Agreement between India and Pakistan in 1972, Shimla has witnessed many more momentous decisions.

The treaty of 1838 between the British and the Punjab government and Shah Shuja was planned here. In the same year (1838), plan to attack and invade Afghanistan was prepared here and 'Simla Manifesto' the declaration of war on Afghanistan, was issued on 1 October 1938 from the Secretary's Lodge, the residence of aide-de-camp of Lord Auckland adjoining the Auckland House.

It was at Simla that Allan Octavian Hume, a retired civil servant persuaded Lord Ripon to agree to the idea of the Indian National Congress which held its inaugural session in 1885. In effect, the idea of forming the Muslim League also gained ground here. The League took shape after a delegation of Muslims had met the Viceroy Lord Minto at Simla. Sir George Dunbar records in the History of India that the viceroy made 'first official acknowledgment of the Moslem claim for separate representation' while replying to a deputation led by Agha Khan III in Simla in 1906.

In 1913-14, Simla was the venue for the tripartite conference with the British, the Chinese and the Tibetans participating. It was held under the viceroyalty of Lord Harding. Sir Henry Macmohan and Sir Charles Bell represented the British. China was represented by Ivan Chen and Tibet by Lonchen Shatra. At the end of six-month long negotiations the Chinese did not agree to the draft agreement, the conference was wound up in 1914 and Macmahon signed a convention with the Tibetan representative. The result was 'Macmahon Line' which was fixed roughly along the Himalayas from the north-east corner of Bhutan to the Isu Razi Pass in the north of Burma. The 'MacMahon Line' adopted somewhat complicated formula whereby inner-Tibet would be controlled by China, while outer Tibet would be an autonomous state, but under Chinese suzerainty and British protection.

From 1930s the flavour of Simla started to change, leaders of Indian national movement started coming here to negotiate with the imperial rulers. Mahatma Gandhi, Jawaharlal Nehru, M.A. Jinnah, Vithalbhai Patel, Maulana Azad, Vallabhbhai Patel and several others came here to negotiate with the British. The Gandhi-Irwin Pact was also signed at Simla.

A Walk Through History

VIPIN PUBBY

It was while writing a book on the former capital of the Raj during the late 1980s that I was overwhelmed with the discovery of some little known historical events that took place in the town and in the area I was living in for the last three years. As I researched for the book, I was stuck by the momentous events and decisions which changed the life and destiny of millions of people forever.

From my study in the US Club (United Services Club), I could see some of the landmarks of the hill town including the Ridge with its famous Christ Church and the Bandstand, the Gorton Castle which once housed the Imperial Government's secretariat and now accommodates the Accountant General's office, the Viceregal lodge which now houses the Indian Institute of Advanced Studies and the historic Assembly Hall where the Central Legislative Assembly held several sittings.

One day I realised that I was sitting in the building, and perhaps the house, which must have been witness to some of these important events. It was a century-old building and a part of the residential building (which might have served as residential quarters for British officers) and shared a common entry for a wing that is now converted into the Chief Engineer's office. The building housed (and still houses) one-bedroom flats, with a drawing room, kitchen and toilets. Mine was the corner flat and as is our wont, one of my predecessors had covered the passage around the flat into three additional rooms—a lobby, an additional bedroom and a dining room. It dawned on me that the officers staying in the flat during the annual sojourn to the summer capital of the Raj must have been part of some of those significant decisions.

Even the US Club area, which comprises several buildings, was the venue of several pre- and post-Independence events. It was the historic venue where the last meeting of the Radcliffe Boundary Commission was held after the conclusion of its public hearings. Sir Cyril Radcliffe, who was given the task to demarcate the boundary between India and Pakistan in about two months, expressed the hope that the final meeting of the four members of the commission would be able to reach a consensus on the boundary between the two nations. However, its four members, two Muslims and a Hindu and a Sikh, disagreed on most of the proposals. Before a photo op at the US Club, Sir Radcliffe said: 'Gentlemen, you have disagreed and, therefore, the duty falls on me to give the award which I will do later on.'

The award was to leave at least ten million dead in riots that broke out after the Partition and displacement of several other millions of people from India to Pakistan and vice versa. The problems created by the Boundary Commission also led to wars and strife between the two countries which continues even sixty years after Independence.

After the partition, Punjab's capital was shifted to Shimla and the US Club played host to several offices. But a little known fact about the club premises is that its library was the site where thousands upon thousands of books were stored after being brought from the Punjab University's campus in Lahore. Even books belonging to the Dwarka Das Library were shifted to the US Club and stored in its erstwhile dining room before moving to Chandigarh.

From the US Club is a virtually parallel, barely a kilometer-long road to the famous Ridge. Often walking on that road, I would imagine British officers walking down to their offices or holding hands of their little ones on their way to the Sunday Service at the imposing Christ Church located at the head of the Ridge. The neo-gothic Church was designed by Col J.T. Boileau in 1844 but consecrated shortly after 1857. The second oldest church in north India is also famous for its five stained glass windows. The inscriptions and signboards in the premises are reminders of the era when it was visited by the high and the mighty.

The Ridge, one of the most popular places in the town visited by every visitor to the town, had remained witness to the making of history. The flat piece of land was the exclusive preserve of the British with only a few shops selling European wares. The entry to the Ridge remains restricted to vehicles and special permission is required to hold functions even now. One of the most significant functions held in independent India was the formal grant of full statehood to Himachal Pradesh in 1971 by the then Prime Minister Indira Gandhi.

But not many who have spent time on the Ridge know that it is only a huge water tank. The water reservoir was constructed some time in the 1880s to meet the water requirement of the town. It has a capacity to store about ten lakh gallons of water and remains one of the largest water reservoirs for the town.

The other landmark on the Ridge is the statue of the father of the nation, Mahatma Gandhi, close to the library constructed in the neo-Tudor architecture. The statue had to be placed on a higher pedestal a few years ago after the local authorities could not cope with the frequent theft of the rounded spectacles on the statue and also to give it more visibility!

The Band Stand constructed during the Raj, where the army band played during the evenings, has now been converted into a restaurant retaining the same shape.

A little down the road is the infamous Scandal Point where the road from the Ridge meets the Mall road. No one has any authentic documentation on how the name of the Point came about. The most common theory is that the then Maharaja of Patiala had allegedly abducted the daughter of the then viceroy or the commander–in-chief (neither the names nor the exact year of the so-called scandal are available) in the early part of the last century. However, there is no evidence to back it and researchers have pointed out that the maharaja was too young (only a teenager) when the then viceroy's daughters visited him during that period. Besides, the situation appears to be too bizarre as any such abduction would have caused a major embarrassment which would have been duly recorded.

The most probable justification of the crossroad point (ironically named Lala Lajpat Rai, well-known freedom fighter, with a small bust of his keeping an unblinking eye on the visitors) being named as such could have been that the point may have been a favourite place to exchange news and discuss scandals in the township. It still remains one of the favourite places to loiter around and meet friends at the junction of the roads from the Ridge, the Grand Hotel, the DC's office and the Mall.

Adjacent to the Scandal Point on the Mall Road is the famous Gaiety Theatre which has just been renovated. The teatre was built in Gothic style by Henry Irwin in 1887, which also happened to be Queen Victoria's Jubilee Year. The formal inauguration of the Shimla Amateur Dramatics Club (ADC), which still exists, took place in 1888 and the theatre has been host to the best of English plays beginning with *Time will Tell*. Among the well-known personalities who remained associated with the Gaiety Theatre were author and poet Rudyard Kipling (who also acted in a play called *A Scrap of Paper* to raise funds for the church), K.L. Sehgal, Col. Bedal Powel, Prithviraj Kapoor, Balraj Sahni, Pran, Manohar Singh, Shashi Kapoor, Nasseerudin Shah, Raj Babbar and Anupam Kher.

The Mall Road, particularly the half-a-kilometre stretch from the Scandal Point to the Combermere Bridge, remains the most common meeting point for Shimlaites. Anyone wanting to meet anyone without the restrictions of time and location can fix up an open invitation for the Mall. A common joke in Shimla is that if you need to find someone, just take a walk on the Mall and there is every chance that you would be successful. There hordes of regulars just walk up and down, waving at friends, stopping for a quick exchange of information or simply indulge in animated discussion while dodging other walkers. One of the best parts is that the stretch is 'sealed' for vehicles and only vehicles used for emergency like ambulances, firebrigade and police besides just the governor and the chief minister are allowed on this stretch which leaves residents to walk carefree on the stretch.

As during the Raj time, it remains a showcase of the latest fashion. It has the best of shops which remain clogged with tourists and do brisk sales. General cleanliness is still maintained with prominent signage which warns that those found littering or spitting shall be fined heavily.

This was the stretch of road which remained out of bounds for 'Indians and dogs' for a long time. Municipal records show that the outbreak of cholera in 1875 provided a pretext to the local officials to prohibit Indians from rebuilding shops on the Upper Mall. The municipality introduced a bylaw in 1891 to prohibit all porters, except those carrying the baggage of European visitors, from the Mall between 4 pm and 8 pm during the period from April to October, when the area was most heavily frequented by the whites.

The area between the Mall and Cart Road on this particular stretch must be one of the most thickly inhabited on any hill station. This is the area which Rudyard Kipling described so tellingly as 'the crowded rabbit warren', a description which holds equally true even today. The houses are cheek-by-jowl and the narrow lower bazaar which links the two entails a climb of almost forty-five degrees.

The Mall is linked to the Ridge, apart from the merger at the Scandal Point, by a couple of flights of steps and a meandering road. The narrow road from the Ridge to Jakhoo Temple (the highest point in Shimla) also has an important landmark related to our history. The house of A.O. Hume, the founder of the Congress party, which later spearheaded the nation's struggle for Independence, is located on this road. Hume held several meetings in his house before founding the Congress in 1885. The particular road also has the private residence of one of the longest serving chief ministers of the state, Virbhadra Singh. There is a project now which would link Jakhu with a Ropeway to the Ladies Garden, the bus stand and the Sankatmochan Temple.

The other road from the Ridge goes to the Lakkar Bazaar and further to Snowdon and Sanjauli. The area between the Ridge and the Lakkar Bazaar is believed to have been the dumping area for the silt that was dug out for the construction of a water reservoir below the Ridge. Thus there had been several instances of land sinking in this zone. The area has been strengthened now and is a favourite haunt of tourists who wish to take gifts made of wood for their near and dear ones. It is another matter that some of these woodwares are made in far-away places like Ludhiana and Lucknow!

I was struck by a particular fascinating reference while researching the book that the Ridge, and for that matter, the legislative building as well as the Viceregal Lodge, were located on the range of hills which marked the watershed for the subcontinent. For the sake of pure illustration, if one spilled water on the east side of the range, it would finally end up in the Bay of Bengal while a similar exercise on the west would merge with the Arabian Sea.

From the Ridge and the Mall, the hub of social activity, the former Viceregal Lodge (now renamed Rashtrapati Niwas and housing the Indian Institute of Advanced Studies) is quite a distance. The huge Scottich Baronial edifice, located exclusively on the Observatory Hill is visible from almost all parts of the town.

Although Sir John Lawrence brought his first entourage in 1864 to Shimla, the official residence for the viceroys was completed only in 1888. The architect of the imposing Elizabethan Renaissance style structure was designed by Henry Irwin (who also constructed the Gaiety Theatre). It was indeed built to impress and no one can remain unawed by the spectacular façade, tapestries, teak-panelled walls and magnificent interiors.

Several important meetings involving the top leaders on the eve of Independence were held in this building. A host of leaders like Mahatma Gandhi, Jawaharlal Nehru, M.A. Jinnah and Sardar Patel met Lord Mountbatten came to discuss the modalities of independence and Partition. It was also the venue of the critical Simla Conference in 1945. Two major turning points in the history of the subcontinent were when Jinnah for the first time made it clear that he was in favour of an independent Pakistan. The second was in May 1947 when Mountbatten showed his first plan for the partition of the country to Nehru. His plan, which he had already communicated to the British government, was to provide a right to all states to choose between India and Pakistan. This was unacceptable to Nehru who said the states should not be given a choice and the transfer should be purely on the basis of majority population belonging to Hindus and Muslims.

Midway between the Ridge and the Viceregal Lodge is the historic Assembly Hall. The Council Building, as it was called, was constructed in 1925 to house the Central Legislative Assembly. The Viceregal Box is now renamed Governor's Box. Vithalbhai Patel was the first elected president (or speaker) of the Assembly from 1925–1930. It was here that he declared after taking over the post that 'from this moment, I cease to be a party man. I belong to no party. I belong to all parties....'

It was in this building that Moti Lal Nehru brought forth a resolution which read that 'India is determined to win freedom, the manner and measure and the time either you determine in a reasonable spirit or else she will determine for herself.'

The chamber was later to house the Punjab Legislative Assembly before it shifted to Chandigarh and finally the Himachal Vidhan Sabha. The speakers continue to occupy the tall teak chair once occupied by Vithalbhai Patel. Incidentally the building is located in the erstwhile Kenedy House, the site of the first ever building that was built by the British in the area.

During my stay at Shimla I had often wondered why the British built government houses and residences of the senior functionaries so far away from the Viceregal Lodge, particularly when the means of transportation were rather primitive. The elegant Barnes Court,

Barnes Court (now Raj Bhawan) in 1882

which is located diagonally opposite and on the other side of the town from the Viceregal Lodge, was the residence of the commander-in-chief of the Royal Army. It derives its name from Sir Edward Barnes who was commander-in-chief during 1832–1833. It now houses the residence of the state governor and is called the Raj Bhawan. The building, located at Chota Shimla, completed its 175 years of existence in 2007.

The most significant event in the post-Independent era was the signing of the historic Indo-Pakistan Shimla Agreement between Indira Gandhi and Zulfiquar Ali Bhutto after the 1971 war. The release of over 90,000 Pakistani prisoners and pulling back of troops from occupied areas was agreed upon here. The table on which the accord was signed is kept in the lobby of the Raj Bhavan. The Bhawan also adorns several rare pictures of the historic occasion including the pictures of the assassinated former Pakistan Prime Minister Benazir Bhutto, then a young girl who had accompanied her father and had become a favourite in India.

The building has been well maintained. In its conference room you can still see old pistols, guns and knives arranged as decoration on the walls. These have rusted with time but they do take one back to the time when it was home to British rulers. Close to it is situated the Elerslie, formerly civil secretariat of the Punjab province and now the Himachal Pradesh secretariat where the chief minister and his cabinet colleagues sit with the top officers of the state. It was in the cabinet room of this building that India and Pakistan burnt midnight oil to hammer out the contentious Shimla agreement. It is still called the Summit Room.

Interestingly, this was the building where the first drafts of the planning for the new capital of Greater Punjab (then called East Punjab), Chandigarh, were discussed. The initial planners for the new capital, Albert Mayor and his colleague and friend Novicki, sat here with a team of young Indian architects and engineers, to map out the location and broad planning for the new capital. Unfortunately Novicki died in a plane crash and Mayor opted out of the project.

Their successor Le Corbusier and his team adopted substantially the basic infrastructure suggested in the first draft and moved down to the plains to bring up the new capital.

Barnes Court was not the only building to have housed commanders-in-chief. Woodvilla and Snowdon buildings too functioned as residences of the top army officers in the country. But perhaps the most well-known of these commanders, Lord Kitchener preferred to stay at the Wildflower Hall, a few kilometers away at Mashobra. In fact it was the favourite of retreat of several viceroys Like Lord Rippon and Earl Lytton. Spread over an area of twenty-two acres, Wildflower Hall has now been converted into a luxury hotel and is popular with the high and mighty of the land.

It is close to the hill resort of Kufri where the slopes are used for skiing by amateurs and tourists. An array of hotels has sprung up to cater to the needs of the tourists who can also enjoy Yak rides and buy traditional handicrafts from the place.

Another interesting place near Mashobra is Naldehra. It is the site of the old golf course in the country and is believed to have been developed during Lord Curzon's tenure. The nine-hole course is considered one of the most challenging courses in the world. It is also the site of shooting for various Bollywood films including *Kudrat* in which two lovers had engraved their names on a tree to re-discover the tree in their next birth. Incidentally that led to almost all trees being engraved by lovers visiting the site at Naldehra.

Very close to Naldehra is the site for the annual Sipi fair. The fair is generally held in the months of April/May and was traditionally known for match-making. Thousands of villagers from far and wide attend the fair which is held in honour of Sip *devta*.

Among the frequent guest to the Mashobra area is Priyanka Vadra, daughter of Sonia and former prime minister Rajiv Gandhi, who is so fascinated with the area that she has purchased land for building her own house in close vicinity of the Wildflower Hall in Mashobra.

Perhaps the last word on the town as witness to momentous decisions is not written yet.

Shimla: As I Recall It...

Ashok Dilwali

'What will be visible from the hill?'
'Why not climb the hill and see for ourselves?'

My innocuous question as a child and the enthusiastic and encouraging answer given by my uncle always did the trick! We ended up climbing small roadside hills and enjoying the scenic beauty. Irritating rashes caused by 'bichchoo booti' notwithstanding, it was always great fun to be with him and explore what was hidden on the other side. He was full of adventure and extremely fond of long walks. We—me and my brother—accompanied him on several occasions. As we trudged behind him, he not only taught us to be careful while walking in the rough country but also told us many things about the flora and fauna of the area. Elder to my father and a bachelor, my uncle Mr R.C. Gupta was wedded to studies. A post graduate in science, he had also completed a Masters degree in Economics. He was a versatile and popular teacher who is still remembered fondly by his students. Small hills that we climbed together to satisfy my curiosity led to an unending quest in me to see what lies beyond. The long journeys in the Himalayan wilderness that I undertook years later to visit far off places started with those small hikes I did as a child in Shimla.

Shimla, for me, is nostalgia. Memories. The place evokes beautiful images of days I can only dream of as they can never come back. As a matter of fact, can any time gone past come back?

My earliest memories of Shimla are of 1952. Shimla and the nearby picnic spots like Fagu, Jakhoo, Tatta Pani, Naldehra and Mashobra where we used to go frequently come alive in my mind and I can feel the fresh air impregnated with the fragrance of pine and deodar trees whenever I think of Shimla. My late father Mr B.K. Dilwali started his career as a professional photographer here in 1929 and established his studio, Shimla Studios, in 1931. Of his six siblings, four are Shimla-born. He used to move to Shimla in the summer months and come to Delhi in winters, thus keeping pace with the British rulers of the day. This perhaps explains the travel genes in me!

Since we used to go during the summers, the dread of doing our school homework in the summer holidays was always upon us and perhaps that was the real thorn in an otherwise good time. We kept postponing it till the last week when my father would admonish us for this carelessness. Holidays over, we looked forward to our return journey to Shimla.

We journeyed from Kalka to Shimla by road as well as by train. I enjoyed both. In fact, more than the journeys I would enjoy the stories that my father and uncle told me about how the road to Shimla was built and how the railway line was made. My uncle told me that before the Kalka–Shimla road was laid (which is now National Highway 22 and is also known as the Hindustan–Tibet Road) it was uncomfortable, cumbersome and exhausting travelling to Shimla. In 1864, when Shimla became the summer capital, the railway line was only up to Ambala from where the British travellers used to travel by a four-wheeled dak-garry (the mail wagon carrying post) to Kalka, at the foot of Shimla hills. Interestingly, these carriages that were generally drawn by horses or bullocks were at times pulled by elephants so that the bridge-less River Ghaggar could be crossed. From Kalka, the gruelling eight hour journey was completed in many ways, each causing more pain than the other. One way was to go by *tonga*, a two-wheeled horse carriage, which was termed a 'greater affliction than a dak-garry'.

The tonga was a crude, uncomfortable but a strong two-wheeled cart drawn by one or two Kabul ponies with passengers sitting back-to-back, and the luggage strapped on to the side over the wheels and a Pathan driver at the reins. Then, there was *dandy* (a sedan chair slung on poles and carried by bearers) and *jampan* or *doli* (the palki) which was a covered type of curtained tiny box-like compartment, carried like the dandy. The jampan was described by one sufferer as a 'jolting, back-aching abomination.' Thank God the present day traveller is spared these horrors and one can travel on a smooth, broad hill road that offers charming views.

I must say that one of the attractions in our childhood was the train journey from Kalka to Shimla. As the track meandered up from Shiwalik foothills at 2,000 feet and wound its way through rolling hills with numerous side valleys up to Shimla at nearly 7,000 feet, vistas of mesmerising beauty opened up and I was spellbound. The journey was always an unforgettable experience. Laying of the rail track to Shimla has its own tales full of human and spiritual wonders. The trace of the railway line known as 'engineering wonder of its time' was 'revealed' in 'visions' to an illiterate vagabond known as Bhalku. One account describes him as a shabby man with long locks and flowing beard swarming of lice. But this unkempt man was a mystery, he guided the team of engineers led by H.S. Harington, chief engineer at every step to build the track that covers the distance between Kalka and Shimla through 103 (now 102) tunnels, 969 bridges, twenty railway stations and five level crossings. It is really amazing that this railway line recorded as the 'greatest narrow gauge in India' in the *Guinness Book of World Records* was built following the trace revealed to an illiterate man by the local deity. Incidentally this project is also recorded as the most surveyed project in railway chronicles of India. A correspondent of the *Delhi Gazette* had first sketched this railway line sometime in November 1847, seventeen years before Shimla was officially declared the 'summer capital' of the British Empire in India under the viceroyalty of John Lawrence.

The work on the Kalka–Shimla route was finally completed in 1903 and it was opened for the general public only in 1906. I remember vividly that while travelling, I always waited for the next tunnel. My father once told me an interesting story about the longest tunnel near the Barog Railway Station. He told me that the station got its name from an engineer named Barog who died here after he failed to align both ends of an under-construction tunnel near here. Even now one can see an abandoned tunnel nearby. Just one kilometre from the present Barog station is the grave of the engineer. Later I was told that had the tunnel been aligned, it would have been the longest tunnel in the world. I was also told that Barog committed suicide. I would always wonder about the man and his effort whenever we passed through this tunnel. Once we were past Solan, I would eagerly wait for our arrival at Shimla and the tiring but exciting walk from the station to the Mall Road.

◆

The Mall Road used to be spotlessly clean with several signs prohibiting spitting and the warning of a challan of rupees fifty! Those were not mere signs; everyone followed them. The signs are still there but the weight these signs carried seems to have vanished and an era has passed. Now nobody appears to bother about these signs. What always strikes me whenever I go to Shimla is the way Shimla has grown. The roads used to be so deserted and devoid of crowds. Today it is a bustling town full of people. Back then, cinema halls were another major attraction and right from my childhood I was fond of Western movies and the cowboys like Roy Rogers and Gene Audrey. We also watched the Walt Disney films on the wildlife of Africa and they fascinated me immensely.

Since I love to take landscapes in wilderness, my uncle's inculcation of this love for nature has done the trick. He walked for miles and for three decades I have gone on countless treks to many nooks and crannies of the Himalayas. My uncle was a strict disciplinarian and his observation of punctuality was to be followed implicitly by us and there were no exceptions.

When I go to Shimla, I can see the place my father used to visit regularly i.e., Gaiety Theatre. He used to tell me that the famous villain of Hindi films, Pran, also began his career in Shimla and he used to be in charge of maintenance at Gaiety Theatre. My father's godfather in Shimla, when he first set up his studio, was the Raja of Jubbal. When the raja built his Woodville Palace in the early 1930s, a very special *machaan* was constructed on a high deodar tree where my father climbed up and took the photograph with his bulky camera. Interestingly, one day my father got a call from him to find out the background of a student named Virbhadra Singh who was doing History (Honours) in St. Stephens College, Delhi. He later got his granddaughter married to Mr Virbhadra Singh who went on to become the longest serving chief minister of the State for about eighteen years!

◆

In my childhood days I went with my uncle to Tara Devi temple and in 2004, I shot an extremely unique photograph of Shimla as visible from Tara Devi. I used a very special technique by shooting Shimla in six parts with a 500 mm lens of Hasselblad and then stitching it on the computer. The strong telephoto has brought the far-off snow peaks right next to the Ridge and this image has been much appreciated for its unique perspective. I can only call it the blessing of Tara Devi and perhaps a reward for a long and arduous trek undertaken by a small kid many years ago!

In a way, I owe my career as a lens man to Shimla. In 1970 fresh from my studies, having qualified as a chartered accountant, I went to Kufri. I saw rolling hills spread out in cascading fashion as far as I could see. The last ranges were covered with snow and were shining in the sun. These snow-covered ranges were so far but appeared so near and I felt as if I could touch them. The view touched me and I was deeply moved. I had an intense desire to capture the view on camera but I still did not think very much of this as a profession! Later when I saw my friend Akshay Sood working in Roshan Studio, I thought perhaps this may be a good avenue to explore. As a photographer of the Himalayas I have found Himachal a very dear subject and naturally very close to my heart. I have published three books on this State and wish to do one more because it has so much to offer. Late Mr Roshan felt indebted to my father as he was instrumental in teaching him photography and he fondly called my father *Guruji*. This is all history as they are both in the heavens now.

In 1945, L.O. Kinsey and his wife decided to go back to England, having worked on their two branches in Delhi and Shimla since 1905. They were very fond of my late father and felt that B.K., as they used to call him fondly, would be the ideal person to keep their flag flying and not change the name of the studio. So in 1945 the proprietorship changed hands. Thus my father had to single-handedly manage four studios, two of his own and two of Mr Kinsey! Sadly and reluctantly he had to close down the Shimla branches as then Shimla was part of Punjab and much later it became the capital of Himachal Pradesh.

My elder brother and I were small kids then, but I still remember the studios. Now when I pass in front of both the studios, I have a lump in my throat! Kinsey Bros. was very close to Clarke's Hotel and my father told me about late M.S. Oberoi who acquired it and became a legend in the hospitality industry. Now I read his biography and realise he is one of my cherished heroes and one can only marvel at his greatness. It was Shimla who gave me some information about him and much later in life I realised the true gigantic nature of this legend.

◆

Shimla hills never fail to spring a surprise or two. Though a little late but nevertheless significant is the acquaintance of Kiarighat and how it came about. In 1973, my wife Manju and I were returning from Shimla in January with our son Rajat, who was just two and a half years, after seeing fresh snowfall when some road repairs were going on at a place called Kiari bangla. We stopped there and the chowkidar was good enough to give us tea. I casually asked if we could spend a night there as it was a PWD bungalow then. He agreed and said that hiring a heater would be nothing less than five rupees! We decided to spend the night there and my driver fetched dinner from Kandaghat. Later on, the Tourism Department took over the property and began running it as a Tourist Bungalow sometime in the late 1970s. My parents used to love the place and would stay there for a month or so regularly; all the villagers around the place got very friendly with him and my parents went for long walks at Kiarighat.

Over time, like any other place, Shimla has undergone change, which is inevitable but she will always retain that special flavour of an ideal hill station and a magnificent fund of unlimited nostalgia. My love for Shimla is as strong as ever and its wonderful people, I can vouch, are the warmest and one of the best humanity can offer for their simplicity, warmth and an ever obliging nature.

'Be Prepared!' A Simla Boy Scout

Ruskin Bond

I was a boy scout once, although I couldn't tell a ship-knot from a granny-knot, or a reef-knot from a thief-knot, except that a thief-knot was supposed to be used to tie up a thief, should you happen to catch one. I have never caught a thief, and wouldn't know what to do with one since I can't tie a knot. Just let him go with a warning, I suppose. Tell him to become a boy scout.

'Be prepared!' That's the boy scout motto. And a good one too. But I never seem to be well prepared for anything—be it an examination or a journey or the roof blowing off my room. I get half way through a speech and then forget what I have to say next. Or I make a new suit to attend a friend's wedding, and then turn up in my pajamas.

So how did I, the most impractical of boys, become a boy scout?

Well, it seems a rumour had gone around the Bishop Cotton prep school (I was still a junior then) that I was a good cook. I had never cooked anything in my life, but of course I had spent a lot of time in the tuck-shop making suggestions and advising Chippu, who ran the tuck-shop, encouraging him to make better *samosas*, *jalebis*, *tikkees* and *pakoras*. For my unwanted advice he would favour me with an occasional free *samosa*, so naturally I looked upon him as a friend and benefactor. With this qualification I was given a cookery badge and put in charge of our troop's supply of rations.

There were about twenty of us in our troop, and during the summer break our scoutmaster, Mr Oliver, took us on a camping expedition to Tara Devi, a temple-crowned mountain a few miles out of Simla. That night we were put to work peeling potatoes, skinning onions, shelling peas, and pounding masalas. These various ingredients being ready, I was asked—as the Troop Cookery expert—what should be done with them.

'Put everything in that big *degchi*,' I ordered. 'Pour half a tin of *ghee* over the lot. Add some nettle leaves, and cook for half an hour."

When this was done, everyone had a taste, but the general opinion was that the dish lacked something.

'More salt,' I suggested.

More salt was added. It still lacked something.

'Add a cup of sugar,' I ordered.

Sugar was added to the concoction. But still it lacked something.

'We forgot to add tomatoes,' said one of the scouts.

'Never mind,' I said. 'We have sauce. Add a bottle of tomato sauce!'

'How about some vinegar?' asked another boy.

'Just the thing,' I said. 'A cup of vinegar!'

'Now it's too sour,' said one of the tasters.

'What jam did we bring?' I asked.

'Gooseberry jam.'

'Just the thing. Empty the bottle!'

The dish was a great success. Everyone enjoyed it, including Mr Oliver, who had no idea what went into it.

'What's this called?' he asked

'It's an all-Indian sweet and sour jam-potato curry,' I ventured.

'For short, just call it a Bond *bhujya*,' said young Tata, my class fellow.

I had earned my cookery badge!

Poor Mr Oliver...he wasn't really cut out to be a scoutmaster, any more than I was meant to be a scout. The following day he told us he would give us a lesson in tracking. He would take a half-hour start and walk into the forest, leaving behind him a trail of broken twigs, chicken feathers, pine cones and chestnuts, and we were to follow the trail until we found him.

Unfortunately we were not very good trackers. We did follow Mr Oliver's trail someway into the forest, but we were distracted by a pool of clear water which looked very inviting. Abandoning our uniforms, we jumped into the pool and had a great time romping around or just lying on the grassy banks and enjoying the sunshine. A couple of hours later, feeling hungry, we returned to our camp-site and set about preparing the evening meal. Bond-*bhujya* again, but with further variations, including Simla mirch.

It was growing dark, and we were beginning to worry about Mr Oliver's whereabouts, when he limped into camp, assisted by a couple of local villagers. Having waited for us at the far end of the forest for a couple of hours, he had decided to return by following his own trail, but in the gathering gloom he was soon lost. Some good folk returning from the temple took charge of him and escorted him back to camp. He was very angry and made us return all our good-conduct and other badges, which he stuffed into his haversack. I too had to give up my cookery badge.

An hour later, when we were all preparing to get into our sleeping bags for the night, Mr Oliver called out: 'Where's dinner?'

'We've had ours,' said Tata. 'Everything is finished, sir.'

'Where's Bond? He's supposed to be the cook. Bond, get up and make me an omelette.'

'Can't, sir.'

'Why not?'

'You have my badge. Not allowed to cook without it. Scout rule, sir.'

'Never heard of such a rule. But you can take your badges, all of you. We return to school tomorrow.'

Mr Oliver returned to his tent in a huff.

But I relented and made him a grand omelette, garnishing it with dandelion leaves and an extra chilli.

'Never had such an omelette before,' confessed Mr Oliver, blowing out his cheeks.

'Would you like another, sir?'

'Tomorrow, Bond, tomorrow. We'll breakfast early tomorrow.'

But we had to break up our camp very early the next day. In the early hours a bear had strayed into the camp, entered the tent where our stores were kept, and created havoc with all our provisions, even rolling out the biggest *degchi* down the hillside.

In the confusion and uproar that followed, the bear entered Mr Oliver's tent (he was already outside, fortunately) and came out entangled in Mr Oliver's dressing-gown. It then made off in the direction of the forest.

A bear in a dressing-gown? It was a sight. And though we were a troop of brave little Scouts, we thought it better to let the bear keep the gown.

Author's note: When I joined Bishop Cotton School in 1943, the junior or preparatory school was situated in Chotta Shimla, a forty-five-minute walk from the senior school. During communal disturbance in 1947; the small boys were shifted to the main school for security reasons. The prep school closed down and the buildings were later taken over by the Tibetan school.

I had gone up to the senior school in 1946 and continued there till 1950, when I did my senior Cambridge exam. Life in B.C.S. was always eventful, but prep school was much more fan, as fur as I can remember. Senior school was tough in those days, but as small boys in the prep school we had more freedom. Boy Scouts forever!

The People of Shimla Town

MEENAKSHI F. PAUL

The residents of Shimla are often told enviously that they live in heaven or *swarg*. A flattering remark, indeed, save this also makes them *swargvasi*—denizens of heaven of course but, necessarily, dead! This tongue-in-cheek view broadly characterises the people of Shimla town and encapsulates their good humour, contentment, unhurried calm and languid pace of life.

Plurality is showcased at its happiest and unconscious best in Shimla's diverse population. This predominantly Pahari town is also home to a range of people from varied places, such as the Punjab, Bengal, Tibet and China. Further colour is added by the sizeable number of people who work in the town for long spells. These are the government servants and ARTRAC personnel from around the country, as well as construction workers primarily from Bihar, and odd-job service providers from Uttar Pradesh, especially from around Bijnor.

Shimlaites know six seasons: spring, summer, rainfall, fall, snowfall and guest fall. The last season is the most capricious of all and, particularly, fills the local inhabitants with trepidation during periods of water scarcity. Interestingly, there are times when Shimla's resident population is completely overwhelmed by the multitude of tourists, as it is on New Year's Eve and during the Diwali and Christmas holidays. At any given time a stream of Hindus, Sikhs, Buddhists, Christians and Muslims, as well as Gujaratis, Delhi-ites,

Bengalis, and Europeans can be seen walking down the promenade of the Mall. Incidentally, the Mall Road is an egalitarian institution in itself as there are no trappings of wealth separating the people. The rich and the poor rub shoulders on this road on which vehicles are not allowed and everyone must walk.

The culture and tradition of Shimla are Pahari and Hindu, the languages of the town are Hindi, Pahari, Punjabi and English and the town in every respect is cosmopolitan and multicultural where diversity is celebrated every day on its winding streets and steep inclines. Not the least by the three-lakh simian population in Shimla who permeate all corners of the town and, although they band together in different groups, together they hold sway over the human population that is less than half theirs. Monkeys are the uncrowned masters of the town and their capers, the subject of many dinner table conversations in homes of all flavours and hues.

A bemused young bride from frenetic Mumbai married into the relaxed coolness of Shimla bemusedly asked her in-laws how people in Shimla found the time to 'stand and stare' for interminable periods of time. The answer lies with the weather gods who reign supreme over the lives of Shimlaites and dictate their lifestyle, conversation and attitudes. Youngsters lounge for hours on the Ridge and the Mall alongside the elderly, who sit companionably on the municipal benches, as they all soak in the warmth of a sunny day. The office-goers stop in the sun to warm themselves before their day begins; others take advantage of office breaks to get their fix of vitamin D and chats with friends and colleagues. In winter, Shimla is a town where all life hushes to a whisper under the spell of a silvery night. Still.

Walks down the curvaceous bazaars of Shimla bring one face to face with the traditionally attired Pahari women, chatting and shopping in gaily coloured headscarves and bordered shawls. The men, in Western or local dress but invariably teamed with the distinctive Himachali cap, stand in groups at Scandal Point discussing the political news of the day. The smartly dressed college students, with unmistakable lilting Pahari accents and the characteristic smooth and rosy skin.

would rather pace up and down the Mall Road with occasional sit-downs for coffee or ice-cream. They exhibit the new confidence of an ascendant standard of living with many of them frequenting the growing number of showrooms selling branded goods. Most of these young people will leave town to pursue higher studies and careers, options of which are limited in Shimla. However, they will return at the first opportunity, even if for a few days, because no true Shimla person can remain away from it for long. Ruskin Bond, the acclaimed writer, who, schooled at Shimla says that the hills never leave a person even if a person leaves the hills. The saying goes, 'once a Shimlaite always a Shimlaite' and the town draws its own as surely as the spring brings back the bright rhododendron flowers dotting the hillsides.

In earlier days, people from different areas surrounding Shimla came to town for education, service, and trade but did not make it their home. Following the yearly visits by the British, Shimla came to be known as the town of quarters. The affluent families had houses in both place, but for the majority home was in the village. However, with the loosening composition of joint families and the exigencies of education and livelihood, people took to building properties and settling in the town. Most families of Shimla from the district and from Kinnaur own apple orchards in the villages. Beside horticulture, they pursue agriculture, tourism, and government service. The capital town also attracts people from Mandi, Hamirpur, Kullu, Solan and other parts of the State, many of whom settle in the town for good.

The earliest settlers in Shimla sizeable in number were the Soods. Many of the shops and stores in the town are owned by the Soods, the leading trading and business community of Shimla. Dewan Chand Atma Ram, Nathu Sweets, Maria Brothers, Hakam Mal Tani Mal, Lehnu Mal, Mela Ram, and such, are names without whom no account of Shimla is complete. During the Raj, it was said that Shimla belonged to the Sarkar and the Soods; in a manner, it continues to hold true even to this day. Originally from the areas in and around Kangra and Hoshiarpur, the Soods follow in the tradition of their forefathers and are leading businessmen, merchants, contractors, commission agents, as well as accountants, doctors and lawyers of Shimla. The Soods are a politically and socially aware community. The Shimla Arya Samaj was founded by eminent Sood leaders, like the redoubtable Rai Bahadur Mohan Lal of Garli, Kangra, in 1882. The members of the Shimla Sood Sabha are committed to social welfare and are also members of the Rotary, various NGOs and the Bar Association. The Shimla Sood Sabha manages the Ram Mandir and Sankat Mochan temples of Shimla as well as a *sarai* at Har ki Pauri, Haridwar, founded by Rai Bahadur Lala Jodha Mal Kuthiala. Lala Jodha Mal was a prominent forest lessee and timber merchant of North India in his days. A larger-than-life figure, he is remembered as a great philanthropist and it is said that he spent ninety-six lakh rupees in charity before he passed away in the late 1950s.

Together with the Soods, the Sikhs also own considerable businesses in Shimla. The Sri Guru Singh Sabha, Shimla was founded in 1886 at the Cart Road and the gurdwara near the local bus stand is a place of reverence for all the people of Shimla. Many Sikhs own shops in Lakkar Bazaar, Lower Bazaar and the Cart Road. Most of them deal in timber, hospitality, wooden artefacts, leather goods and cloth. The Sikh population is varied: from landed aristocrats, building contractors, educationists, and transporters, to government servants, tailors, and carpenters, the community has them all. The Sikhs observe their festivals with characteristic abandon and high spirits. The *langars* on festivals and Sundays at the main gurdwara are popular with the people of all classes in Shimla and it was only natural that the commemoration of the 400 year of the Guru Granth Sahib brought together the entire population of Shimla in devoted festivity.

Another major trading community of Shimla are the Muslims from Kashmir, Uttar Pradesh—especially from Saharanpur, Bihar and Delhi. The Saharanpur traders are mostly migrants and chiefly deal in fruit and wooden goods. Most of them return to Uttar Pradesh during the winter. Usually, only the men and boys travel to Shimla around March to sojourn here for a few months. The boys are sent to local schools but, to the teachers' exasperation, are seldom promoted to the next class because they usually leave for home in November and do not sit for their final examinations in December.

The Kashmiri Muslim merchants deal in timber, woollen shawls, cloth, dry fruits, and semi-precious stones. About four hundred families own houses in the town while others are migrants who descend on Shimla in summer and autumn. A considerable number of Kashmiri Muslims are porters. Hardy and well-built, these 'Khans' are indispensable for carrying heavy and bulky goods up and down the steep slopes of Shimla and for clearing snow in the winters. They also, often, double up as hotel agents. The gas agencies almost exclusively work with Khans who strap two or more gas cylinders to their back and nonchalantly trapeze up and down the precarious paths to light the hearths in the valleys and peaks of the town. The closely-knit community is predominantly Shia and most of their children study at the madarsa at Boileauganj. One is reminded of Khan Muhammad, a tall, handsome railway porter in the 1970s who spoke impeccable English and Hindustani, wore clean and ironed shalwar-kurta and black sandals polished to a shine everyday. He had two Masters of Arts degrees from Kashmir University but had not found a job in Kashmir despite them. The degrees were of no use outside the State because the medium of instruction in his university was Urdu, a language that had been replaced with Hindi or English in other Universities. He came to Shimla to earn for his family because he could earn as a coolie here without his family's knowledge back home. A striking figure, he was the favourite of the tourists, especially those from overseas who often asked for him by name. It was some years before he found suitable work and left Shimla for always. The Khans of Shimla are the heroes of the town and easily outshine the Bollywood Khans in the imagination of the people.

With the Khans, many porters and labourers chiefly from Sirmaur and Bilaspur, also make their livelihood in Shimla. Less robust than the Kashmiris, they are also less savvy and, therefore, cheaper to hire than the Khans. They have followed those rickshaw pullers and coolies who were indispensable to maintaining the spit and polish of the British Raj at Shimla. Most of the rickshaw sheds of that period have disappeared and the labour hostels are disbanded or decrepit. The uniform of turban, kurta-pyjama and cummerbund has been replaced by terrycot shirts and trousers and an occasional pair of inexpensive jeans. The rickshaws have given way to pony rides on the Ridge, popular with children and tourists. Most of the pony owners are from Hamirpur and some are from Mandi and Bilaspur. The dozen or so ponies also double up as mares for the bridegrooms during the wedding season. The horses line up near the big horse chestnut tree that stands sentinel to the northern winds on the Ridge. The tree would be desolate without Rattan Lal Gautam, from village Jhanduta in Bilaspur, who sits under the tree and in every season, for the last thirty-two years, has sold his paper cones of savoury peanuts, chickpeas, and potato chips together with mouth-watering churana. The balloon sellers from Uttar Pradesh and Punjab add to the festivity at the Ridge as do the softy ice-cream cones from Sardar ji's Loveena.

The last of the rickshaw-pullers, Malu Ram and Devi Ram from district Bilaspur became coolies and could be seen sitting outside the Grindlays Bank building (now ICICI Bank), in all weathers till the 1980s. They were remnants of an age where courtesy and polite comportment were imparted together with humiliation and domination. Shimla has lost much of that colonial style, its genteel charm, finesse and understated elegance as well as the prejudice. They have been replaced by exuberant confidence and a *joie de vivre*, immensely added to by the regular influx of excited tourists: honeymooners, pilgrims, and—determined to have a good time—groups and families. The one thing to be lamented, though, is the utter disregard of sanitation in a town legendary for its cleanliness round the world in bygone days. Unplanned urbanisation with the breakdown of infrastructure and the loss of green cover are also mourned by the residents but not really addressed by them in any substantial way as they go about their work.

Shimla's reputation of its roads being clean enough to eat from, rested almost entirely on the Balmiki Samaj in the days of the Raj.

Pamela Kanwar writes in *Imperial Simla* that every summer the Balmikis came to Shimla from villages of Jullundur and Hoshiarpur following the viceroy's government. They lived atop the Lal Pani neighbourhood near the Ladakhi Mohalla of the labourers and artisans from Ladakh who worked at construction sites. These settlers from Punjab were mostly landless peasants in the villages and, gradually, some of them made Shimla their hometown. They are recognised for their earthy exuberance and hardy vitality in Shimla.

The first major additions to residential buildings and the concurrent divisions of the bungalows and cottages of the British happened when, at the partition of the country, several families from Lahore, Peshawar and Para Chanar in North West Frontier Province (NWFP) of Pakistan moved to Shimla. Most of them opened shops in Lower Bazaar and Middle Bazaar, while some retailed on the Mall. The Frontier Sweet Shop was a landmark of Lower Bazaar till the mid-1980s. A close-knit society, the migrants have preserved their distinct culture, language and lifestyle. Even though they send their children to elite English-medium schools they prefer to marry within their own community and have maintained their distinct culture to this day. Statuesque and milky-complexioned, the Peshawari and Para Chanari women easily stand out in the crowds milling the bazaars.

The aforesaid residents of Shimla also have Bengali neighbours. The first of the Bengalis came as clerks and appendages of the British government for its summer sojourn at Shimla. It is said that a young Bengali clerk working in the viceroy's government was asked about the renowned town in a letter by his eager bride. He gave a snapshot of the town in words to the effect that everywhere there are dozens of trees wrapped in swirling mist with an occasional man huddled in woollen clothes walking through them. It is most likely that the bride did not insist on accompanying the husband on his subsequent visits to the town. Not all Bengalis were dampened by the cold, though, and a few gradually began to acquire property and settle here. Dr Rash Bihari Ghose, the freedom fighter and the moderate face of the Congress, bought Grasmere and made it his home. Well-educated and politically motivated, the Bengalis favoured government services, administration and teaching to trade and commerce. They exemplified the bureaucratic character of Shimla that till recently considered shopkeeping as plebeian. Interestingly, the once famous Bengal Crockery, by the fish market, is not owned by Bengalis but seems to be ingeniously named for the Bengali customers who came to buy the fresh river fish brought from Bilaspur next door.

The Kali Bari is the focal point of the Bengalis. The Shimla Bangia Sammelan is an association of the nearly fifty families who celebrate festivals from Baisakhi to Saraswati Puja in authentic Bengali manner. The Shimla Kali Bari Trust runs a subsidised guest house and canteen in the Kali Bari complex. It is the choice destination of most tourists from Bengal who throng the town in the hundreds during the Puja holidays. Shimlaites swear by the fish curry of the Kali Bari canteen, which is delectable and reasonably priced. Although the fish is procured from the local market, it is cooked by proficient Bengali cooks to give it genuine Bangla flavour. Durga Puja is celebrated with great fervour by the Bengalis of the town. The carnivalesque atmosphere of Kolkata is mirrored by the enthusiasm palpable at Kali Bari. Images of the goddess, resplendent in brilliant silk, are placed in the hall through the navratris for the devout to pay obeisance. The immersion of the idol, *visarjana*, is performed with great revelry and devotion at the ITBP lake below Tara Devi.

The Brahmo Samaj of Shimla was founded in 1876 by a few Bengali leaders some years after Keshab Chandra Sen expounded its principles to the people of Shimla during his visit to the town. The Bengalis, together with other government servants from Punjab, South India, and the United Provinces were also instrumental in founding many amateur dramatic and cultural clubs. The rich tradition of drama in Shimla is as much a progeny of these clubs as it is of the Amateur Dramatics Club founded by the British at the Gaiety Theatre. Regular drama performances and festivals are still a feature of the Kali Bari hall. The Bengalis of Shimla actively engage in debate, literature, and cultural pursuits. Although the Bengalis are few in number they add vibrant colour to the rainbow comprising the inhabitants of Shimla.

Similar to the Bengalis, the Jains of Shimla also founded the Jain Sabha in 1904. The Digambar Temple premises at Middle Bazaar also house the Jain Hall, a *dharamshala*, and a charitable dispensary. The Jain traders are a small but significant part of the business community of Shimla. The shops, Gainda Mal Hem Raj and Munshi Ram Nanak Chand are central to a child's fantasy of exotic sweets and chocolates. Jains also take up government jobs and service in the private sector and are recognised for their financial acumen and competence. Jains have extremely close-knit extended families. Dancing and singing are prized talents in the women and Jain weddings are a riot of colour, jewellery, and dance.

Another small but very visible constituent of the population of Shimla who are integral to the town are the Christians. There are about one hundred and fifty families belonging to the main churches—Christ Church (Church of North India) on the Ridge, St. Michael's Cathedral (Catholic) near the district commissioner's office, Seventh Day Adventist Church at Chaura Maidan, Baptist Church and Evangelical Church of India on the Mall. Most of these families are second-or third-generation Christians from Kotgarh hills and Kangra district. Many of them have retained their family names—Chauhan, Rathore, Sharma, etc. They follow the Pahari lifestyle and are rooted in their soil. There are also Punjabi Christians most of whom changed their names at the time of their baptism and adopted a composite culture of Anglo-Punjabi mix. The Catholic Church has some South Indian members, most of them in service at Shimla and also a couple of Chinese families who own shops of handcrafted shoes. Education is extremely important to the community and most of the renowned educational institutions of Shimla belong to it. Most Christians opt for government service, teaching and nursing. They are the least politically active members of society but are involved in social work and welfare activities, in which the YMCA and the YWCA play a pivotal role. Interestingly, there are more women than men in the families of Christ Church, which is reason to cheer in the state that has a falling female sex ratio. Marriages among Christians are a simple affair and, other than a few wedding gifts, no dowry is ever given. The few English and Anglo-Indian women who lived on in Shimla even as their families and friends moved away, passed the last days of their lives in the Hardinge Home near Bemloe and the last of them died two years ago.

Apart from these old churches, there are new house and cottage churches or congregations that have come up in recent years. These churches are evangelical in nature and, unlike the old churches, do not follow a set liturgy or sacraments, such as the Holy Communion. Their emphasis is on singing, praise and prayer. New churches draw large numbers of people from all communities and are not limited to the Christians.

The mosaic of Shimla's population would be incomplete without the Tibetans. Stout, good humoured and laconic, the Tibetans have made Shimla their home since the 1950s. Most of the young Tibetans have never visited Tibet and only heard stories of their homeland from their elders. Tibetan colonies at Sanjauli and Chhota Shimla house most of the population. The monasteries and the Central School for Tibetans are the hub of the community. The older generation wear their traditional dress but the new generation has taken to wearing Western and Indian clothes. Handheld prayer wheels are rarely seen in public anymore. The Tibetan Emporium on the Mall is popular with the tourists and the youth. The award-winning documentary maker from Shimla, Vivek Mohan, made *Spot the Difference* on the owners of the store and the Catholic Chinese family, Ta-Tung, which zooms in on the easy way of living together in Shimla. The Tibetan Bazaar on the road from the Scandal Point to the Rivoli Theatre caters to the local population's demand for reasonable readymade garments, shawls, bags and trinkets. Tibetan women are extremely enterprising and run their makeshift stalls with flair while their fingers keep busy plying wool to make socks, caps, baby mules, and friendship bands. Tibetans are alive to their demand for free Tibet and regularly hold rallies, meetings, and candlelight marches to remind themselves and the world of the issue. The birthday of H.H. the Dalai Lama and the Tibetan New Year, Losar are observed with great fervour by the Tibetans of Shimla. They participate enthusiastically in the Republic Day, Independence Day and Statehood Day functions as also in the famed Shimla Summer Festival.

The emotional warmth of the people of Shimla is borne out by the special relationship they share with the figures in stone and metal that dot the town. Mahatma Gandhi at the Ridge and Lala Lajpat Rai at Scandal Point are affectionately regarded as elders of the town. Many anecdotes in the people's lives revolve round them and most Shimlaites choose to wait with them for appointments on the Mall and the Ridge. The figure of the hill woman made by Prof M.K. Saxena held court at Daulat Singh Park and was the dream woman of many Shimla lads, till she was removed for the ongoing renovation work at the Gaiety Theatre.

With such geniality in their attitude, the inhabitants of the capital of the Land of the Gods, cannot but be deeply religious. The numerous places of worship of all communities fulfil the essential function of spiritual solace and social bonding for the residents scattered over the hills. Mahashivratri, Navratri and Diwali, are the major festivals celebrated in the town. Eid, Guru Nanak Divas and the birth of Gugga Zahar Pir are also eagerly observed. Christmas has turned into a winter festival with the residents and tourists joining in the revelry and joy of the yuletide. Zen Buddhism is becoming increasingly popular among the people of Shimla in recent times. The devotees of Zen, Sri Sathya Sai Baba, Radha Soami Satsang, Sri Sri Ravi Shankar's Art of Living, and many others hold regular formal and informal gatherings for chanting, prayers and singing devotional songs in the town, which are attended with fervour by all people.

However, the different communities largely limit themselves to their own in matters of marriage and cultural and religious observances. Interfaith initiatives are few and far between. Although there are occasional all-faith meetings and seminars attended by the leaders of the various communities, by and large, live and let live is the policy practised by the residents who do not evince more than passing interest in the culture and lifestyle followed by people from different origins living around them. Yet, there is complete acceptance of the differences and the people of all communities foster strong neighbourly and friendly relations with each other. The people of Shimla are people at peace. Surrounded by the beauty of nature, blessed with simplicity of the heart and, relationships nurtured in serenity—yes, it can be said that the people of Shimla are truly *swargvasis*.

Real Shimla in Reel Shimla

USHA BANDE

'Ah, Shimla! You know, we have also seen your Simla... in *Love in Simla*, of course!'

Expressions such as these were often heard when you said you came from Shimla. That was in the 1960s. *Love in Simla* had captured the cine-goers' fancy across the country with the 'sweet Bengali boy' (Joy Mukerji) and the 'cute little girlie' (Sadhana), playing the lead roles and cooing love lyrics across the historic Mall Road. Concepts like travel, weekend getaways, and taking a quick break being unknown in those days, very few people could visit Shimla. Moreover, Kashmir was the hot favourite with film producers and the viewers, by and large, were satisfied with the romantic visions of the hills—be it Srinagar or Gulmarg. But once Bollywood discovered Shimla and its splendour, they could not but return to it again and again. Besides its exotic charm and the colonial ambience of its setting, Shimla offered a peaceful working environment to the film-units. The local people, disciplined and peaceful, were usually content to stand patiently watching the shooting—a patience one could hardly find in other cities. Wish we could say this now. Frankly, Shimla of the new millennium is not the same. Remember, how Shahid Kapur and Kareena Kapoor were mobbed here during the shooting of *Jab We Met*? Times change and so do towns and cities. Change becomes obvious when we juxtapose the old and the new, and it is here that the old movies vis-à-vis the new provide clues to the changes that have come over in the last half-a-century.

From the 1960s—*Love in Simla* and *Tere Ghar Ke Samne*—to the recent ones like *Jab We Met, Kareeb* and the action-based love story *Badal*, a large number of films have depicted Shimla in its myriad hues and many moods—romantic, brooding, thrilling and chilling. But it is its 'romantic' aspect that holds on; the picture of a dream-like place where starry-eyed lovers sing amorous songs, dance around the verdant slopes and forget the fret and fume of a more protean existence. Every town has a personality—a *Sthalapurana*, as Raja Rao, the novelist terms it in his novel *Kanthapura*. This means every place has some myth or legend attached to it. The legend ascribed to Shimla is of 'romance'. Since the early British days Shimla signified ball-dances, frivolities and flirting. Go to Rudyard Kipling's writings, the letters of Emily Eton and the diaries of many British officers or their wives and you get an authentic glimpse of the social life here. The image stuck on and it was sustained conveniently by Bollywood. The early light musicals started depicting young couples/lovers carefree and euphoric, lolling among the wild flowers, shuffling on the lush green grass, reading love poetry, and sliding down the snow-covered slopes of Kufri and the town soon became synonymous with love, fashion and romance. Within this framework, the more subtle aspects of its everyday life have found no takers. The celluloid world found another attraction in Shimla—its old, huge colonial-type abandoned houses and lonely wooded walks. These were used as ideal settings for suspense and rebirth movies. On the more profound side, its colonial ambience helped in giving potency to thought-provoking themes as in *Black* (2004) and *Mein Aisa Hi Hoon* (2005).

Roughly, the movies depicting Shimla can be grouped as: (i) those fully shot in Shimla in which the theme and the locale complement each other; (ii) those partly portraying Shimla either in the first half or the second; and (iii) those in which Shimla has only a minor role to play as a backdrop for a song or two. The scenes flit past rapidly as the song and the singers move on, but surprise and joy may be the dominant emotion when familiar sights and landmarks are caught sight of.

Shimla is recognised immediately because of its prominent landmarks: the Mall, the Ridge, Christ Church with the thickly wooded Jakhoo Hill in the background. These have been fully and pleasantly exploited in many a movie. Other favourite locales are the ice-skating and the roller-skating rinks, Kufri in snow, the green slopes of Naldehra and the picturesque Chharabra valley. These locations figure in almost all movies showing skiing or song sequels. Among the educational institutions, Sacred Heart Convent popularly known as Tara Hall School, Chelsea that is the Convent of Jesus and Mary, and the Indian Institute of Advanced Study have played significant roles in films showing residential schools or working women's hostels and other institutions. Oberoi's Clarke Hotel, a favorite with the 1960s–1970s movies, Woodville Palace Hotel and Wild Flower Hall have lodged film personalities. In addition, reaching Shimla is a romantic experience and road or rail journey is portrayed with vim and vigour.

To find an excuse to set out on the journey, usually the hero or the heroine needs to go to Shimla—either for recuperating or to meet an old relative or for some music or dance performance. So, the 'reaching there' process begins with an exciting journey through the thickly wooded mountains. In *Love in Simla*, Dev (Joy Mukerji) boards the narrow-gauge train to reach Shimla to meet his fiancée. He is alone in his first class compartment and is at liberty to sing 'Dil Tham Chale Hum'. The film ends with his journey back, this time with Sonia, his newly-wedded bride. In the 1961 Shammi Kapoor starrer *Boy Friend*, Shammi in his inimitable style hops atop a Kalka-Shimla train drawn by a ZF locomotive. The song 'Mujhe Apna Yaar Bana Lo' continues till the train comes out of 103 tunnel and we feel the thrill. In *Dhadkan* (1972), Roopesh Kumar abducts a child from a moving Kalka-Shimla train; in *Daag* (1973) Sharmila Tagore travels with her little son aboard the Railcar—a heritage carriage; and in *Dost* (1974), Dharmendra travels to Shimla to visit his guardian, a priest in a local church. He nostalgically sings 'Gaddi Bula Rahi Hai' and remembers his father singing it to him in his childhood.

The road journey may not be as exotic as rail journey by the toy train but in some movies it is pictured convincingly and sometimes comically. In *Tere Ghar Ke Samne*, Dev Anand travels from Delhi to Shimla by scooter. He crosses Kethlighat valley and we see the fascinating road with wide open valleys on both sides. The road was free of hoardings and buildings in the 1960s, it is not so now. Reaching Shimla he stops at Oberoi's Clarkes, and hobbles to the reception bow-legged making a hilariously amusing sight. In *Woh Kaun Thi*, Manoj Kumar drives through mist and lashing rain on a zig-zag road when he meets the ghost (Sadhana's look-alike). In *Sanam Teri Kasam*, the protagonist Kamal Hasan is going to Shimla for a live music/dance performance. Reena Roy and her friends buy all the tickets of the last bus and the hero is directed to perform his journey on a mule. Since the movie is coloured, the scenery looks attractive—light green cheel pines, the lush green grass and the azure blue sky dotted with fleecy clouds.

So, we reach Shimla with the hero or the heroine and experience the vibrant town. Forgetting the hurly-burly, high-speed crowd far away in the plains, the characters imbibe in the salubrious surroundings. A typical Shimla scene is the rickshaw-drive through the Mall. Rickshaws have disappeared from Shimla roads since long but their presence in the old movies is reminiscent of the bygone era. In *Kudrat*, the heroine rides in a rickshaw in a shot showing her earlier birth. In *Love in Simla*, Joy Mukerji pulls the rickshaw with Sadhana sitting smugly in it. Singing, he runs past the Shimla Club, the thickly wooded road past US Club, the Ridge, the Scandal Point and on to the Mall through the Town Hall road. The row of shops like Ta-Tung, Rama, Hugh, and the fire station glide past and the Mall with very few pedestrians around looks somnolent. At the end of the rickshaw drive, the town vanishes but the director does not let us forget that we are in Shimla—there are intermittent references to Shimla gentry, Miss Shimla contest which obviously the heroine wins, *Simla News* (a bulletin) and the snow blizzard. One notices a few obvious changes that have come over the town—the Ashiana Restaurant was an open band stand, there was no Daulat Singh Park or the extended terrace of Padam Dev Complex. The Ridge was just one vast open space from north to south. The indoor scenes were shot in Raj Niwas—Peterhof near Chaura Maidan and one of my friends, whose father knew R.K. Nayyar, remembers how she and her sisters would run to Peterhof after school to see Sadhana and Joy Mukerji. *Love in Simla* brought real life romance in Sadhana and R.K. Nayyar's life. They got married soon after.

In more recent times, Shimla is the vibrant presence in Sanjay Leela Bhansali's *Black* (2004). Shot in Tara Hall School, Indian Institute of Advanced Study and Woodville, *Black* is a serious rendering of the emotional maturity of a special-need girl. Starring Amitabh Bachchan and Rani Mukherji, the film exploits the locale to the full to bring out the best in both—the theme and the site. The torrential rain of Shimla, the misty heights and the colonial nuances of the houses and Michelle McNally's dark world—all synchronise to produce the desired effect. Woodville, with its sprawling gardens, period furniture and the manor-type building is an ideal setting where Debraj Sahai (Amitabh Bachchan) tries to lead the deaf, dumb and blind Micheel (Rani Mukherji) into the world of light of knowledge. Sacred Heart Convent (Tara Hall) is the girls' dormitory whereas the massive and impressive Viceregal Lodge (Indian Institute of Advanced Study) is a university.

Another special need person's story set in Shimla is *Mein Aisa hi Hoon*, starring Ajay Devgan, Sushmita Sen, Esha Deol and Anupam Kher. As the autistic father Ajay Devgan fights with circumstances, his dim mental world matches the locale—dark at times and full of exuberance and light at others: like when his daughter's birthday is celebrated on the fun-filled Ridge. The movie is shot in the Convent of Jesus and Mary, Tara Hall (Sacred Heart Convent), the Woodville Palace Hotel and the Ridge. Some of the Tara Hall teachers recall how the school library was converted into a big book shop and how

The Toy Train

meeting the renowned stars was an exciting experience. While the Cecil Hotel was converted into hospital, Ashiana Fast food joint became Coffee Café Day. One feels intrigued when the hero rotates the cup to bring the Coffee Café Day emblem on the screen every time he serves coffee to some customer. Shots of Summerhill station and of Chaura Maidan with Dr Ambedkar's statue in the background provide a few more glimpses of the town.

Even those films that are partly shot in Shimla have an authentic sampling of the grandeur of nature and the appeal of the town. Let us take, for example, *Sanam Teri Kasam, Daag, Aa Gale Lag Ja, and Banarasi Babu, Khiladiyon ka Khiladi and Arzoo. Arzoo* has some of the most beautiful and powerful skiing scenes. These vigourous skiing shots are given by Prof M.L. Sharma, a veteran skater and skier of Shimla. Ask the lively professor and he will reminisce how he doubled for Rajendra Kumar during these shootings wearing identical clothes. The orphanage where Sadhana works after her paramour fails to keep his promise, was actually lodged in an old colonial bungalow atop Longwood hill, which is now a residential house. In *Woh Kaun Thi*, the ice-skating rink becomes the dominating presence all through the song 'Shokh Nazar ki Bijlian.' Prof Sharma and many Shimla skaters can be recognised during the skating sequel.

Colour photography lends charm to the scenery as the abundance of indigenous flora, the blue of the sky and the deep green grass under the massive trees present a fascinating view. In *Sanam Teri Kasam*, the Mashobara-Karignano hillside opens up a panoramic view as Reena Roy and Kamal Hasan dance through the expanse of wild white daisies before moving on to the Naldehra's velvety golf course. Though the scenic splendour generates a romantic atmosphere, one wonders how they could enter the golf course, entry to which is banned. In *Kudrat*, the hero and the heroine emboss their names on the trunk of a huge pine. So powerful is the visual effect of the scene that tourists often make a bee-line for the spot just to have a look at *the tree*. In *Daag*, Sharmila-Rajesh Khanna duo dance on the snow-covered slopes of Kufri, going on to Naldehra and other picturesque locations, while in *Aa Gale Lag Ja*, Sharmila-Shashi Kapoor pair lose themselves on the snowy heights of Kufri with predictable results. After these brief spells of heavenly bliss, the stories take a turn and Shimla no longer remains the focal point.

In *Tere Ghar Ke Samne*, the camera focuses on the Ridge, thence to Café d' Park below and to the Mall Road. Dev Anand stands on the Ridge near the Band Stand end (Ashiana Restaurant) and throws a half-eaten apple at Nutan sitting on a bench in the sun. Embarrassed, she sends her companion to get some chocolate and comically, the companion, who under command not to leave Nutan alone, just shouts, '*Chocolatewalle, Ek chocolate dena.*' This is humorous because we know there is no 'Chocolatewalla' on the Mall hawking his wares. We get a faint glimpse of a few shops in the background when the camera turns to Café d' Park. Later, in another situation, Dev Anand loiters on Shimla streets on a misty night, singing the famous S.D. Burman-Hasrat-Jaipuri number '*Tu kahan yeh bata, Is nasheeli raat mein...*'. The setting is tenderly romantic but it is not Shimla, only a made-up set.

In *Banarasi Babu* (1973), Dev Anand is again on the Ridge, this time with Yogita Bali. To tease his beloved, he flirts with a young collegiate out of the crowd standing there. These were local SDB College students. And, many Shimlaites, particularly college students of the 1970s watched this movie umpteen times to see themselves on the screen. There was a small joke in Shimla that the movie earned revenue because of these enthusiastic youngsters.

Lootmaar (1980), with five top villains of the Bollywood film industry—Amjad Khan, Kader Khan, Prem Chopra, Ranjit and Shakti Kapoor—was also shot in and around Shimla. One of its hit songs was '*Jab chhaye mera jadu, koi bach na paye.*' Among the new movies, Shimla makes its presence felt in *Jab We Met*. Kareena works in a school in Shimla after her heartbreak and stays in a working women's hostel—Tara Hall School converted as such. The movie also has shots of the Ridge, the Mall and the Town Hall. Interestingly the hero, Shahid Kapoor is seen in a taxi parked on the Mall.

The impact of Shimla on the thematic structure of the movie where the town plays only a nominal role may not be great but it cannot be denied that the overall effect of the town lingers on for long. For example, in *Kabhi-Kabhie*, Rishi Kapoor and Neetu Singh sing the familiar duet of poet Amit (Amitabh Bachchan), '*Kabhi kabhi mere dil mein khayal ata hai*' on the Ridge standing at its north end. The scene shifts to the Skating rink and within a fraction of a second to Kufri—a place that takes at least an hour to reach from Shimla.

Politically important as the summer capital of the British Raj, Shimla figures in movies dealing with the partition and freedom struggle themes. *Gadar*, based on the partition of India, was shot at the Convent of Jesus and Mary and in the Gaiety theatre. The sonorous song filmed here '*Ek mode aya, main dil chhod aya*' became an instant hit. In *Gandhi*, the Mahatma treks to Vice Regal Lodge to attend a meeting. He walks the distance partly because he likes to take long walks and also because he protests being driven in the man-drawn rickshaws.

Other movies that deserve mention are *Paanch Quaidi*, *Mukaddar ka Sikandar*, *Badalte Rishte*, *Kareeb*, *Anamika* and *Dillagi* known for their Shimla stint. In the Bobby Deol-Neha starrer *Kareeb* the Town Hall façade is converted into a civil hospital whereas the Fire Brigade office has a dry cleaner's board. *Kudrat* by Chetan Anand, *Raju Chacha* by Ajay Devgan, and *Badal* by Raj Kanwar have the salubrious setting of Woodville Palace hotel as also *Kaun Kaise*, *Bade Dilwale*, *Chori-chori*. Woodville Palace has a billboard showing photographs of the film personalities who visited it or stayed here and the staff can regale you with stories of the 'shooting' days and their interaction with the *filmy* personalities.

A 1975–1976 movie *Main Tulsi Tere Anagan Ki* shows Nutan going up the lift—a wonder of Shimla in those days—and heading for Bandeliers (a big shop on the Mall) to sell her *mangalsutra*. At the counter, Prof M.L. Sharma is the sales person who dissuades her from taking this extreme step. Of the forthcoming movies, *Wapsi* and a murder mystery *Ssshhh!* are set in Shimla. Also, a film on the life of Dhananjoy Chatterjee who was sentenced to death for raping and killing a minor girl is slated to be shot here. It is titled *Mera Jeevan Kora Kagaz*. To mention a few more films: *Manzil, Anjana* (new), Sunil Dutt-Mumtaz hit *Gauri*, Nana Patekar starer *Aanch*, Shah Rukh Khan's *Maya Memsa'b*, and O.P. Dutta directed *LOC-Border II* are all located in and around Shimla. In *Mujhse Dosti Karogi* (2002), Hrithik Roshan, Rani Mukherji and Kareena are residents of Shimla, and while the locale moves to London, for a major part of the film, Shimla holds its sway.

Shimla may be a distant place for South Indian movie-makers, but after MGR-hit *Anbe Vaa*, many Tamil and other language films accepted Shimla as an exhilarating locale for a few shots. The latest to be shot is *Desamuduru*.

No piece of writing on Shimla and films can be termed complete without the mention of the stalwarts who belonged to Shimla and who took pride in recounting the carefree life they enjoyed here. These are Amrish Puri and Prem Chopra, the dreaded villains of the film world. Prem Chopra studied in SD School and later in B.M. College. He often speaks nostalgically of his 'Shimla days,' recollecting how his interest in extra-curricular activities formed his personality and helped him in getting into the film industry. Amrish Puri loved the Shimla of the 1940s and 1950s when he was studying in DAV School and in B.M. College. Shimla was then a small town having a lot of community feeling. Another Shimlawalla to make his mark in Bollywood is Anupam Kher. Studying in Government College, Sanjauli in the 1970s, he was often more interested in dramatics than in classroom studies and his professors still remember taking him to task for bunking classes to make a dash for rehearsals. Vijay Kashyap, a student of SDB College, first made his presence felt on the small screen in *Tenali Raman*, a TV serial, before getting into the celluloid world. Late Manohar Singh could often be seen strolling with a cheerful mien and a light gait on the Mall, in summers. Parikshit Sahni was known to visit Shimla during holidays where his father,

Balraj Sahni had bought a house. He recollects his time spent in Shimla as full of fun and frolic.

Of the women actresses, the youngest, Shreya Sharma of *The Blue Umbrella* fame is at present a student of class X in Tara Hall School. Then, there is the all-time favourite Preity Zinta, a student of psychology at St. Bede's College, Shimla. Her teachers speak proudly of Preity who was also Miss Shimla. Ranjita and Priya Rajvansh studied in Shimla. Those living in the erstwhile Central Hotel near the High Court remember Ranjita as a school girl. Among the seniors, Mona Singha, popularly known as Kalpana Kartik, was studying in St. Bede's College in the early 1950s when Vijay Anand chanced to meet her. He introduced her in *Baazi* opposite Dev Anand. In his autobiography *Romancing with Life*, Dev Anand recounts his early days with Mona when they were madly in love. Very few of us probably know that Meera Nair, the director of *Salaam Bombay* is the product of Tara Hall School.

Not only the major landmarks, but even the crowd, a glimpse of someone wearing Himachali cap, or someone draped in Shimla shawl, an HRTC bus whizzing past—all add to the excitement of seeing Shimla in the tinsel world. Indeed, so prominent and profound is the presence of Shimla in the celluloid world that when the town flits past on the screen, it is always 'Look Shimla... Shimla!' from all those who stay here and also from those who have visited it maybe only once.

Quite the Adopted Child—the Legacy of Shimla's Architecture

RAAJA BHASIN

One didn't realise that then, but we were riding the steadily thinning tail of one of history's more extraordinary episodes. India was independent. The colonising British had been gone for a decade and some. Among the dozens of things that they had left behind, were 'Irish ish-tew', (not stew, and of which one critical ingredient was Marmite), kut-less (not cutlets), kus-tur (not custard) and there were sahibs, lesser sahibs and still lesser ones of assorted colours that ate all this on a regular basis and approved. Serviettes were not called napkins and Sunday morning breakfast of a plain *paratha* topped by a fried egg was eaten with a fork and knife. Almost needless to add, when we went for elocutions and debates, we were told to 'speak for God's sake, not sing'. A part of that big huge jumble generated by British presence in India, was in the towns and houses which were well on their way to being as much of a hybrid and as much a part of everyday life as the food or that sing-song lilt could be.

My parents, both of whom worked, needed to procure an *ayah* to take care of me when I came along. The lady that found an altogether brief employment in the house, claimed an added qualification when she took a look at them and declared: 'I have never worked for dark people before.' My mother (whose complexion is fairer than many 'whites'), I believe, as mildly as ever said: 'None of us can help the way we look. That is normally decided by Someone Else.'

But then that was the Simla that had still not acquired that 'h' after the S for the postmen to call 'Shimla'.

When I was all of ten and some five feet tall, and the snow fell and a path for pedestrians was cleared on the Mall and the Ridge, I still could not see over the top of that cold trench. Perhaps we looked at Shimla that way too. We could see only what we could in that furrow that steadily filled with slush while the sides turned greyer and oddly dustier with every passing day. At best, one could look up every once in a while and see a sky that could turn from bright blue to dark and sombre within moments and the deodar branches weighted down by snow.

For an Indian, especially one with no claims to the pecking order, the fifties and the sixties were perhaps the best time to have lived in Shimla. The town was free of a measure of the snobbishness and social divisions of the Raj. And it was still free of all the pressures that arrived with burgeoning urbanisation that drove one tourist who came to savour the 'peace and beauty of the hill station' to remark that 'today's Shimla was nothing but a Ludhiana on a hill top.' While that industrial town of the Punjab may well have more than just noise, congestion and factories that churn out woollies and lathes to recommend it, Shimla was fast losing the grace and elegance that it was once known for. The 'Queen of Hill Stations', where the word 'queen' was used in its older and corrector sense, could with the passage of years also be taken to mean the jaded and tired and sad 'queens' one knows of now.

The architecture which was to give Shimla its distinctive character, slots itself into reasonably clear time-frames. The first period began when the 'Gurkha wars' came to an end in 1816. In 1821, Charles Pratt Kennedy, the newly appointed British 'Political Agent' to the Hill States built Shimla's first 'permanent' residence—though we are told that there were 'a few miserable shepherds' huts' in the area.

Within a few years, the hills around Kennedy House were dotted by houses built mainly by European invalids from the plains.

In 1828, the commander-in-chief, Lord Combermere visited the hill station and his acutely observant aide-de-camp, Captain Mundy noted of the typical house in Shimla, a pattern that later varied but did not really alter, 'The houses of the English residents are neatly and scientifically built of unmortared stone, intersected horizontally, at intervals of two feet, by pine beams dove-tailed at the angles. Many have flat roofs covered with a red clay, which requires many days labour to beat it into a solid cake impervious to rain. Others have sloping or gable roofs, formed of fir planks or of flakes of clay slate, of which there are plentiful quarries in the vicinity. Outhouses, stables and huts are commonly erected in the compound material styled "wattle and daub", and thatched with the bark and even with the dried leaves of the pine.'

(Interestingly, a decade later, Governor-General Lord Auckland's sister, Emily Eden observed that the 'beaten earth' of the roof was not all that 'impervious to rain' and residents often had to move around the house with open umbrellas—and even dined or read under them.)

While his stay was brief, Combermere built the town's first water tank and bridge over the stream which was then named after him. He also traced the path that Shimla's Mall was to follow and form the core of the town's character—and is believed to have paid for the expenses from his own pocket.

The Mall steadily developed as the town's commercial street and the hub of its social life. This road, which is some five kilometres in length, starts in the west at the gates of the former Viceregal Lodge, the present-day Indian Institute of Advanced Study and ends at Chhotta Shimla, 'small' Shimla, in the east. The route has bends, as one would expect any hill road to have, but it essentially follows a wide sweeping curve along the hills. The primary aspect is south facing and affords a view of the valley below the town and of the foothills that reach out to the plains. In pockets, snatches of the northern aspect spring up for a dramatic view and hold woods of pine and Himalayan cedar—the majestic deodar.

At the beginning—or at the end—of that road, lies the former Viceregal Lodge. This is easily the grandest building in Shimla—and may well rank among the more magnificent creations that the British Empire sprinkled over the world. It was from here that for the better part of every year, one-fifth of the human race was governed for well over five decades.

Atop 'Observatory Hill,' the site for Viceregal Lodge was selected by Lord Lytton, who was viceroy between 1876 and 1880. The original residence of the governors-general and viceroys was 'Peterhof', on the neighbouring hill. Like Peterhof, Observatory Hill (where an observatory had stood in the 1840s), is a watershed and figuratively stands astride India. The waters from one side pour down to the Bay of Bengal and from the other, find their way to the Arabian Sea. In Lord Dufferin's tenure (1884-88), the plans were redrawn, and the Lodge built. He occupied it during the final months of his stay in India. The structure that finally rose from the ground had a style of architecture of what was loosely termed as 'English Renaissance' and drew inspiration from the forms of the Elizabethan era—though elements of Scottish castles are quite overwhelming. The building is of light blue-grey stone masonry with tiled pitch roofings.

With wrought stone-work embellishment, the main block has three storeys and the kitchen wing has five. A tower strikes above the rest of the building and its height was increased during Lord Curzon's tenure (1899-1905). In Lord Irwin's time (1926-31), a public entry building was added in 1927. By this date the character of the building with all the strength of its limbs, fine features, or distorted architectural grimaces—depending on the point of view, was formed and remain to the present day. This was the first building with electric light in Shimla and for the interior, a massive shipment of teak was summoned from Burma to create the ornate panelling. Apart from the fact that this was where the viceroy and his council took their decisions, it was here that several momentous meetings and conferences also took place. This was the venue of the Simla Conference in 1945. In 1947, many of the discussions that led to the partition of India took place within the walls of Viceregal Lodge. After Independence in 1947, the building became the property of the president of India and was renamed Rashtrapati Niwas. At the instance of the president of India, Dr S. Radhakrishnan, on 6 October 1964, the Indian Institute of Advanced Study came into being as a Society. The following year, on 20 October, the Institute was formally inaugurated at Shimla by the president and housed in the Lodge where it remains.

The core of the Mall is the row of shops that take the approximate mid-section of the road and traverse this for about a kilometre and a half along its length. At one point of time, this was regarded to be as fashionable as the finest streets of London, Paris or St. Petersburg and every morning, the tarmac was washed down by *mashks* carrying goatskin bags full of water. Architecturally, this stretch is often likened to an English small-town marketplace. Elements of Tudor framing, a varied roofline, assorted columns and numerous decorations have given this row considerable character. The row also has a variety of windows that range from bay, to sash-barred and to diamond-cut panes and some unusual elements also find expression and take the form of Mughal-inspired cupolas that hold bay windows. Reminiscent of Italy, acroteria of urns can be found on a couple of structures. While decorative devices abound, the aspects of safety were hardly neglected. The presence of 'fire walls' between buildings ensured that fires remained contained and did not spill over to the adjoining structures.

Apart from the shops, where several buildings still retain elements of a bygone lustre, the street holds the famous Gaiety Theatre whose neo-Gothic structure was completed in 1887 and once towered above the town. The theatre itself is modelled after the prize-winning design of a bijou theatre and is remarkable for the quality of its acoustics that allow the lowest whisper to carry to the farthest corner of the hall. Adding to the Mall's ambience, are the Municipal Offices housed in an impressive dressed-stone building. The General Post Office and the spire of Christ Church on the Ridge, add their own touches of background atmosphere—even if the post office was once described as 'wild west Tudor'. At the crossroads where one arm reaches to the Ridge and another to the Post Office, is the famous 'Scandal Point'.

The southern slopes immediately below this row of shops are regarded to be one of the most densely populated hill slopes in the world. Over a hundred years ago, the celebrated writer Rudyard Kipling described this stretch in *Kim* as, 'The crowded rabbit-warren that climbs up from the valley to the Town Hall at an angle of forty-five. A man who knows his way there can defy all the police of India's summer capital. So cunningly does veranda communicate with veranda, alley-way with alley-way, and bolt hole with bolt hole.' The description holds true even today.

A major determinant of the town's character and social ethos, the Mall has modified its colonial and rather snooty ambience to reflect the Indian market-centric lifestyle. Yet, the original colonial architecture, somewhat crumbling, somewhat forlorn and yet, almost unforgivingly still its spine, the street remains the town's social hub and for many, also its economic core.

The finest of Shimla's architecture was created when it officially became the 'summer capital' of British India in 1864. This coincided with the time period that is often called the 'high noon' of the British Empire. From a sort of cold storage that had begun even before the Second World War, the drastic alteration and the erosion of the character and environment of Shimla began in the 1970s.

Imperial edifices were built with all the grandeur, complacency and aggressive display of colonial power. Architects like Sir Swinton Jacob, Henry Irwin, the Colonels Boileau and Abbott, created remarkable structures like the Viceregal Lodge, the Town Hall, the Norman Baronial district courts, the rather gaunt Imperial Civil Secretariat at Gorton Castle while the various churches drew on assorted aspects of the Gothic vocabulary.

A superb example of mock Tudor framing still exists at Barnes Court, the present-day Raj Bhavan. Cast iron for both structural and decorative purposes was extensively used at Ellerslie—the present-day Secretariat of the government of Himachal Pradesh, the Army headquarters and most remarkably, in the Railway Board Building.

At times regarded as the monuments to a collective ego, the imperial structures of Shimla are more than just that. Derived from mainly European models, these buildings were the *baba-log* of their pure-bred parents. These children were the embodiment of colonial power, the knowledge of that power and the aggressive assertion of that power. If Shimla represented colonial and imperial authority in India, the buildings were a constant reminder of that authority to those with it, and to those without. If these structures were disposed of the function of fortresses, they maintained that aspect if only for visual and psychological reasons.

Somewhat away from imperial architecture, were the houses of colonial Shimla. The primary function of the bungalows, cottages and flats was residential—although some also functioned as offices and depending on a host of seemingly unconnected factors like the occupant's position, appropriate dimensions, suitable variations and assorted embellishments were added on. Constraints of terrain, climate, sun and wind orientation, woodland and the fact whether the property was owned by the government or by the individual were also considerations.

The most notable characteristic of these houses is that the composition is European, while the structural elements are vernacular. This is quite unlike the theme of domination that is apparent elsewhere. Shimla's domestic architecture stands out for here, two schools with totally different backgrounds have met as equals on the same plane and have intertwined quite happily. In most cases, local workers, working with local materials on local principals have created buildings as diverse as country manors and neo-Tudor dwellings seen in the British Isles, to Swiss-Bavarian chalets from the Alps. Mature and efficacious structural methodology from the Himalaya was modified

Earlier view of the GPO, the Mall, Town Hall and the Church

or redesigned to suit different requirements and markedly different lifestyles. The result was a curious mingling of forms from all over the world, and each abode was highly aesthetic, functional and at one time, quite inexpensive to build. If the imperial structures of Shimla created the face of the town, these houses gave it the body and character.

The local timber-framed structure—*dhajji*—was extensively used. Conditioned to a European floor plan, the load-bearing wooden posts were set into a shallow but stable foundation of stone. The vertical members were then spanned by horizontal beams creating a mesh of wooden framework. Within each square, normally two feet by two, corner to corner wooden planks were fitted in a diagonal cross. The open space was filled with stone held together by a mortar of clay or slaked lime or cement. This was then completely plastered over, completely on the inside, and at times only partially on the exterior leaving the main wooden frame decoratively exposed in the Tudor fashion. Variations were made by mixing pine needles or straw into the mortar, and this provided greater binding power as well as insulation.

The practicality and desirability of the relatively easily maintained *dhajji* construction can be gauged from the devastating earthquake of 1905. Shimla rests on a seismic anti-cline and it was the inherent 'elasticity' of this building method that prevented extensive damage to both life and property. Nearby Dharamsala, built almost entirely with stone was virtually destroyed.

The floors and ceilings were invariably made of deal planks, though as a variation wood parquet was sometimes used on the floor and *papier mache* or plaster mouldings and recessed panels were used on the ceilings. Fireplaces were built into almost all major rooms. The roofs were of shingle or slate, but when in 1843, the mass production of corrugated galvanised iron sheets began in Britain, it was only a matter of time before this became the standard norm for almost all roofing in Shimla—and in almost every other 'hill station' in the country.

The bungalow was already an evolved and developed form by the time it arrived in Shimla. The typical one was built as a single level on a standard floor plan. There was a porch or verandah, then the entrance hall: the dining room was on one side and the drawing on the other, with bedrooms at the back. Where the house was double-storied, the bedrooms moved upstairs. Dimensions, the addition and location of a study or morning room, maybe a billiards' room and a library were the only real variations.

Kitchens and their smoking fireplaces were often relegated to the outhouses, reached through a covered passageway connected to the pantry. As the number of servants was large—a dozen or more were attached to an 'ordinary' household—the system functioned fairly well. In later years, the outdoor kitchen moved in, and it is interesting to see a house that has rooms of large proportions and a tiny kitchen—often a converted pantry. Adjuncts to the main house were rows of servants' quarters, a rickshaw shed, stables and occasionally a cowshed.

The constraints of terrain and the absence of an adequate number of naturally flat spaces, as well as the difficulty of transporting materials created their own innovations and every single structure was somehow different. For example, if the site lay at a drop from the path, the main access was provided at the second or even third level of the building: a short bridge connected the road and one climbed down—instead of the normal up—to many rooms. In some cases, a covered stairway or rough path climbed precariously down the hillside to provide individual accesses to every floor. Another variation was that the main door was placed at the back of the house while the windowed front with no provision of ingress or egress, faced the valley.

One of the interesting peculiarities of the old houses of Shimla, is that almost none is designed, at least internally to face the bitter winter. This was the direct result of the annual migration to the plains in early November when the government shifted to Calcutta and later, New Delhi and remained away till late March. The skylights, ventilators, *louvres* and large rooms with high ceilings could have belonged to the 'civil lines' of any colonial station in the plains. Yet, the presence of fireplaces and the basic insulation of the materials used, mitigated the cold to a considerable extent.

While *dhajji* remained the most popular form of construction, it was by no means the only one. Locally available stone and brick were also used to impart strength to taller structures, at times, stone was used for the first level, brick for the second, *dhajji* for the third and wooden planks for the attic—and this successively lightened the load.

Apart from the bungalows, there were also shop-houses, flats and smaller cottages. Almost all the larger structures of Shimla of the twentieth century were constructed in these mediums. In place of *dhajji*, many of them have stone or brick—sticking to wood for the floors and ceilings, and many have wooden tiles or planks set over concrete floors.

While the interior of every house was inevitably different, ranging from the Spartan bare-minimum to the richly elaborate, it is the external ornamentations—both practical and decorative—that are worth observing in detail. Gables with finials and decorated bargeboards, skylights and dormer windows break the monotony of the lines. Many of the long low houses have their canopies and deep eaves richly decorated. One of the more remarkable embellishments was of the finely turned and corbelled features that are seen on Alpine chalets. Valances on the south facing windows and verandahs were seldom plain; if they did not have a jewel-like tasselled fringe, they were at the very least, modestly fret-worked. Gothic revival occasionally cropped up on voussoired windows, and Doric or Corinthian columns on porches and even alongside windows and were often preferred to simple wooden members. Balusters and engrailed arches covered whole ranges of design.

Windows were richly varied. While the bay window—often acting as a door to the verandah or terrace—was very popular, there are examples of sash, Venetian and Georgian windows too. Glass panes and even art-deco stained glass were used in all sorts of patterns, and the diamond cut was not uncommon.

One has lived in houses both solid and stolid. Those that have stood a quake or two and with walls wide enough to take two chimney flues back to back. So thick were they, that going from one room to the next, one felt that one was passing through a short corridor and my pre-teen arms could not touch them end to end. Today's corridors may be built of row upon row of concrete blocks and one may howl and wail all the way from Tuttikandi to Sanjauli and still have laments left over for Bhattakuffar and Rhuldubhatta. Shimla has changed, and it will change some more...and then some. What will that change be...something to make us yet again a littler older, and yet again no wiser....The legacy of Shimla's colonial architecture seems so much like that dearly loved 'adopted child.' 'Mine, but not mine.'

My Job, Paintings and Mexican Scholarship

SATISH GUJRAL

The agonies of Partition left their impact on all those who were witnesses. Over time, the horrific scenes I saw no longer created in me the same intensity of revulsion I used to feel in the beginning. My senses succumbed to a gradual hardening. No calamity seemed to affect my numbed perceptions, which had frozen into a block. During those days I worked for rehabilitating refugee women with my parents.

After Partition, my father's membership in Pakistan's parliament had been transferred to the Indian parliament. My mother was unwilling to abandon the women under her care and let them go to government-run refugee camps which had rapidly become like brothels. My father had very little choice in the matter. He could not think of being separated from his wife and spending part of his life away from her in Delhi. He decided to make his home in Jallandhar. He resigned from the Indian parliament and started the Nari Niketan (women's home) in Jallandhar. It was gradually opened to women other than victims of the Partition.

Once the work of rehabilitating refugee women was over, I began to look around for a job. My father could no longer afford to support me. There was no question of my starting another graphic art studio of the kind I had earlier set up at Lahore. The best I could hope for was to get a job as a graphic artist. Fortunately, my father's friend Dr Gopi Chand Bhargava was elected the first chief minister of the Indian half of Punjab. The department of public relations which employed graphic artists was directly under him. In the summer of 1948, I joined this department at Shimla.

The job was a reasonably well-paid one. With it came a house that was too large for my needs. However, my joy at being able to earn my own money was short-lived. A government office is not the best place for an artist to give free rein to his creative faculties. My immediate boss, Lajpat Rai Nair, was an erudite man but not sophisticated enough to appreciate art. He also had his own problems. The director-general of the department was Shri Virender, a scion of the family which had founded the Urdu newspaper *Pratap*. He was the eldest son of Mahasha Krishan, its chief editor and member of the Congress party in the Punjab Assembly. His status empowered him to boss over our department.

It did not take very long for my superiors to conclude I was a misfit, and would not be able to draw pictures of the kind appreciated by Urdu or other vernacular papers of the time. They began to look for excuses to get rid of me. I gave them a convenient one soon after I joined the department.

I was asked to design a poster against the hoarding of food grains and profiteering in general. The man I portrayed as the prototype of a black marketeer had an uncanny resemblance to the state food minister. Though I had designed the poster many weeks before the fellow was elevated to ministerial rank, he was incensed by the adverse publicity he received. Even before he took the oath of office he had decided to teach me a lesson. He found my superiors more than willing to oblige him. They were devious in the way they went about it. They knew that if I was sacked for drawing the minister's likeness, they could be in trouble themselves. So they dug into my past to see if they could discover some skeletons in my cupboard. They found what they were looking for in police files: my association with the Communist Party. I was proud of my leftist past and foolish enough to brag about it. Isher Singh Majhail, the minister in question, was an Akali and had many scores to settle with the Communists. He found me an easy prey. I no longer had the protection of Dr Bhargava who had been replaced by Bhim Sen Sachar. I was ordered to either resign or be fired. I chose to resign.

During my years in Shimla I had plenty of spare time to paint. I began with scenes of the Partition and its horrendous aftermath, which were still fresh in my mind. This theme was closest to my heart. It is possible that had there been no Partition I might have invented some traumatic and overwhelming scenario to express the anguish in my heart. I was ploughing a lonely furrow. I knew no one who could assess the quality of my work.

Fortunately, one day in 1950, I ran into my old friend and mentor, Sardari Lall Prasher. Having lost the Mayo School of Arts to Pakistan, he had come to Shimla to try and set up something of the same kind in the half of the Punjab that came to India.

I had not met Prasher since I left Mayo five years earlier. Renewing my acquaintance with him proved very worthwhile. He was surprised to see my work. He was not a man of many words, so the little he said in the way of encouragement bolstered my sagging spirits.

In 1949, there was a lot of talk about building a new capital for the Indian Punjab. Shimla was then the temporary seat of the Punjab government. It was swarming with the top brass of anglicised civil servants who feverishly imitated the lifestyle of their erstwhile rulers. They were pressurising Nehru to invite a foreign architect to design the new city. Leading the group was P.N. Thapar, the senior-most ICS officer in the state, who held the post of financial commissioner (development). Thapar had recruited P.L. Verma, the chief engineer of Punjab, and Avatar Singh Malhotra, the finance secretary; both men shared Thapar's enthusiasm for everything Western.

Pandit Nehru resisted the pressure put on him by Thapar. He had earlier criticised the grandiose designs of the Viceregal Lodge and the secretariats by Lutyens and Baker in New Delhi. If it had to be a foreign architect, Nehru's preference was for the American, Albert

Mayer. Mayer was in India during the Second World War and had established a bond with leaders of the freedom movement, including Mahatma Gandhi and Pandit Nehru. He had impressed them with his ideas about building model villages and reviving cottage industries. Prior to Mayer's arrival in the Punjab, Thapar and his associates had tried to hire the American Frank Lloyd Wright as chief architect. Wright declined the offer on grounds of age and failing health. Mayer suggested the name of the Polish-American architect Javersky, a young man of surprising sensitivity towards Indian culture and architecture. Prasher and I, who had the privilege of meeting Javersky and seeing his early sketches, were impressed by how much he had imbibed the atmosphere prevailing in India's bazaars and bylanes.

Young Javersky was not destined to have a hand in the designing of Punjab's new capital. On his return flight to India, he died when his plane crashed at Cairo.

Thapar and his friends persuaded Nehru to accept three Euiropean architects to work with Mayer. They were Charles Edouard Corbusier, popularly known as Le Corbusier, who brought with him a team consisting of his cousin Pierre Jeanneret, Maxwell Fry and his wife Jane Drew, who was an architect in her own right. She was also the chief reason for Corbusier agreeing to accept an assignment to work in the remote land of heat and dust. Her liaisons with Corbusier and many others were as famous as Corbusier's buildings round the globe. When Corbusier was appointed, Mayer left. Corbusier set up his office in Shimla. Young aspiring architects from all over India came in swarms to seek employment in the new venture.

At the time I was living in the YMCA where many of these hopefuls were staying. Among them was an American named Ted Bower. Bower had been a student and the alter ego of Frank Lloyd Wright. He had come to Shimla to get acquainted with his mentor's bete noire, Corbusier, and study his plans to build a new city—or as he put it, 'to witness the seeding of a foreign culture, in an ancient land'.

According to Bower, Corbusier disregarded indigenous styles and never made a secret of his contempt for anything which did not fit in with his preconceived notions.

Bower's analysis of the trends in architecture proved to be prophetic. Corbusier based his plans for Chandigarh upon the time-worn cliché of 'form follows function'. His admirers treated it as a sacred mantra. What they called functional architecture turned out to be more his own concepts rather than the users' or clients' notion of what they wanted. In common parlance, this phrase meant architecture for the sake of architecture. His buildings exhibit a marked indifference towards local cultures around which communities have traditionally created their habitats, in the way birds construct their nests according to the shapes of their own bodies. Architecture that ignores this time-tested rule becomes artificial. Even decades after its construction, Chandigarh continues to manifest a duality of cultures: the culture of its inhabitants and the culture of its architecture. The two never seem to reconcile.

Corbusier's acolytes never ease to praise his pioneering work in India. They describe him as Pandit Nehru's own choice for the project. There is no truth in this assertion. Even if it had been so, it does not change my opinion that what Corbusier built has little relevance to the Punjabi ethos.

In a letter addressed to the then governor of the Punjab, Nehru wrote:

> Last night Mr Corbusier had dinner with me. In answer to my question as to what Indian style of architecture Chandigarh was going to have, he replied, 'You wear trousers, drive autos and have adopted the Westminster style of democracy and yet you ask for an Indian style of architecture. There is no Indian style.' this man worries me. Please keep an eye on him.

This letter still exists in the archives of the Prime Minister's Secretariat.

Sometime late in 1951, before I lost my job with the Punjab government, I ran into Charles Fabri and his Indian wife Ratna Mathur who had been with me at Mayo.

The most widely discussed artist at the time was Amrita Sher-Gil, whose untimely death a little earlier had elevated her into a cult figure. There were scores of women artists who dreamt of filling Amrita's shoes. One of them was Ratna Mathur. She intended to join Bhubesh Sanyal's studio but he had more students than he could accommodate. Charles Fabri persuaded her to abandon the idea. She was completely taken in by Fabri's claim that he had made Amrita Sher-Gil the greatest figure in the art world. He convinced Ratna that he could do the same for her as she had the same potential as Amrita. He promised to raise her to great heights.

Ratna joined the Mayo School. Fabri took her under his wing. Ratna was convinced that Fabri had the magic formula by which he would open vistas of future greatness for her. Fabri came to see her in her classroom almost every hour and left her in high spirits. She applied herself to her work with demonic zeal and eagerly awaited his next visit.

Ratna was like one in a trance. Despite her father's strong opposition, she became Mrs Charles Fabri. Both of them died tragically. Charles' last days were full of financial difficulties; his age and falling health did not allow him to take on more work. He took his own life. Ratna died a few years later while still in her prime and busy as ever.

My first meeting with the Fabris in Shimla was very significant. I invited both of them to see my work. Fabri's comments were most flattering; he was prone to exaggerate and write in superlative terms when he liked something. I was not aware of this at the time. He talked of the great murals that were being painted in Mexico and compared my canvases to the best in that country. That was the first time I heard of Mexico as the home of mural art.

My earlier acquaintance with Mexico was through the myths of Mayan culture I had heard before I became deaf. According to *kathas* narrated by pundits in the Mohalla Chowk in Jhelum, Mexico was the *firangi* (foreign) name of *patal*, the underworld. I was fascinated by the idea of this mythological subterranean country. The significance of *patal desh*, according to these pundits, was that the Pandavas had migrated here after realising the hollowness of their victory in the battle of Kurukshetra. The legend was given a 'scientific' gloss by a fraudulent anthropologist, Chiman Lal, who had been in jail with my father. In his book *Hindu America*, he propounded the thesis that the Inca and Aztec civilisations of Latin America had Hindu origins. According to him, the Pandavas had named Argentina in honour of their warrior sibling Arjuna, and Yucatan, the coastal area of Mexico, was a distortion of the word 'Yogistan'.

After listening to Charles Fabri, I began to conjure up a new image of Mexico. More so as Fabri thought it was the place I should go to for inspiration. At about the same time I came across an advertisement issued by the ministry of education announcing a scholarship to study painting in Mexico. The year was 1952. I decided to apply for the scholarship. When it came to filling out the application form, I realised that I had nothing to support my claim except a diploma from the Mayo School of Arts. Fortunately, I remembered my connection with Charles Fabri, who had settled in New Delhi and was writing regularly on art for the *Statesman*. On a hot June afternoon, my brother Inder and I knocked on the door of Fabri's apartment in the Shahjahan Road barracks.

As we pushed through the half-open door, we were astonished to see Fabri standing stark naked. Without being in the least discomfited he asked us to sit down and took his seat in front of his typewriter, which he had left to answer our knock.

I told him of the Mexican scholarship and asked for a recommendation. Without wasting time on formalities he pushed a fresh sheet of paper into his typewriter and hammered out words which remain engraved in my memory. It was a glowing tribute to my talents as a painter. After handing me the testimonial he warned Inder not to build up too much hope about my chances.

Armed with Fabri's recommendation, we went to India Coffee House to show it to our friends. To my pleasant surprise, they suddenly began to see in me talent they had never before suspected. Among these regulars at the Coffee House was an old classmate of

Inder's—a stenographer on the board which interviewed applicants for scholarships. He did not pretend to have any influence but promised to keep us informed of what transpired at the interviews. Considering our limited contacts, we were delighted with this offer.

A few days later, our stenographer friend told Inder that the Mexican cultural attaché, who had the final say in the selection, had recommended my name to the ministry as his first choice. The cultural attaché was none other than the celebrated Mexican Poet Octavio Paz, who later won the Nobel Prize for literature.

The next hurdle was getting a passport. I knew that I would never get clearance from the Punjab Police. I had to think of other ways to obtain it. In June 1952, Nehru made a minor reshuffle in his cabinet and inducted Mr R.K. Sidhwa as head of the ministry of home affairs. Sidhwa had been in the same jail as my father. My father took me to see him and explained my predicament.

Sidhwa advised me to apply from Delhi. In the normal course of things, the passport officer in Delhi would have referred the case to the Punjab Police, which would have taken a long time. Using this as a pretext, Sidhwa effectively sidelined reference to Punjab and had the Delhi Police give me a clearance. A passport was issued to me.

The news of my getting a scholarship to Mexico got around. I began to be taken more seriously by the Coffee House crowd. One of the regulars was S.H. Vatsyayan. He was impressed by my work and suggested I hold a one-man exhibition in Delhi before leaving for Mexico. He and his wife-to-be, Kapila Malik, made arrangements to exhibit my paintings in the annexe of Freemasons Hall, located between Hotel Imperial and the main building of the Cottage Industries Emporium on Janpath. Vatsyayan wrote the introduction to the catalogue and persuaded Humayun Kabir to inaugurate the exhibition.

The Punjab government changed its attitude towards me and offered me a loan to meet the travel expenses not covered by my scholarship. I went to Shimla to collect the money and regain a little of the respect I had lost with my dismissal from my old job. The visit did much to inflate my ego.

However, there was one thing I did not accomplish on this visit. I was hoping to win the heart of a young lady I had seen soon after my arrival in Shimla in the summer of 1948. I had spotted her strolling on the Mall. She appeared to have a high-spirited nature and was conscious of her good looks and aware of men ogling her as she slid through the crowd. Basking in the attention showered on her, she would walk up and down the stretch between the Clark's Hotel at one end and Scandal Point at the other.

I was not the only one under her spell. She had a horde of admirers and was known among them as 'Miss .303' after the make of the rifle used during the Second World War. She was the epitome of vivacious sensual charm and was also said to be mature well beyond her eighteen years. As the summer wore on, my infatuation for her increased. It persisted through autumn and the snow and ice of winter. Instead of strolling on the Mall, most people went to the ice-skating rink. Miss .303 was a regular skater. I did not particularly enjoy skating as it was too rigorous a form of exercise for me and I liked to stay in my warm bed till mid-morning. But there I was, up at the crack of dawn, taking a quick bath and arriving at the skating rink by 7.30 a.m. Once a day was not enough. I was there again in the evening, and did not leave till the girl departed at closing time.

All my efforts to attract her attention were in vain. Miss .303 scarcely noticed my existence. I fantasised about her, converted my fantasies to imaginary conquests and boasted about them to my friends. She remained beyond my reach. She was always surrounded by admirers who dwarfed me by their physical strength and social status.

On my last visit to Shimla I felt that since I had become a minor celebrity, I stood a better chance of making her acquaintance. I was out of luck. She had left for England. Shimla was thick with rumours that she was infatuated with a Pakistani and intended to marry him.

Snotty Shimla: Past Imperfect, Future Tense

Deepak Sanan

I am yet to come across a really satisfactory explanation for the name Simla or Shimla as the locals have always called it. There are references to a temple devoted to a Shyamala Devi in some records as a possible source but hill folk have no memory of such a deity. Though the surveyor Gerard mentions a nearby village called Shemla—when the British first came on the scene—my favourite is a story that may not appeal to all sensibilities. The first British explorer to stand on the famous Ridge and gaze awestruck at the splendid autumn view of snow-capped peaks looked around and asked the first local he saw for a place name. A peasant woman cutting grass nearby was then in the act of helping clear her son's runny nose. 'Sheem la' she said and so it became even though she was only asking her son to blow his nose and get rid of the 'sheem' (snot for local hill folk).

For close to two hundred years now we have been adding much more to these hillsides than the snot that peasant lady wiped on the grass that day. There is another snotty perception on when the rot really set in. For upper-class old timers Simla (the official name change to Shimla was effected only in 1983) was a beautiful *Chota Vilayat* in British days and the change for the worse is of recent vintage. Pamela Kanwar's excellent account of 'Imperial Shimla' does much to expose the blind spot in this nostalgia. As she notes, 'the abiding impression is of a well-planned town, sparkling window panes and washed roads even though the majority lived in crouched subservience in the bazaar'.

From its early beginnings, Shimla was an enclave for the expatriates of the day that required a manifold number of natives to service their needs. The British lived in hotels, estates and cottages scattered along the forested spurs radiating north, west and south from the Jakhu hill. From thirty-odd buildings in 1830 to about a hundred in 1850 and something over four hundred by the turn of the century, this was the sum total of properties in the *gora log's* spread out domain. Their number in an 1898 count was 4,124 but the supporting cast of locals was 29,048! The latter were cramped into five bazaar areas occupying less than a tenth of Shimla's area. The memories of 'la dolce vita' in Shimla are recorded by those fortunate enough to live in those expansive acres of wood and meadow. It was they who breathed the cool, scented air in home and street kept clean and sanitized by the native hordes largely sequestered in the crowded squalor of bazaars that for the British were a vile excrescence on the fair face of their refuge. In the twentieth century, upper-class Indians progressively took over more and more of the British enclave and added their bit to those wondrous tales of Shimla as it once was since their world too was far removed from the wretchedness of the bazaars.

The British were almost paranoid about the overcrowding of Shimla. There was a dread that the cool, clean and disease-free hill station would become 'unhealthy' and 'unsanitary'. The municipal memorandum (1871) echoed this fear, 'Shimla is overcrowded, and was really very unhealthy this year, it will never be a good hill-station. However, we should do what we can to make it bearable'.

The overcrowding in the bazaars was unbelievable. Val Prinsep aptly describes the situation in his *Glimpses of Imperial India*. 'It is most thickly inhabited; and at night, coming home from dinner, one is astonished at the number of inanimate bundles lying on step, shelf or roof, all of which represent so many sleeping men.'

'I regard Simla in a general way, as vastly overbuilt and overcrowded in the summer season...' the sanitary commissioner reported in 1898. The 1904 municipal census revealed that Lower Bazaar had the highest population density in the Punjab, with an average of 17.4 persons per house compared to 5.7 for the province as a whole. The poor drainage and sanitation system, congested lanes and unwashed bodies engaged in day-long toil, combined to produce the stench that sickened the refined noses that usually stepped out in the evenings to take the air on the Mall. But even more serious was the public health dangers lurking in these conditions. A cholera epidemic in 1875 took 184 lives. While measures to improve sanitation followed thereafter, the problem was never really solved.

The *Simla Times* reported on the Municipal Report of 1917: 'The overcrowding of Simla is a serious problem and whereas Government is grappling with it as regard its officials the Municipality is doing its best to solve it in the case of the ever increasing Indian population... The conversion of latrine sanitation from the old fashioned method to the modern flush system is regarded as an ideal which ought to be extended to the whole of Shimla. For ourselves, while we disclaim any authority to speak on sanitation, we are not so sure of the healthiness of flush system.'

Shimla as a whole was then never that unblemished jewel that it is often remembered as. In effect, there were two Shimlas in British times; a sylvan Eden for the colonial masters and their favoured 'comprador' and a set of smelly, unsanitary enclaves, often visible but seldom visited, for those who served them. Independent India has created a new, more inclusive Shimla. Imperial India dictated the existence of old Shimla as two demarcated zones. Democratic aspiration has led its expanding boundaries and many suburbs along a more composite path. The native inroads into the exclusive expatriate acres were restricted in British times. Native princes were the first to be let into the charmed circles. However, from 1890 informal orders were issued asking the Indian princes not to 'hang about in Simla', they were allowed to come on formal visits. Later wealthy merchants, civil servants and professionals 'who could fit in' were allowed but reluctantly. Post-independence, the invisible barriers that prevented ingress by more ordinary folk lost their bite. But it was 1966 and 1971 that were the real watershed years in the town's existence.

In 1966, Shimla, till then in the state of Punjab, became part of Himachal Pradesh and in 1971, Himachal Pradesh became a full-fledged state. For those first twenty-four years after 1947, Shimla's destiny was still guided by outsiders, first by the British and then by civil servants and interests representing Punjab and to some extent the Centre. After 1966 and 1971, Shimla has finally become a town that belongs to the people of the hills. Its character and social composition has changed forever. It was a town ruled entirely by the seasons. It waned to almost an eighth its summer time size come winter less than a hundred years ago and now it waxes no more than a fourth its winter time numbers each summer. The summer influx of tourists still holds importance for a section of Shimla's inhabitants but for a majority it is incidental, perhaps even a nuisance. It is a town that increasingly serves its own hinterland, as the seat of government and as the centre for medical attention, education and commerce related needs. The apple-rich valleys of Shimla district dominate the eastern suburbs but the town as a whole is now home to people from all over the State.

Shimla's problems stem from sheer numbers. Its population jumped from 18,345 in 1941 to 46,150 in 1951 and then to over 1,50,000 in 2001. Add to this the daily commuters from ever-widening feeder zones and the tourists, and you have a recipe for urban nightmare. While its permanent population increased almost six times compared to the ideal of '25,000 *souls*' for which the British planned it, basic infrastructure and facilities have failed to keep pace. Shimla residents and planners seem to have almost forgotten that the city lies in a highly sensitive seismic zone. Utter disregard to nature, despite existing rules prohibiting felling of trees; congested, expanding hotch-potch of suburbs that starve for civic facilities are putting tremendous pressure on Shimla.

This change in Shimla's essence and character is yet to permeate the consciousness of those who make or influence policy for the city. As a result, a dominant strand guiding thought and action is one that continues to visualize Shimla as a summer time retreat for people from the plains. Preserving the tourist enclave and facilitating visitors are seen as the key drivers for the city. The old expatriate core of the town, variously called the green area or heritage zone, is at the heart of urban-planning debates. Expenditure on basic services and civic amenities is disproportionately weighted in favour of this old Shimla. Regulations on building, felling of trees and even lopping of branches, dating back to the British, find their strictest expression in relation to this area. Decongestion and mobility figure as issues primarily in relation to reaching Shimla from the plains or visiting the tourist spots beyond rather than in the context of linking mushrooming suburbs with their city centre.

This failure to recognise the reality of contemporary Shimla complicates even more a challenge endemic for much of urban India today. A popular thesis runs along the following lines. The fact that a preponderant majority of Indians and specially the poor live in the villages has seen a primary focus on rural development. But India as a whole will be over fifty percent urban in a decade or so. The cities are the generators of wealth and prosperity and magnets for the poor in the rural heartland. These cities are bursting at their seams. Their infrastructure needs have seen woefully little attention in the past. Investing in urban infrastructure is the need of the hour. The challenge then is to make the resources available. But this is only the easy part of the story.

Perceptive observers point out that the investment that has taken place in the past has often been misdirected or has seen inadequate utilisation. Instances of this kind abound across India. Water supply schemes in many Indian cities produce as much or more water per capita than many European towns. Delhi produces over 250 litres per capita per day of water and yet water is perpetually in short supply and most poor residents rely on sporadic availability from public stand posts or tankers. Shimla with a daily production of over 150 litres per capita per day seldom makes available more than half an hour of water per day to its residents. For many even this may flow only once in two days or even in three. In contrast, a city like Paris with a similar 153 litres per capita per day of production is able to ensure water twenty-four hours a day-seven days a week to its inhabitants. There are no accurate estimates of how much water is wasted in Shimla but those responsible for delivery estimate that unaccounted for water could be in excess of fifty per cent! Yet the response to Shimla's water problems continues to be a search for more water by laying pipes from new sources rather than fixing the plumbing.

The sanitation story reflects even greater wastage of resources but gets less attention. Water is understood to be a basic necessity and shortages are highlighted daily. Sanitation is more distant in the public mind and only when plague hits Surat or jaundice stalks through large swatches of Shimla, does it draw attention. When funds are sought for sewerage networks and treatment plants, few stop to consider what has happened to the existing investment in sanitation infrastructure. The fact that Indian cities abound in sewerage networks that carry little sewage or empty directly into rivers or have sewerage treatment plants unconnected to any sewerage system is seldom realised. Shimla is a classic example of inadequate utilisation. Sewer lines are meant to serve large parts of the town and take the waste to a network of nine sewer treatment plants. The actual utilisation of the system is nine per cent of is capacity!

In such a scenario, increased investment could become a case of pouring more water into a leaking bucket. The key challenge, many of us feel, is to alter the institutional arrangements to make cities accountable for delivering services and not merely creating infrastructure. City level accountability would be facilitated if a city had the incentives to think and act as a city responsible for itself. This is inhibited by the relationship that history and statute have created between different tiers of government in India. Despite a history of municipal bodies dating to early British times, the real responsibility for infrastructure and services has always vested with higher tiers of government. Independent India's Constitution clearly placed local bodies in the list of subjects under state government control. The 74th Amendment to the Constitution, carried out in 1993, has ensured that local bodies will be elected every five years but has not really succeeded in reducing the principal agency relationship between the state and local bodies that dilutes the latter's accountability for delivering services and local governance. There are few functional responsibilities that are clearly vested in local bodies. State government agencies in the shape of departments, boards and authorities overlap even in spheres like water supply, sanitation, roads, housing and regulation of construction and land use, typically regarded as core local body functions. Control over key staff positions is usually exercised by the state government and not by the local bodies. The ability of local bodies to raise their own resources is usually severely constrained by statute and instructions. A considerable amount of funding comes through Central and state schemes. These schemes often tie funds to projects and emphasize infrastructure creation rather than the delivery of services through the efficient utilization of assets. They also end up encouraging ad hoc infrastructure creation instead of a comprehensive approach to issues like sanitation, mobility or housing.

Shimla is an archetypal example of all the ills of a system that prevent a city from being responsible for delivering services to its inhabitants. Despite being given a municipal body in the nineteenth century, it was largely governed through Central direction in British times. It now has a municipal corporation but responsibility for the town, in both public perception and in fact, vests largely in the hands of the state government. The state department responsible for water supply looks after bulk water supply and all infrastructure creation in both water supply and sewerage. But a large part of the city is still based on onsite sanitation systems and nobody really looks after that. Roads, housing, regulation of construction and land use are a messy area of overlap and divided responsibility. All senior positions in the

The Ridge in the mid-twentieth century

corporation are filled by the state government and a provincialization of the services of all cadres of municipal employees in 1994 means that even the lowest-level employee is ultimately controlled by the state government. The corporation has no control over rates of revenue sources vested in it. Even routine operations are funded out of dispensation by the state government. In recent times there are two classic examples of project-based funding executed by the state government department concerned with virtually no utilization. The water supply distribution system has seen a Rs 40 crore investment through Central funds but the pipes buried in various parts of the town have virtually no link with the distribution system managed by the corporation. The under-utilized sewerage system that has been mentioned earlier, was a Rs 73 crore project that drew on substantial grant funding from external sources.

Water supply represents an extreme case of the cycle of infrastructure creation with little or no regard to improved service delivery through accountable utilisation of the existing infrastructure. Shimla has always been seen as a water deficient town. The first houses came up close to spring sources but as numbers grew, the bazaar areas and the Mall sprang up, the idea of a managed water supply system was logical. Tunnels into the Jakhu hill and reservoirs to store spring water were initial responses. Piped supplies to key locations from the reservoirs were an early innovation. In the nineteenth century itself, prospecting for water led the British further afield. The springs on the south-western flanks of the Mahasu ridge were tapped and water brought to a reservoir in Sanjauli and another on the Ridge. In the twentieth century, when demand outstripped the ability of the catchment forest springs (despite the large-scale plantation to protect and recharge them) came the first lift water supply for Shimla. The massive lift from Nauti khad to Craignano near Mashobra, constructed in the 1920s, was an engineering feat of its time. Post-Independence, we have continued to scout further afield to supplement water as demand increases and the maintenance of existing systems lacks both glamour and the ability to attract funding. First came the additions to the Nauti khad scheme, then a new lift from the Ashwini khad on the southern side of Shimla. This has recently been followed by a scheme that will lift water from the river Giri over thirty kilometres away. Likely to be commissioned by April 2008, this will result in an unprecedented production of over 250 litres of water per capita per day for Shimla. This should be enough for Shimla even if it grows to twice its size, if the accountability issues were to be addressed. But the prospect of possible Central funding for a new scheme means that another project to tap the Pabbar river near its source, almost 180 km to the east has already been announced!

Urban India's fortunes may be changing. Increased investment in infrastructure still leads in the search for solutions. But policy change to empower cities to think for themselves is also evident in recent Central initiatives. But for this to gather weight, assertion at city level is important. This process could gather force if there was recognition, by city-level opinion makers, that cities must chart their own course. Leadership is needed to bring inhabitants together on issues that concern them all. Inhabitants need to be convinced that the answers ultimately lie with them and not in patronage-based handouts from above. All this is a tall order in any city. The blend of colonial legacy and the overwhelming weight of contemporary state local body relations makes it even more difficult in Shimla. It is doubtful that Shimla can be in the vanguard of a movement for change in the direction of assertive self-dependent cities, conscious of their own needs and willing to address them. Meanwhile, Shimla dwellers will continue to look to the new 'Imperial', the state government for answers to the monkey menace and the jaundice scare.

The Bagpipe Trek

A Trek to the Chur in the Shimla Hills

Harish Kapadia

It often happened that I had to visit Delhi for a short visit from Mumbai. Dealing with *babus* and the bureaucracy in the capital city can be quite exhausting and so to relax, I would meet my friend, philosopher and guide, the famous writer, Bill Aitken. As we had lunch, watching cricket and talking mountains, he would make several suggestions, enough to fill a year of trekking. Bill specialises and believes in 'A Lateral Approach to the Himalaya'[1] and would firmly suggest 'more of the lesser'. I would tuck the information away in my mind and when an opportunity arose, I would go on these small treks from Delhi. Some were ten days and some were only four days (return). We called them 'The Bagpipe Treks'.

This name has an origin too. While on a trek in Kumaon, a villager sat and chatted with us. It transpired that he was a retired soldier from the Kumaon regimental band. His speciality was to play bagpipes. He did not need much persuasion to play for us as he anyway played at several local marriages. The hills vibrated with the high pitched sound of the pipes as he serenaded the mountains—no wonder they are also called Highland Pipes. We walked ahead and he walked with us, still playing in an amazing show of breath callisthenics.

---

[1]See his article in the *Himalayan Journal*, Volume 57, p.1

This walk firmed my resolve to enjoy more such walks where the sound of music and a gentle breeze matters the most.

No place is more suitable for such an experience than the Shimla Hills. As the road climbs up from Kalka, several side valleys open and each one leads to small villages, now mostly connected by roads. The old world charm still rules and the simplicity of villagers is intact. The monarch of these hills is the Chur. Sitting in a veranda of a hotel in Shimla one can view the blue hills rolling on, range after range. The most prominent high point is that of the Chur. For that matter, the Chur can be seen from Mussoorie, Chandigarh and Saharanpur and other faraway places. Its ridges are the watershed between the Satluj and the Yamuna valleys. To give a wider scale, water draining south into the Tons, Giri and Yamuna flow to the Bay of Bengal, while water draining to the north from the Chur is carried by the Satluj and Indus to the Arabian Sea. Thus the Chur, as the 'highest peak of the lesser Himalaya' has an important role. It is of great geological importance as many fossils are also found here.

The British called the peak at the foothills of Shimla as 'the Choor' or the Chaur, 'the ridge of the sweeper'. But the more apt and romantic name attributed to it is 'Choor Chandni', the 'ridge that shines in moonlight', as it evidently does when there is snow covering its summit. The Choor according to Lt. White 'is the most lofty eminence belonging to the secondary Himalaya, running south of the great snowy range from whatever point it may be seen forms a grand and prominent object, towering majestically amidst host of satellites'.[2] He describes it as 'hill on hill, and alps on alps arise' which is rather apt as you approach the summit via never-ending lower slopes. The best eloquence he bestows on the Chur is writing about its flora and fauna:

> Another beautiful variety frequent the most shady and secluded dells, sheltered by overhanging rocks festooned with ivy and creepers, and diversified by clumps of holly and wild cherry;

---

[2] *Touching Upon Himalaya*, Bill Aitken, p.19.

here and there an open space of greensward, a few yards in circumference, surrounded by patches of wild rose, scenting the fairy dell with delicious perfume. A little silvery stream bubbles from the rocks above, and trickles over the elastic turf, its murmuring course defined by a belt of violets and cowslips, whilst ferns of every variety are dancing gracefully in the breeze, and dipping their feathered heads in the tiny wave as it sparkles on its way.

The romantic old English language tells us what the Chur possessed, what we may have lost and what we still have.[3]

I was to first see this grand peak in tragic circumstances. Our family friend Major Navneet Vats was killed in action in Kashmir. He belonged to Chandigarh and had often talked to me about going to the Chur in Shimla hills. While we talked of other high ranges, his fondness for this mountain made it come alive for me. For someone in Chandigarh, 'the Chur is just there'. To offer condolences I had flown from Delhi to Chandigarh. These flights go at lower heights as less of a distance is to be covered. Looking out of the window I could have my first view of the Chur, a prominent hill and the first peak of prominence rising above the plains of Punjab. I tucked away this view somewhere in the corner of my mind.

One early November, keeping in mind five days of free time in Delhi, we planned a quick trip to Churdhar, a well-known point with historical significance and easily approachable. A taxi from Kalka carried us to Rajgadh, which in the early autumn light looked serene and beautiful. The Shimla Hills are now well developed with roads reaching many of the remote places. While obnoxious fumes are the price one has to pay, this development offers the advantage of trekking deep in the valley in a short time.

Soon we were alighting at a small PWD rest house of Nohradhar (2,160 m). A local meeting was being held in this two-room rest house. One could watch the 'administration' listening to the problems of

---

[3]*Himalaya Mountains*, Lieut. George Francis White, pp.184–85.

the 'commoners'. There were gentle nods and both sides knew that nothing would happen in a short time but it was important to keep talking and listening as something might happen someday!

That evening to acclimatise we took a small walk to the temple of Kudon devta. A small boy, who appeared from nowhere, accompanied us as our self-appointed guide. He was talkative and made for good company. As we reached the temple he stopped at the steps below and would not come up with us. When I motioned to him, 'Why don't you come up?', he smiled and stayed away. He said villagers would thrash him if he came up for he belonged to a lower caste. Even when we told him that these are attitudes from the past he nodded his head, 'Not in this part of the world'. Even the next generation was not ready to break traditions or was too scared to do so.

Early next morning we climbed up the steep ridge behind the bungalow. The climb was steep and spread over different slopes. With several trails it was confusing to find the correct way. Some of us were lost, some took a longer detour but finally we assembled on the upper ridge. The trail proceeded along this gentle and lightly wooded ridge. It was forested and with a good view towards the south. There were marks of shepherds having moved on this ridge many times and traces of their campsites were visible. By late evening, we were at one such campsite, Tisri (3,180 m) for the night. Shepherds had built three huts and we settled quite comfortably. No sooner our Kumauni porters had a roaring fire going with hot sweet tea than all rigours were forgotten. There was light snow around making the night magical. One of our companions, Soham an accomplished musician, played raga Hansdhawani on his flute. If Lt. White had paid a tribute with his romantic English, here our friend musically invoked the magic of the Choor.

Lt. White had also written about the storms on the Chur; 'to be overtaken by a snow-storm in crossing the Choor, proves one of the least agreeable varieties in a tour through these hills'. This is true as the Chur, being the first high peak from the plains, any disturbance or storm chases the peak with ferocity. Except for during autumn when you have clear views at other times when it is colder, the Chur remains snow-covered or mist-covered for many months.

From Tisri the climb to Churdhar (3,647 m) was steep and more tiring because of snow. The pilgrim route is from the north where there are large dharamshalas at Nahura. We made our way to the top easily to a stupendous 360° view. A statue of Shiva adds another five feet to the peak making it 12,000 feet high. Our Parsi companion Kekoo sat at the statue's feet, giving the atmosphere a secular feel. The locals narrated the importance of *Shirgul Mahadeo*, the story of a local chieftain whose faith and worship of Lord Shiva led him to salvation. We were at the high point of the Shivalik range. We could see the hills of Shimla, and the town itself to our northwest with Chandigarh to our southwest. The wide expanse of view from the summit almost makes you feel as if you are on the high Himalaya and not on the lesser one. The ranges from Dhaula Dhar to Nanda Devi and Trisul were in front of us. The best views were in the centre, that of Deo Tibba, Indrasan and peaks of the Kullu Himalaya. Slopes of conifers plunged down the Giri and the Tons on all sides. After an hour, one had to come back to reality and hot tea.

From Chur top there are several trekking options. One popular trek is to Sarain village on Chopal side. This picturesque village has the ancient temple of Bijat Maharaj which is very popular with the people of erstwhile Mahasu area. There is a forest rest house here located in a thick grove of trees overlooking the village. Almost level walk of about thirteen kilometres kms takes one to Manalag, another small village in idyllic surroundings. Chur top and the surrounding area is part of Churdhar Wildlife Sanctuary. You may encounter any of the following the animals or birds on way to the top: goral, barking deer, musk deer, panther, black bear, monal, koklas, kalij and chakor.

During the Raj days Chur was a popular trek. The fifty-four mile distance from Shimla was covered in eight stages with halts at Fagu, Kot, Digtali, Bhujjil, Bahla, Madhainghat and Kalabagh. The final ascent of one mile was undertaken from Kalabag camping site.

While the British romanticised about Chur, the mountain of the silver bangle and the beautiful forest around, the locals have several captivating stories associated with the Chur, Shirgul devta, Bijat Mahadev and other local deities.

Locals say that on top of the peak, there is a small aperture near the cairns and if a coin is dropped in it, jingling can be heard for quite some time as the coin falls deep into the secret path used by the gods. Another legend has it that Churdhar was the nearest point from Delhi where snow could be found even till early summer. The Mughal *badshahs* (kings) sent horsemen who would pick up snow from Churdhar, carry it sealed in animal skin, riding in rotation to the Red Fort in Delhi so that the *badshah* could have a chilled drink in the evening. Whatever may be the truth, the snows of Churdhar cannot have a better tribute.

I Feel I Belong Here

Emily Hansen

I was in Thailand, sweating in forty-degree heat, sick of pineapples, palm trees and sex tourists. And then it happened. I watched *Himalaya*, the film by Michael Palin who had always made me laugh, but had never made me want to buy a plane ticket! Yet, in this one film, he fully romanced me, all the way to the travel agency, with images of plumed waiters in colonial uniforms at the English Coffeehouse, and visions of the Gaiety Theatre. I wanted, like him, to roam the same streets as Rudyard Kipling and Amrita Sher-Gil. In fact, at the time, I could not imagine dying without having had this experience. My decision to come to Shimla because of Michael Palin might have seemed to another person as insane as throwing one's underwear on stage at a guitar-playing celebrity, but it struck me as completely logical. I will never know if it was just the lao-lao I'd consumed, which made me envision Shimla as my future Paradise, but my first day here, was confirmation that sometimes the best choices are impulse ones.

As I hoisted myself down, through the paths of the Lower Bazaar, past the roving spice clouds, second-hand sweater mines, and a Holy Cow anchored in its unlikely spot outside of a washroom stall, eventually settling in a cliff-hanging *dhaba*, I felt like I had truly arrived in the Queen of the Hill Stations. It was freezing, but I didn't care, because it was the first time I'd felt cold in almost a year. In fact, I felt mildly heroic, enduring frostbite like dust in a desert sandstorm. It was nearly Christmas, and I was a snow girl, liberated from English-teaching slavery and tropical heat. It didn't matter that the waiter was so disenchanted with his work, that if he could have thrown the meal from the kitchen, he would have. I didn't care about service, and it didn't bother me that my toes were being numb. I had arrived, in a place filled with character and magic.

In my guesthouse, where the owner reeled me in the door, with promises of 'too much hot water', 'too much', in Indian terms, meaning, 'just enough', I felt like I occupied a palace. Even as the paint peeled off the walls, and my backpack sat where a television had been ripped from the wall, I sat happily, with blankets covering me from head to toe, sipping my tea and gazing at the mountains through the window, feeling frosted to perfection, like a margarita glass.

Other than the Michael Palin's movie, I didn't have a clue about Shimla. I didn't even read the guidebook. I watched so many Monty Python Movies that I thought, well, if Michael Palin likes it here, then so will I (although I suppose in the end I was right).

The Gaiety Theatre smelled exactly as I had expected it to smell, old, dark, and rich with the tale of history. I could imagine a time when women pulled up their stockings beneath long starched skirts, and when men would put on their hats to go out. I could imagine a bunch of pampered colonials, laughing and pronouncing 'lovely' with crisp British accents after seeing one of the plays. I imaged, for some reason, that Rudyard Kipling would sweat a lot on stage, and that his father who created the stained glass windows of the Christ Church, would have been quite impressed.

Even the English Coffeehouse was better than I'd thought it would be, and as a small bonus, I'd discovered the matrimonial section and the hand-rolled indulgences that *bidis* are, so I was able to read and smoke at leisure, something that Palin had never mentioned in his movie. This coffee house, which puts Starbucks to shame, is the resting place of locals and experts in enlightenment alike. Never underestimate the adventure of having your fortune told at ten a.m., while reading the matrimonial section of the paper, over a dose of caffeine.

Truth be told, my first visit here, I wasn't even aware there were monkeys, until I was pleasantly surprised to discover I couldn't escape them. Even as they steal my underwear hanging to dry, my lunch, and the glasses off my head, I still maintain a soft spot for these plotting, mischievous Hanumans, which seem as many as there are people. Like almost everything in Shimla, I love them. They are as much a part of the landscape as the Mall.

Now, having spent time here—even though I can claim to be a long-term resident of Shimla with an Indian partner—I have to be a private detective, searching for hints and tiny nuances which will open up the people and the place, so that I may come to more fully appreciate my life here. It is impossible to pick from a small purchased poly bag of ideas, to define, exactly, what is Shimla. It is not that Shimla is particularly big, or even particularly exciting in that Taj Mahal glittery sort of way, but it is that it is incredibly dynamic. It provides examples of local life, ape life, and tourist life, spinning brightly and dizzily, as if three colours of a pinwheel.

The stimulant rush will leave you braced for bargaining at the Lower Bazaar, as you haggle in the company of sari-purchasing ladies, and three porters lugging up the hill, some mysterious substance in an oil drum. *Ladoos* and *samosas* abound, at the local chat shop which provides refuge from entrepreneurs of all sorts, beckoning you to 'Come in, and sit', while they prepare a cup of *chai*, dragging out gorgeous fabrics in a range of epileptic colours. For the foreigner, this can all prove to be a wonderful adventure, and for locals, a taste of daily life.

And the locals are no less interesting. On any given day you may run into an ice-skating mathematician with a penchant for poetry, a chatty *sadhu*, a politician, a barman who will buy you angora sweaters and try to seduce you on your twenty-ninth birthday, or a social justice activist who will invite you to his cousin's wedding in Kathmandu. Walking out the door in the morning, one never knows what to expect, and this, dear readers, is a fabulous thing.

While I appreciated all the crazy quirks that downtown had to offer me, it was through my many hikes in Shimla, that I forever fell in love with the place. Coming from the city, where entertainment is shopping and going for martinis with friends, I had always thought my father's plea to feel my 'communion with nature' was yet another unfortunate sign that he'd ingested too much LSD. But, as I sat in the woods, with nothing around me, but evergreen trees and resurrecting bars of sunlight I could doubt my connection to the natural world no more, and its ability to enchant me.

On one of my walks I noticed a sign on the road, which read: 'The Allah of Islam is the same as the God of Christians and the *Ishwar* of Hindus'. At the time, I saw it to have religious significance, but now as someone settling into a new country, it means more to me. What the sign is talking about is division, something, which all people, including myself, can identify with. I started thinking about all of our social divisions, whether it be x religion/y religion, man/woman, foreigner/national, East/West, and how, in prioritising one over the other, they chip away at our sense of individual and collective dignity. It is my struggle as a foreigner, to look through all the imagined divisions and find commonality, instead of animosity towards some of the new dynamics that make me uncomfortable.

Sometimes I find it hard to cope with my new environment. I don't want to be seen as an aardvark on the Mall, or a troublesome '*firangi*', with all the clichés attached, but rather, an integrated part of what goes on here. I want to have real and meaningful discussion with local people, instead of random picture taking, hand shaking, and shouted how-are-yous.

Nevertheless, being misunderstood is the plight of immigrants everywhere but in Shimla I have had many experiences where I have felt like a person first, and a foreigner second. The *Karva Chauth* festivities in Shimla were one such example. As I fasted for the long life of my loved one, and waved my hennaed hands at the women who'd attended the gathering on The Ridge, I felt at once, part of this wonderful celebration of shared womanhood. While a few people felt it blasphemous that I had taken up the rites and rituals of a married Indian woman, most commented positively on my choice to observe this day, and welcomed me into the evening's activities. I felt that I may one day, if I get married here, truly feel a part of this society.

I have my theories about connecting with the people here. For men, I look at turban colours and how they treat the monkeys. A bright turban, while not only a mark of religion, is almost always a positive sign, but relentless monkey-beater, for example, is unlikely to be a man at all.

For women it is the 'bangle theory'. Bangles, in India, can give me small indications as a foreigner, about the women who wear them, and the society itself. Depending on how many, and how expensive, they may signify whether or not the woman is married, or if she is rich, poor, or middle class. I have learned that even personality traits, can be foreshadowed by the mighty bangle. Red and noisy bangles usually signify that the woman is joyous, but those in lethargic, sombre colours, a more melancholy character. If a woman wears no bangles, I would conclude that perhaps she is a bit eccentric, a blazing antenna, perhaps, in a city full of gray buildings.

Every woman wears her signature, in every place around the world. My Norwegian grandmother wore polyester polka dots from the 1950s, and 4711 cologne. My mother's defining characteristics are her bright red lipstick, and head full of short spiky hair, which she keeps a natural grey, 'because,' she says, 'there is no shame in growing old'. My choice of signature is probably that, drawing inspiration from Taiwanese fashion models, I dress like a twelve-year-old, and accent with a pair of Eiffel Tower earrings, that remind me of being a German exchange student and walking in nearby Paris. My boyfriend's mother here in Shimla wears the most incredible armfuls of crimson and gold glass bangles, which make the most wonderful chiming sound. When I hear her clink around the house, it makes me think of New Year's champagne, and cheering glasses, which gives me the feeling that she is in a permanent state of celebration.

Unfortunately, because she is deaf, she cannot hear the sound they make when they smash together while she is cooking, bringing the food, cleaning, or washing the dishes. Since we cannot speak much, except in my limited sign language or by writing things down, our interactions are more intuitive. Without contempt, without judgment, we search through one another's culture waters through doing, not speaking. Once in a while, I bring some food from Canada; she teaches me how to cook masala. I stare right through her eyes, to see what comes next. One night, she gave me some of her bangles. They were pistachio green, with gold trim. I remember thinking that I should one day return to Canada, amidst the tune of clanking bangles. I felt very lucky, not to have something new, but to have received something of a personal nature, which meant that we had passed the point where we were merely symbols of two separate foreign cultures; we were joined, with her signature.

While Shimla seems forever awash with a Holi rainbow of colours, her signature, and thus, her essence, stands apart from the crowd. Not everyone, despite their circumstances, can carry in their step, and on their wrists, a marching band. Mostly, however, I look at what the women do, because I am one, and because you can tell a lot about someone's culture by looking at its women, the performers of three-quarters of the world's work. We are birds of a feather, in this sense, yet, I see so many variations in women's lives compared to home. In Shimla, the women always look busy with children, cooking, or other household tasks. Sometimes I do not even see them. They are inside, tending to their duties. As a foreign woman, I often find myself accidentally surrounded by men, which I suppose is both flattering but very strange for me. Sometimes when I sit in the pub to have a beer, something that most Canadian women do to relax, I see only men; because of that, I find it hard to get to know women here, as their domain is the household, and not always that of the outside world.

If I want to get to know them, I have to learn how to cook Indian food, and sadly, I have been known to explode even basic *dal* in a pressure cooker. Culinary finesse and motivation comes about as easily to me as quantum physics. I hate household work, and sometimes, even, my house. Evidence of this is a string of flashing Diwali lights, which remains up long after Ram has seen his way home. I am too lazy to take them down, so now, when the neighbours ask, I term them 'Christmas lights', and after January, 'disco lights', so that I will not appear even more of a domestic nincompoop than I already am.

Where I come from, women and men are less divided in terms of income, occupation, and status. In Canada, we also have a strong concept of 'the individual', and our society is built around that. Here in India, I find the situation, particularly in more traditional families, somewhat opposite. Rarely, am I asked about my passions, my personal feelings, my history, my job, my travels, or my education, and nor do most people here reveal them either. I am most frequently asked if I am married, if I can cook, where my house is, and if I have children. These are the questions that remain important for many women in India, the very core around which local life revolves; since this is the case, I hardly know how to answer.

However, I get a feeling that I belong here. One evening as I was walking home, I became overwhelmed with the beauty of Shimla at night. The cars seemed fluorescent in the moonlight, the stars like nature's hieroglyphs, burning through the sky. I closed my eyes. Like a hundred piece accapella band, the stray dogs were barking, yelping and howling. I wanted to sing with them, in the sombre rhythm and blues that is their story, and the raw glory of life. I thought if all of our voices could be heard, as part of a melody, we would never feel alone, and we would give up this grand hope of ego and identity, which limits our human potential for connection.

Even if I had no purpose coming here to begin with, except a silly movie, it has grown far ahead of that. Michael Palin might have motivated me to come here, but he only touched the surface of where my journey would begin. As the old proverb goes, 'A bird does not sing because it has an answer, it sings because it has a song'. While I cannot attempt to define exactly what Shimla is, or my experience as a foreigner, I can at least, appreciate it.

Of Kuccheris and Kings

Deepak Gupta

The history of Shimla is closely linked with that of judicial evolution in the hill station, in ways that provide interesting insights into its overall development.

Shimla as we know it today, came into existence because the English who then ruled over India, found in this region the cold and misty climate of the homeland they missed so much.

However, before it donned its British robes towards the beginning of the nineteenth century, Shimla was overrun by the Gurkhas, an aggressive and overbearing people. To rid themselves of their tyranny, the harassed rajas of the hill states collectively sought the protection of the British.

Brigadier General Sir David Ochterlony, who was the British resident commissioner at Delhi, was asked to subjugate the Gurkhas, a task he managed to do with efficiency. According to the author William Dalrymple, General Ochterlony was a 'white mughal'. This meant he dressed and ate like an Indian nobleman and true to local custom even harboured a number of *Bibis*, or wives! Nevertheless, his essential loyalties remained British to the core, and the town which he helped wrest from the clutches of the Gurkhas, was to epitomise everything British and later became one of British India's main bastions of power; a British enclave in letter and spirit.

In return for the favours of protection given to the rajas of the hills, the English, as was their wont, sought their pound of flesh.

This took the form of relieving the hapless rajas of their judicial powers. Although the kings were permitted to administer justice to their subjects, they were now obliged to take the approval of the commissioner of the Simla hill states in order to confirm a death sentence. This act was the first infringement by the British upon the sovereign powers of the hill chiefs. However, the rajas themselves were not exactly the most able administrators and were known to display a large number of idiosyncrasies. Some kingdoms that form part of the state of Himachal Pradesh such as Chamba, Sirmaur, and Mandi were known to be well administered and had a fine legal system. However, there were other kingdoms where the rulers were autocratic and often behaved like despots.

A number of interesting anecdotes illustrate the high-handedness of such members of royalty towards the administration of justice at that time.

Once, just before the country became independent, an advocate of the high court also happened to be the inspector general of police in one of the small kingdoms. As demanded by custom, every evening he called upon the raja to pay his respects and inform him about the law and order situation in the State. On one such evening, the raja demanded to know how many people the inspector general had managed to throw into jail. The inspector general proudly replied that since the law and order situation in the State was so good, there were no inmates in the jail.

Upon hearing this the raja was incensed and instead of congratulating the inspector general, severely reprimanded him for keeping the newly constructed jails empty when they should have been full by then. He then immediately ordered that the inspector general be put behind bars so that the jail would have at least one prisoner. The shocked and bewildered policeman sought for time to remedy the situation. Rushing out of the palace, he seized the nearest beggars who were loitering casually around a temple, threw them behind bars and in the nick of time spared himself the ignominy of taking their place in jail.

Another interesting incident concerns a leading lawyer in Shimla who was representing an accused in a criminal case, before one of the chieftains of the area. As the story goes, the raja was holding court at a small village not far from Shimla. To attend court, the lawyer had to ride on horseback. Unfortunately for him, however, his client failed to show up. Therefore, he drafted and gave an application to exempt his client from personal appearance.

The hill chieftain, who was virtually illiterate, was not impressed by the absence of the accused and took this as an affront to his person. Thundering in his local language, he ordered that in case the accused was absent, his lawyer should be arrested and put behind bars until the accused himself turned up.

The shaken lawyer, wanting to make his escape, observed that there was no armed guard with the raja. He then quickly mounted his horse and galloped at full speed towards Shimla, not stopping till he had reached the British territory, where he was safe.

As the visits of senior British officers to Shimla increased in frequency, the importance and population of this town also grew. Soon, the need for a formal legal system could no longer be denied. The courts of Shimla were thus established around 1850.

The local *kuccheri* was set up just above the original village, (from which Shimla derived its name) Shamali. This building, which still houses the district courts, was earlier known as Gaston Hall. Doz, an author well known at that time, reports in his highly irreverent book *Simla in Ragtime* that the need for members of the legal fraternity grew at a rapid pace keeping in view the nature of the people visiting Shimla. Doz explains his own 'ABC' or alphabet of the 'bunch of human afflictions that plague Shimla.' These include 'V' for the 'vakil' 'you get by the gross'! The situation remains unchanged even today when you can hardly cross the Mall at any time of day without bumping into a number of black-coated 'vakils'.

Keeping Shimla's importance in view, some very senior and competent judges were appointed to the courts. A number of highly competent lawyers also made their mark here and soon the town developed a capable and independent bar of its own.

After Partition, large areas of West Punjab and Delhi, which fell within the territorial jurisdiction of the high court of Lahore in Pakistan, were left with no high court. Therefore, a decision was taken to set up the high court of Punjab at Shimla.

The courts were housed in Peterhof, a building situated towards the western side of Shimla upon Inveram Hill. Peterhof had initially been constructed as a residence of the viceroy. Although it was a picturesque house, Peterhof was not thought to be well situated for a court since there was no room large enough to hold one.

One of the most important cases to be heard at Peterhof was the appeal in the case of the murder of Mahatma Gandhi.

The trial of this case was conducted at the Red Fort in Delhi. The accused were Nathuram Godse and seven other persons including his brother. The trial court convicted seven of the eight accused, Nathuram Godse and his friend Narayan Apte were sentenced to death and the remaining five convicts were awarded life imprisonment. One of the accused, Vinayak Savarkar was acquitted.

The appeals filed against the convictions were heard at Simla. Since the case was so important, the ballroom of Peterhof was converted into an imposing courtroom. When the hearing started on 2 May 1949, the courtroom was full to capacity.

Nathuram Godse declined to be represented by any lawyer and argued his appeal himself. According to Justice Khosla, 'His small defiant figure with flashing eyes and close-cropped hair offered a remarkable and immediately noticeable contrast to the long row of placid and prosperous looking lawyers who represented his accomplices.'

Godse, in his appeal, did not challenge the conviction imposed upon him on the charge of murder. He did not even question the propriety of the death sentence passed against him. His sole contention in the appeal was that he alone was responsible for the murder of Mahatma Gandhi and none of the other convicted persons had conspired with him. He wanted to exhibit himself as a fearless patriot and a passionate protagonist of Hindu ideology. He remained unrepentant of his crime believing it had been his 'dharma' to murder the Mahatma since he had shielded Suhrawardy and other Muslims who, according to Godse, had heaped carnage upon Hindus.

Nathuram Godse spoke for several hours before a full bench of the court. Justice Khosla observed, 'The audience was visibly moved. There was a deep silence when he ceased speaking. Many women were in tears and men were coughing and searching for their handkerchiefs. The silence was accentuated and made deeper by the sound of an occasional subdued sniff or muffled cough. It seems to me that I was taking part in some kind of melodrama or in a scene out of a Hollywood feature film.'

Despite the fervent lecture, the high court dismissed the appeal. He and Apte were hanged in Ambala on 15 November 1949.

The court of the judicial commissioner for the state of Himachal Pradesh was constituted on 15 August 1948. Upon the reorganisation of the state of Punjab in 1966, the hill areas of the erstwhile State were merged into the State of Himachal. Thereafter the jurisdiction of the High Court of Delhi was extended to the entire area of Himachal Pradesh from August 1967.

The building known as Ravenswood was chosen as the seat of the Circuit Bench of the Delhi High Court. One of Shimla's most ancient buildings, Ravenswood has an interesting and chequered history. In 1867, it was bought by a dental surgeon Dr O'Meara, the nephew of Dr Barry O'Meara, Napoleon Bonaparte's medical assistant. When Napoleon died, the doctor planted a weeping willow over the dead man's grave. Doctor Barry O'Meara then sent cuttings of the tree to his nephew in India. A few of these cuttings were planted in a number of properties in Shimla including Ravenswood. This was how the weeping willow first came to Shimla.

Later Dr O'Meara sold the property to the financial secretary to the Indian government. It then went to the Raja of Faridkot who spent a king's ransom to turn it into a palatial residence. Ravenswood then became known as Faridkot House and after Independence, became the Circuit House of the Punjab government till the High Court was established in May 1967.

Although Ravenswood was, regrettably, torn down much later to make room for a towering concrete structure to house the high court it might be said that the achievement and the role played by the court have been equally towering. On 25 January 1971, Himachal Pradesh attained statehood and it was on that day the high court of the state was established. Hon'ble Mr Justice M.H. Beg was appointed as the first chief justice of this Court. He was followed by Hon'ble Mr Justice R.S. Pathak. Both rose to become chief justices of the Supreme Court of India. Chief Justice Pathak also has the rare distinction of being a judge of the International Court of Justice.

The High Court of Himachal Pradesh has also played a pioneering role in the field of Public Interest Litigation, helping to make some sweeping changes in the State even before the concept caught the fancy of the rest of the nation. Thanks to the effective and bold application of this tool, forestland has been saved, unauthorised construction stopped, the town cleaned up and beautified, streets paved and encroachments removed besides other notable improvements.

Shimla: An Educational Profile

ASIF JALAL

After its discovery in about 1819, British dignitaries and officers started visiting Shimla to escape the scorching heat of the plains, and to soothe their homesickness in this seemingly extension of Primrose Hill of England. By 1864, this 'Jewel of the Orient' was thrust with the status of the summer capital of the mammoth British Indian Empire. During this period, the '...land of brooks of water, of fountains and deoths...' witnessed the growth of all supporting structures and institutions like municipal committee, theater, library, police station, etc. across the forested hillsides. Soon the leading educationists and Christian missionaries committed to the spread of modern education in the Empire, sensed situation and sprinkled this awesome and varied Himalayan landscape with the best of the public schools.

Bishop Cotton School

The Bishop Cotton School, according to some documents, was established as Shimla Public School by Bishop George Edward Lynch Cotton in July 1859 and started functioning from March 1863 at Jutogh in the old native Cantonment. However, Jutogh Cant was found unsuitable for the school and the founder Bishop Cotton looked for an alternative site in Shimla. The south end of Knollswood Spur, the place where the school is ensconced today, finally enamoured Cotton and he acquired this area for the school.

The founder of one of the oldest boarding schools of Asia, Bishop Cotton was one of British India's eminent educationists. Educated at Britain's leading Westminster School and Trinity College, he was an associate of Thomas Arnold, the founder of the British public school system. After a career at Britain's leading public schools, Cotton was hand-picked by the Empress of India, Queen Victoria, as the bishop of Calcutta and Metropolitan Bishop of India, Burma and the Island of Ceylon. In India, he realised a need for quality educational institution for the Europeans and the Anglo-Indian boys. Soon he drafted a scheme of education for the Anglican churches in India. The viceroy, Lord Canning (1856–57), who established three universities in India, also convinced him of the necessity of establishing schools for the European boys in India.

In 1867, the school built in neo-Gothic architectural style on the plan of Engineer Crawford Campbell was renamed after Bishop Cotton to commemorate his contribution as an educationist when he drowned on 6 October 1866 while disembarking from the governor's yacht on the river Gorai in Assam.

The school, first to start the house system and the prefect system in Asia aimed at preparing the candidates for the Junior and Senior Cambridge Examinations. Though opened mainly for the English and the Anglo-Indians, the school allowed Indians to enroll and the first Indian to do so was Suren Tagore in 1881.

In May 1905, an enormous fire tore through the school buildings consuming everything except the Head Master's Lodge and a few other structures when most of the students were on leave. The school buildings were rebuilt by the government and the school was reopened in 1907. The main school building, reconstructed in 1907 after the cataclysmic fire, is in Gothic architectural style. The Holy Trinity Chapel at the campus makes the spiritual centre of the school. Rebuilt in 1908, it is a living memento of the history of the school. Its stained glass windows, polished pews, faint aroma of the oil, parquet flooring, pulpit and a soft strand of music make it look like God's most blessed place within the Bishop Cotton School.

The Irwin Hall named after the viceroy and the governor-general of India, who inaugurated the Hall in 1930, is used for school functions, lectures, theatricals, debates and cinema shows. During the partition of India, the headmaster addressed the Muslim boys from here before their departure to Pakistan. The school's alumni list looks like India's virtual Who's Who register. The names in the list range from the heads of state, to Supreme Court and High Court judges, a chief minister, air chief marshal, generals, ambassadors, civil servants, members of parliament of India and abroad, famous writers like Ruskin Bond, industrialists and sportsmen.

The Lawrence School, Sanawar

The only residential co-educational institution probably in the world, the Lawrence School, was founded in 1847 as Lawrence Military Asylum for the children of the British soldiers serving in India. One of the walls of the gymnasium bears a quotation from Rudyard Kipling's *Kim*: 'Send him to Sanawar and make a man of him'.

Founded by Sir Henry M. Lawrence, a British soldier and statesman, and his wife Honoria Marshall, the objective was to establish a chain of schools to provide education to the children of the deceased and serving soldiers and officers of the British army in India. During his lifetime, Sir Henry set up one Lawrence Military Asylum at Sanawar and another at Mount Abu (1856). After his death, two more such institutions were added to his mission, with one in 1858 at Lovedale, near Ootacamund and the other in 1860 at Murree in Pakistan.

Along with the elite Eaton and Shrewsbury, the school was presented Kings Colours by Lord Dalhousie in 1853 and registered itself as one of the six schools and colleges to be so honoured in the entire British Empire. On the 150th year of its foundation, it received felicitations from the Prince of Wales, Prince Charles.

With 'Never Give In' as its motto, the level of military training imparted at the institution was incomparable. During the First World War, several contingents of the students were enrolled for military service directly from the school and dispatched to the theater of war. In appreciation of the exemplary feat by the students, the school was renamed Lawrence Royal Military Academy in 1920 and two years later the Prince of Wales, Edward VIII, commended it with new Colours. The school's contribution to the armed forces continues to be exceptional even in the post-Independent India as it churned out many distinguished and celebrated officers including Arun Khetarpal, a Param Vir Chakra awardee.

The centenary year of the school in 1947, presided over by Governor-General Lord Louis Mountbatten, witnessed large scale departure of the school staff and students to the United Kingdom. The administration of the school thereafter changed hands from the Crown to the Government of India. The same year, the school was re-designated for the third time as the Lawrence School, Sanawar, and made a new beginning as a public school. In 1953, an autonomous Lawrence School Society, with the Education Secretary of the Government of India as its chairman, was constituted, and took control of the school. In 1956, the last English headmaster of the school relinquished the charge and Major Som Dutt took over as the first Indian headmaster and laid the foundation of the school as it is today. However, the school is still proud of its English connection.

Spread on an independent hill, in an area of 139 acres at an elevation of 5,780 feet amidst densely forested pine and cedar, seven hundred students are divided into four houses namely Himalaya, Nilagiri, Siwalik, and Vindhya; each House making a small family with its contingent of boys, girls and teachers. The spiritual nucleus of the community is a century and a half old, grey-stone built chapel designed in gothic style, with stained glass windows. The Birdwood School Buildings make the hub of academic activity and Barne Hall, situated in it, hosts all plays, shows, films and lectures. The school commands a solar-heated indoor swimming pool and an indoor sports complex, squash courts, firing range and gymnasium. The school also has its own printing press, poultry farm, and a sixty-bedded infirmary.

Sanawar, in its 160 years of spectacular existence, produced several prodigal figures. The roll of its alumni include the former Chief of Naval Staff Admiral Vishnu Bhagwat, Param Vir Chakra awardee Lt. Arun Khetarpal, politicians Omar Abdullah, Maneka Gandhi and Sukhbir Badal; film actors Sanjay Dutt, Rahul Roy, Puja Bedi; and business professionals Rana Talwar, Pankaj Munjal, Jeh Wadia; sportsmen Shiva Keshwan, Ajeet Bajaj; filmmaker, Bunty Walia, artist, Illoosh Ahluwalia and many more.

St. Bede's College

St. Clare, a young educationist and missionary during her visit to India in 1902 realised the need of a training college where the members of the Congregation of the Religious of Jesus and Mary could be trained by qualified professionals for teaching and spreading the message preached by. As a number of schools were being opened to provide modern education based on the evolving concept of public school system, trained and competent teachers were required and the idea of starting a Catholic Training College for the religious was prophetic.

Shimla, the hill top in the Central Himalayas with evergreen coniferous forests all around, being the Summer Capital of the British India and one of the centres of missionary activities, looked a natural choice. Thus, St Bede's college, located amidst century-old towering fir, oak and spruce trees in the most picturesque part of Shimla, was founded by Mother St. Clare of the Congregation of the Religious of Jesus and Mary in 1904.

The Sisters of the Congregation of the Religious of Jesus and Mary, founded by St. Claudine Thevenet in 1818 in Lyons, France, is an international congregation of Catholic sisters. They came to India in 1842 with a mission to educate young girls.

Set up amidst centuries-old mountains, the college was named after St. Bede the Venerable, a Benedictine monk and priest born in 673, who spent his life teaching and writing in the monasteries of Wearmouth and Jarrow in England.

The motto given by Mother St. Clare for the college was Non Nobis Solum or Not for Ourselves Alone. It sought to raise the standard of education in north-western India and to produce a generation of integrated personalities. The college aimed at higher education of the Catholic community in India and preservation of their faith and practices. It also laid emphasis on training young women to be able to fulfil their traditional obligations as wives and mothers at home and society at large.

The wall of the college library and its visitor's book boasts of pictures and signatures of dignitaries like Jawaharlal Nehru, Vijaylakshmi Pandit, Lord and Lady Mountbatten, Jacqueline Kennedy, the Beatles, Benazir Bhutto and Indira Gandhi with Sanjay and Rajiv.

Set in Tudor-styled majestic buildings against the snow-draped peaks of north-west Himalayas, the college has been the alma mater of leading Bollywood actresses, models, civil servants, artists and one Miss India. Among the best-known alumni are film actress Preity Zinta; models Ayesha Prem, Moeveea Dhanda, Anjana Kuthiala; civil servants Harinder Hira, Satwant Atwal Trivedi, Punita Bhardawaj; journalist Ruchika Mehta and many more.

The college housed in a single block started functioning in 1904 with fifteen students. The first principal of the college was Mother St. Gregory Canty (1904–32). Till 1947, it worked as a Teacher Training College but in 1948, graduate classes for Arts and Science were also started and the college which till now catered only to Christian girls, opened the portals of its sprawling campus to students of other communities also.

In 1967, the college authorities decided to close the college as they thought that the students would be better served in the newly opened Jesus and Mary College, New Delhi. However, St. Bede's being a leading institution for women's education in Himachal Pradesh, an appeal was made by the then Himachal Pradesh chief minister and several local dignitaries to Bishop Alfred for rethinking the move. Finally, the college with its distinguished tradition stayed and till today it continues to give shape to the vision of St. Claire.

In 1970, when Himachal Pradesh University was opened, St. Bede's College was affiliated to the university and its graduation courses were recognised by HPU.

What began amid 'sorrow, sacrifice and opposition, has done and still continuing to do much good for souls and keeping the flag of...Congregation flying unsullied.'

Convent of Jesus and Mary

The Congregation of Jesus and Mary, apart from rewarding Shimla with St Bede's College for the training of nuns as qualified teachers, also gave it one of the best boarding school for girls, the Convent of Jesus and Mary in 1864.

Located at the spur amidst the dense deodar-covered dreamy hills near Navbahar in the sprawling twenty-six acre Chelsea Estate, Convent of Jesus and Mary, one of the oldest educational institutions of the hill city, was founded primarily as an orphanage for the children of British soldiers, but, in course of time, boarders were also admitted for education and the institution graduated into a full-fledged convent for girl students.

With St. Lewis Gonzaga as the first superior, the convent ran on the monthly contribution of the members of the British armed forces. The school's colonial-style premises, originally a place for the congregation of the Nuns of Jesus and Mary, was expanded in 1869 to accommodate the soaring demand for Western education for the daughters of the officers of the British Raj.

The imposing Chelsea Convent Chapel, with spires peaking through the towering deodars, was erected in 1873, and in the following years large playgrounds and more buildings were added.

After the year 1880, military service regulations reduced the period of stay of the British regiments in India to a few years and consequently, the number of orphans at the convent began to dwindle. With the changed conditions, a demand for converting the institution into a boarding school for the daughters of officials was forwarded to the authorities of the Congregation and they responded positively to the demand.

The foundress of the Congregation of Jesus and Mary, Marie Claudine, wanted to take care of the abandoned children and orphans, and to bring the love of God into their hearts; and to fulfil this deep urge, she created the Convent of Jesus and Mary. She defined the philosophy of the Convent as: 'Let us so form these children that they may become serious minded, well balanced, home-loving women that they may cast their blessing in every home they enter'.

Loreto Convent Tara Hall

Loreto Convent Tara Hall School was founded by Mother Gongaza of Loreto Convent at two buildings, Belle Vue and Tara Hall on Kaithu spur having a view of the distant Greater Himalayas in the year 1895. Though the school was set up first at the Townsend building situated en route to the Jakhoo temple in 1892, it was shifted to the present location in 1895.

Run by the Irish branch of the Loreto Sisters, belonging to the Institute of the Blessed Virgin Mary, a religious order founded by Mary Ward of England in 1609 for emancipation and education of women, this school was also an attempt to give modern education to the daughters of the officers of the Raj. The Sisters first landed on the Indian shores in 1842 and established convents all over the Indian subcontinent including the premier hill city.

The school, like other girls' institutions of the period, aimed at training the young English girls to become fine ladies and good mothers and wives though the foundress of Loreto Sisters envisioned a modern mode of religious life for women. According to an alumnus's impression of the school, the teachers concentrated more on the way the girls walked and talked than on the learning of mathematics or biology. However, in the early 1960s, the mission of the school was expanded and it endeavoured to enable the girls to take larger roles and responsibilities of State and society.

No wonder the school produced personalities who broke the most obstinate glass barrier and achieved unprecedented success in every field. A few examples are Naina Lal Kidwai, the first Indian. woman to graduate from the Harvard Business School and third World Top Woman in Business in Asia; Nonita Lal Quraishi, a noted golfer; Pratibha Singh, Preneet Kaur, both Members of Parliament; Priya Jhingan, the first lady officer to be recruited in the army as judicial adjutant general; Komal G.B. Singh and Usha Alberquerque, the media personalities; Mira Nair, New York-based film director; Pamela Rooks, the noted film maker; Ms Justice Abhilasha Kumari, judge High Court, Himachal Pradesh and countless daughters of the princely and noble families of the former Indian Empires.

Cased along gigantic, dark green cedar in colonial style courtyard planning, the school constitutes an intrinsic part of the hill city's architectural heritage. The school gets its name from the Hill of Tara of Ireland, which is an ancient seat of political power and a sacred place for the dwelling of gods. The school building was rebuilt in 1930 and two more buildings, 'Wheatfield' and 'Darbanga', were added to the main complex of the school in 1960.

St. Edward's School

St. Edward's School founded in the red-roofed stone building on the cool strawberry hill of Shimla by the Irish Christian Brothers, a community of religious brothers working for evangelization and education of youths, in 1925 was a successor of St. Michael's School at Milsington Estate, Shimla.

With the dioceses of Shimla and Agra separated in 1910, the catholic St. Michael's School that existed at Milsington Estate was closed. Then the people of Shimla requested the first Archbishop of Shimla diocese, AEJ Kenealy to give them a substitute for St. Michael's School.

The Archbishop Kenealy, honouring the wishes of the Shimlites, invited the Congregation of the Irish Christian Brothers, a religious community based in Ireland and dedicated to teaching the disadvantaged youths, to start a catholic school for the boys at Shimla. The Brothers, reciprocating the request, visited Shimla in 1924 and founded St. Edward's School for the boys on the Milsington Estate.

Though dedicated to the Catholic community only, boys from other communities were also admitted to the school. With an objective of casting men out of young kids capable of responding to the challenges of life with joy and faith in God, self and fellow men, the school is credited to have produced the incumbent vice president of India, a chief minister, judges, lieutenant generals, ambassadors, super-cops including K.P.S. Gill, chief secretaries and commissioners, writers, poets, musicians and highly placed business executives.

In 1948, faced with a large-scale withdrawal of students in the backdrop of turbulence of partition and exodus of the British, the school management transformed the school into a day school. Apart from that, kindergarten classes were also introduced to fill in the space vacated by the boarders.

The motto of the school 'Lumen Sequere', 'Follow the Light', scripted on the school's crest, inspired the generations that straddled through its campus to pursue excellence and to grow as persons.

Auckland House School

'A home away from home', Auckland House School, standing on 7,200 feet high Elysium Hill, was founded in the spring of 1866 at Holly Lodge on Jakhu. The project for starting a school to provide Western education to girls in north-west India on Christian principles was initiated by J.B.D Aquilar in 1864. On the intervention of Mrs Cotton, the wife of Bishop Cotton, it was decided to found the school at Shimla as the Punjab Girls School.

The school headed by Mrs Mackinnon as headmistress began functioning with thirty-two students from 1866. In 1868 the school authorities looking for a better site to house the school purchased Auckland House and shifted it to its present site of Auckland House complex on the Elysium Hill, one of the seven hills constituting the 'British Jewel of the Orient', Shimla, in 1869.

This House, a scene of many a brilliant ball and amusing theatricals, has an amusing background. In 1828, one Dr Blake of the East India Company built a large house on the north-eastern spur of the Shimla range and after almost seven years sold it to the then Governor-General Lord Auckland. Later this house with deep green valleys on the one side and snowy mountains on the other, came to be known as Auckland House.

The hill on which Auckland House School stands received its present name Elysium Hill in 1838 as a compliment to Misses Eden, Lord Auckland's seven sisters, including Emily Eden the famous English novelist, who accompanied him during his deputation to India.

At this one-storied building with a flat roof composed of a thick coating of earth, Lord Auckland held durbar in which all hill chiefs and Punjab's Maharaja Ranjit Singh participated. The plan leading to the botched First Afghan War was also given a shape under the roof of this house. As per one report, during a heavy downpour of rain, the water settled down on the roof of the principal rooms and dripped down. The inmates moved to different corners of the room seeking refuge and wrote and dined with umbrellas held above their heads. It is also recorded that fleas were terrible problems in the rain; for several nights the occupants of the house were not able to sleep and the more the rooms were cleaned, the livelier those pests became. The house also served as a residence to Auckland's successor Lord Ellenborough and Lord Hardinge.

However, the school received a massive blow when, in 1905, an earthquake struck Shimla and almost completely destroyed the landmark mansion. The governors of the school pulled down the remaining piece of history and in 1921 put together a new edifice, specially suited for establishing a boarding school. The fine teak timber of the Auckland House was preserved and used in the new structure.

From 1908 to 1952 the St. Hilda's Society, a society of lady teachers working under the diocese of Lahore, provided the school with principals and other members of the staff.

In 1960, the school acquired the Belvedere Estate with a view to accommodate the rising number of students, and classes from nursery to fifth standard were shifted there.

The objective of the school was providing education based on the life and teaching of Christ. The '*Altiora Peto*' i.e. 'I Seek the Higher Things' as the motto of the school, each girl within the campus surrounded by blooming red rhododendron and shrubberies inculcate the higher values and proudly walks out as an accomplished lady.

Arya Girls' Senior Secondary School

In the year 1882, when France inaugurated free, compulsory and secular education, the founders of Arya Samaj in Shimla started the Arya Prathamik Pathshala in the regal Shiwalik Himalayas. Inspired by Swami Dayanand's vision of social and religious reform, the first girls' school by the Indians functioned as a primary school catering to the needs of the Indians for whom the campus of the English schools like the Auckland Complex was impermeable.

But founding a school for girls was not seen as a prudent move in nineteenth-century India and the orthodox section of the community put up solid resistance to this undertaking. However, the Arya Samajis stuck with their conviction to open the avenue for the Indian girls where, unlike the missionary schools, the traditional Indian cultural values were respected and promoted.

In 1932, the school was upgraded to middle level and the year 1945 saw the school moving up to the high school level. And in 1991, with about 800 young pupils on its roll, the school got accredited as a senior secondary school by the HP School Examination Board.

The school came into existence at the grandiose red Main Block building which is now more than a century old and with the surge in the number of students and upgradation of the school to higher levels, two more blocks were added to the existing block. Funding was always a problem and the school owes almost 125 years of its successful existence to the generous contributors who even today contribute more than sixty per cent of its total budget. The school's faculty who worked more out of their commitment to build a better society than for monetary remuneration also share the credit for building this institution. The principal Kailash Gupta (1978–1997) worked wholeheartedly to raise the academic standard of the school and bring it at par with any missionary school.

A typical day at the school begins with prayer and recitation of the Gayatri Mantra, 'We meditate on the glory of the Creator...May He enlighten our Intellect'. The students also perform yajna twice a week to nurture the divine within. The school's motto is to shape young girls for taking on the role of an ideal wife and mother as prescribed by the Shastras. Besides the modern subjects, the school prepares the students in dharma shiksha, yoga, Sanskrit, the ten principles of Arya Samaj etc. For girls in the region, this school was a boon.

These educational institutions made the British summer capital a major educational and cultural hub of the Empire. They attracted students from all corners of British India, from Lahore to Bengal to the South. As this period also saw a revolution in public school education in England under the educationist Thomas Arnold, Shimla, under the British became an experimental turf for testing new concepts in education, and became an immediate beneficiary by the founding of such leading schools.

Motoring in Shimla Hills

H. Kishie Singh

For a town such as Shimla steeped in history, romance, intrigue and conspiracies, there are numerous stories to fire up the imagination. There is the story of the phantom rickshaw, how Scandal Point got its name and the shenanigans that went on in Lovers Lane. A lot of stories have been lost in the fog of time. Others have been distorted and lost their relevance. There is one story, however, which remains true and unadulterated. It is as accurate today as the day it happened. It's the Clippity-Clop story.

The time was sometime in the mid-1930s. The Raj was at its zenith. England had defeated Germany in the First World War. The economy was booming, Britain ruled the waves and the sun never set on the British Empire. They virtually owned their colonial possessions. They ruled; they did not govern. Their arrogance knew no bounds. It was not unusual to see a sign outside All White Clubs, 'Dogs and Indians not allowed!'

It was this attitude that allowed them to pass a law in Simla. No natives were allowed to walk on The Mall especially in the evenings. At five o'clock offices gave over. The 'burra-sahibs' would head for The Mall. The 'memsahibs' would be walking on The Ridge. A band would be in attendance. A band stand had been especially constructed for this purpose. Opposite the band stand were stables where the burra-sahib's horses waited. Syces were allowed. Rickshaws waited next to the band stand. Four 'jhampanis' were allowed for each rickshaw. After all they had to pull the memsahibs home in the rickshaws. The men folk would either walk or ride alongside.

After a leisurely stroll on The Ridge or The Mall, it was almost mandatory for a quick drink at the Green Room. Again it was an all-white affair. There were no Indian members at the Green Room. It was high-handedness on part of the British and stifling for the Indians. After all rajas, maharajas, noblemen and gentry did live in Shimla and were denied the right to walk on their own soil! It belonged to the British!

One day some ladies, all Indians, had met for a cup of tea at a friend's house. One of the ladies present, a prominent socialite, was told by the host, 'You had better leave as you have to cross The Ridge to get home. It's getting onto five o'clock!' The statement rankled. It was anathema to the free thinking, liberated and rather rebellious lady. 'We should do something about it,' said she. And told herself. 'If you don't, I will!' And left for home.

On the way home she figured out a plan of action. The very next day she put it into action. The first stop was Daffadar Duli Chand. Duli Chand made the best saddles and accruements for horses. He also made the best hand-stitched riding boots. That done, she walked down to Jones, tailor and draper to the viceroy, governor and a host of other VIPs. Jones' specialty was trousers. The lady ordered a pair of riding breeches, hand-stitched, made to measure from beige cavalry twill. As the name suggests, it is a special fabric favoured by the cavalry. It does not collect horse hair. Not that the horses in Shimla shed any hair. They were brushed, massaged, shod, maintained and predicured as any memsahib. The finest breed of horses was to be found in Shimla and there was no shortage of syce, staff and servants to keep them in fine fettle. It was a matter of pride for the British that their cavalry was considered one of the finest in the world. Possibly the Cossaks from Russia were better. Reputedly, the Cossaks lived, drank and slept in the saddle.

Next stop for the lady was Rankin's. Again a tailor of great repute with shops in London, Delhi and Shimla. He stocked the best imported material from England for coats and suits. She selected a hounds tooth design and had a riding jacket made. Double breasted with twin slits at the rear. It allows the rider to sit comfortably in the saddle. Exactly the same that the memsahibs wore.

When the riding gear was ready, the lady put her plan into action. In the afternoon she came and sat in the library on The Ridge. Her syce brought the best horse from her husband's stable. A handsome, large, seven-hands high black Arab stallion. At five o'clock she left the library and mounted Black Boy, as the stallion was called. Clippity-clop came the sound from the slow methodical walk as Black Boy was urged on. Past the Christ Church she took the road down to The Mall, past Ladies Park and down to The Mall. The road meets The Mall right opposite Duffader Duli Chand's shop.

Clippity-clop! She did a left turn and headed towards Chotta Shimla. She kept to the specially designated track for horses but the sound from the hooves, like canon shots, could be heard by all. The Indian shopkeepers were aghast, they stood at the entrance to their shops and wondered what would happen. Nothing happened.

Clippity-clop. The lady continued till Combermere Post Office and bridge. She hesitated and did an about turn. Back up The Mall, past the Gaiety Theatre, the Town Hall to Scandal point, down the other side, past the General Post Office and all the way to the Chaura Maidan.

About turn again, Clippity-Clop all the way back to Scandal Point. She took the upper road to The Ridge past the Town Hall, the Band Stand and the manificent chestnut tree. Clippity-clop and she disappeared in the direction of Lakkar Bazaar. The echo of the hoofs was mesmerising.

There was deafening silence as she left. There was not a whisper, not a whimper. Shimla was simply stunned! I have heard this story umpteen times. Last week I heard it again from the lady herself. She is my mother!

◆

Another association I have with Shimla is skiing. The first time I saw a pair of skis and ski boots was the winter of 1952 to 1953. My father's friend Panchi Sen had just been posted to Shimla as the manager of Grindlays Bank. He had been holidaying in Europe, learnt how to ski and had brought his skis back to India. My father had a Second World War jeep and its four wheel drive was ideal for snow. So we bundled into the jeep, skis and all, and took off for Kufri. The Potato Research Institute had a huge slope and this served as the ski run. Here were no facilities, just a beautiful snow-covered slope. Panchi Sen was of course the instructor and the occasion was more fun than skiing. My greatest thrill was that I got to drive the jeep. As the skiers got to the bottom of the slope I would collect them and drive them back to the top of the hill.

I tried to ski but after falling repeatedly, ending up in the snow, face down, I gave it up! I enjoyed driving the jeep up and down the hill in the snow. That love of driving a four-wheel-drive vehicle has stayed with me till today.

Four-wheel-drive vehicles have opened up a whole new dimensions in Himachal but sadly skiing is non-existant. Considering that Himachal has massive snowfields, skiing should have become one of the most exciting attractions for tourism. Narkanda has a ski centre but it is an apology for a skiing facility. Solang has a ski slope but it features more snow scooters than skiiers. Considering that Himachal has seventy-one high peaks and of this thirty-six are over 6,000 metres above sea level, skiing, climbing, hiking should have been Himachal's foremost offering to the fun- and adventure-seeking tourist. Sadly, it is not so.

However, where Himachal has very successfully exploited its natural resources is car rallying. Here again it would be thanks to the four-wheel-drive vehicles. Himachal offers thousands of kilometres of rugged 'kutcha' tracks for rallying through its hills, forests, along its mighty rivers and over its famous passes.

The credit for introducing motor sports to North India in general and Himachal in particular, goes to Nazir Hoossein, a charismatic man with a rallying background. In 1980, Nazir brought the first Himalayan

The Ridge. The frescoes surrounding the church's chancel window was
designed by Lockwood Kipling, Rudyard's father

Rally to Himachal. It grew in stature and in a few years could boast of being the only international sporting event in the country. It was part of the Asia Pacific Championships and hosted drivers from Australia, New Zealand, Holland, Belgium and England.

The back roads of Himachal provided perfect roads for rallying. There was little traffic and though at first there was opposition from the locals when roads were closed, bus schedules and life disrupted, attitudes have changed today. Little known villagers are suddenly on the international radar. Today the same people whole-heartedly lend support to rallies passing through their little-known villages. They await the gaily painted cars, mostly four wheel drive Gypsys to go roaring through their villagers. The sound of the rally-prepared engines reverberates through the hills as the villagers line the road and cheer them on. There has been a sea change in the lives of these simple people who have taken up rallying themselves. Some of the best-known rallyists today are Himachalis.

As the Himalayan Rally grew in size and stature, Nazir Hoosein introduced a new format of motor sport, the Raid. The Raid is a long-distance rally. The rallies being run at that time were two, may be three day affairs and were never more than three or four hundred kilometres long.

The year 1988 was when the National Great Desert Himalaya first ran in Himachal. As the name implies it was an event that introduced the Raiders to the great desert of Rajasthan and the great high-altitude desert of Himachal and finally Ladakh.

The event ran for a few thousand kilometres in Rajasthan. The Raiders tackled sand dunes and swollen rivers in Rajasthan, cut through Haryana to Himachal to Simla and onto Manali. The Himalayan Rally ran till 1991 and for reasons not quite clear, fizzled out at the last moment. There was a gap of seven years and Vijay Parmar of the Kargil roll over fame came onto the scene.

Manjeev Bhalla and Atul Handa also came on to the scene. The total experience of those three would exceed fifty years of rallying experience. They gave the world of motor sport, the Raid de Himalaya.

All three are Himachalis and the Himalaya is their playground. The Raid de Himalaya is the longest, roughest, toughest, highest and coldest motoring event in the world!

The first event was run in 1999 and the ninth edition was in October 2007. The event flags off in Simla and winds its way, through Narkanda, Sainj and crosses over to Kullu district and moves across Jalori Pass to Manali. Then it traverses over Rohtang Jot to Gramphoo at the bottom of Rohtang in the Lahaul Valley. A sharp right turn takes the event over the Kunzam Pass, 16,000 feet above sea level into the Spiti Valley and to Kaza and Tabo.

From there it doubles back to Gramphoo, Koksar, Keylong, Patsio and the final destination is Srinagar via Leh and over the high passes. It has made to Srinagar a couple of times but on a few occasions had to be terminated at Bara Lacha La. Some said the snow conditions were abominable; others like me and a hordes of die-hard Raiders say that the conditions are simply marvellous. There is no place on this planet like Himachal to have motor sports events. It is a supreme test of man and machine versus mountain. You come out a better person with a respect for Mother Nature. This is the magic of the magnificent Himalaya.

◆

If you long for some old-world charm and the magnificent deodar forests, the place to motor to is Chail. Situated at a height of 2,150 metres which is higher than Shimla, Chail is set on a hilltop amidst towering pines. Since Chail is off the beaten track, it has remained untouched by the wanton destruction that cement and concrete have wrought on Shimla.

Chail was built by the Maharaja of Patiala at the turn of the last century. The Maharaja was known as a cavalier king who pretty much did as he pleased. It was because of one of his shenanigans in Shimla that the British banned his entry there. Undeterred, the Maharaja set out to build his own summer capital. He chose Chail. It was secluded, set in a mighty deodar forest and in pristine Himalayan surroundings.

The Chail Palace was built and today is the Chail Palace Hotel, a prized property of Himachal Tourism. One of the attractions of Chail Palace Hotel is the numerous walks amidst the forest surrounding the property. The Maharaja was a great sportsman and he built a cricket ground in Chail and its claim to fame is that it is the highest cricket pitch in the world. It is also the fastest. The pitch is cement and with jute matting on it, the rarified air providing little resistance to the ball, even a medium pace bowler becomes a cannon.

One of the most dramatic drives in Himachal is from Chail to Kufri via Chini Bungalow. It's only about twenty-five kilometres but the road provides a fantastic panoramic view of the great Himalaya. The road is cut along the side of the mountain with a precipice on the 'khud-side'.

From Chini Bungalow the road drops down to Kufri on the National Highway. Today it is a well-maintained black top road but it is actually the 'Hindustan-Tibet Road of olden days. Narkanda is almost fifty kilometres from Kufri.

The area around Narkanda is steeped in history. Thanedar, as it is called today, is derived from Thanda (cold) and Dhar (mountain). The cold mountain. A Christian missionary from Pennsylvania, Samuel Evans Strokes came and settled here. His mission was to introduce Christianity to the locals and convert them to the way of Christ. However, the hunter became hunted. Samuel Evans fell in love with a Hindu woman and converted to Hinduism and became Satyanand Strokes! He also made one of the greatest contributions single-handed in Himachal. He introduced apples to Himachal and changed the life of every man, woman and child for all times to come.

In 1956, when it was decided to extend the road, it had to be re-aligned. Till then, the mules were the only mode of transport and the animals could take the steep gradient. Motorised vehicles could not come up the steep slope. The new alignment was through Oddi, Kumairsain Kingal and Sainj.

On my various motoring expeditions on this stretch, one of the joys of travelling are the numerous eateries. The dhabas serve an excellent meal at all times. '*Karhi*-rice' is the standard fare and of course the Himalayan speciality 'bread *pakora*' with a mug of sweet tea makes sure the traveller is always happy! *Aaloo* and mushroom stuffed paranthas are available easily since both *aaloo* and mushrooms are grown locally in the area.

At Sainj the road comes down to meet the Sutlej river, India's fastest flowing river. There is a rather fancy restaurant, or rather an up-market dhaba that has come up in Sainj. It has an interesting *a la carte* menu to cater to an empty stomach and that one offering that appeals to any traveller and it's not on the menu—clean toilets!

The drive to Rampur, forty kilometres away, is along the Sutlej river. Rampur has been an important trading post for centuries. Traders from Tibet used the Shipki La pass and it is here that bread *pakoras* give way to *momos* and *thupka*. The architecture also begins to change. The flat slate roofs, so typical of Himachal change to the pagoda style roofs, an import from Buddhist Tibet.

Our destination is Sarahan. Jeori is twenty-five kilometres away and from Jeori a steep twenty kilometre climb brings us to Sarahan. Sarahan being almost 2,000 metres above sea level was the summer seat for Rampur Bushahir. The famous Bhima Kali temple is in Sarahan and is one of the oldest temples in Himachal. The architecture is unique. It is built entirely of wood and in the pagoda style. The courtyard is of slate. The most outstanding feature is the main gate which is made out of silver.

The Hotel Srikhand is a fine place to stay and one gets a view of the snow-clad Srikhand range from the bedroom balcony. There was a beautiful small British-style bungalow that was part of the hotel complex. It has also been torn down to make way for a modern building.

◆

There is another side to Shimla. It is the wanton destruction of one of the most beautiful towns. From being the Queen of the Hills, it has degenerated to near slum-like conditions. The Queen, now a doddering dowager is clothed in tattered clothes—her tiara is askew, the jewels are gone.

Some of the finest buildings like Kennedy House, the first English-style bungalow built in Shimla, the Secretariat and Peterhoff, home to governor-generals and viceroys of India have all been consigned to flames.

What has made matters worse is that the rebuilding of these buildings has been entrusted to the PWD, the Public Works Department. They build roads and lay sewage lines. They cannot build hotels like Peterhoff. Peterhoff today is a monumental disaster. Built out of stone and marble brought in from Rajasthan, the material is completely unsuited for the hills. The traditional Himachali material was ignored. Wood, slate and chiseled stone is what was required to 'restore' this building.

Two of my favourite bungalows, that did not perish in fires, have been pulled down. History is being razed. Peach Blossom in Fagu was pulled down to put up an ugly concrete and marble hotel. The original bungalow where I have stayed many times was an English-built rest house. It could have been retained as a reminder of the Raj. Indians with feeling and foreigners for a trip back in time would have loved the ambience of wooden floors, rickety doors and the old-world charms. It's gone, lost forever. We have a very poor apology in its place.

But, for me, there is a Himachal that exists in the senses. It is not possible to forget the valleys full of floating mist, white clouds against a crisp blue sky, the eternal snow of the Himalayas, smoke drifting up from a wood fire in the early morning cold, the smell of fresh-cut wood, freshly turned earth in the orchards, the resinous odour of the conifers, the damp smells of foliage that only the monsoon can bring. Himachal lives!

And Himachal lives because of its magnificent mountains. Nowhere are these mountains praised better than in the Buddhist prayer.

They are my mother
and my father
They are the earth
and the sky
Darkness and light
Sun and Moon.
Life and Death
They give me Food
They give me Water
They are my children.

Under Another Sky

Pankaj Mishra

I spent much of my twenties in a little Himachali village north of Shimla called Mashobra. It was a serene and fulfilling time; and like most good things in life it came about with a minimum of fuss, with no anticipation or planning.

Beauty is Truth: A glimpse of Mashobra

I had gone to Shimla in the spring of 1992 in order to find a cottage I could rent cheaply for a few summers. For the first couple of days, a lethargic estate agent showed me around a few sunless houses with damp cement walls, and it became clear that the silence and seclusion I associated with living in the mountains weren't to be found in the city's aggressive favela-like squalor. I had given up on Shimla; and that morning, when I took the bus to what had been described as a 'nice picnic spot' in my guidebook, I was hoping only to kill some time before taking the train back to Delhi.

The half-empty Himachal Roadways bus never stopped groaning, as it travelled through the broad open valley that slumbered peacefully in the pale sunshine. After about half an hour, we were surrounded by damp pine trees, and didn't regain our freedom for some time. Miniature mountain ranges of snow sat muddied beside the rutted road; at tea-shacks in dark little clearings, men in woollen rags hunched over pine cone fires.

The bus left the highway, stuttered down a steep road cramped by tottering houses of wood and tin, and then abruptly stopped. The driver killed the ailing engine, and everyone got out.

I was the last to leave. After the warm pungent smells of the bus, the cold came as a little shock. I saw that I was on a long ridge, facing a vast abyss filled with the purest blue air. The overall view, extending far to the east, was clear and quite spectacular: a craggy row of white mountain peaks, watching over, along with its minor underlings, the layers and layers of hills and ridges, a deep wooded valley.

The cliché fantasy broke with renewed force into my mind: wouldn't it be wonderful, I thought, to live here? I wondered if I should ask someone about places to rent. But the bus had emptied fast—I had been the only tourist on it—and there was no one around. It was then that I noticed the red tin roof of a largish house, and the steep spiralling dirt path that seemed to lead towards it.

The house was indeed big and handsome, if in an old-fashioned unostentatious way—it had been built, I later learnt, in the early '70s, when wood was plentiful and cheap. Flowerpots with peonies hung from the eaves; on the wide sunny porch, some red chillies lay quietly drying on a bright yellow sheet.

A window on the second floor was open; so was the main door that opened, I could see, on to a wooden staircase. I knocked and then heard the thump of bare feet on the floor. Someone appeared in the second floor window: a boy. I tried to explain what I was looking for. He disappeared and then a little later Mr Sharma came down the stairs.

He was a tall man, and seemed even taller in his fez cap, which I didn't see much of as the years passed, but the air of somber dignity it gave Mr Sharma that morning deepened by itself and became an air of mourning.

Road to Solitude: enroute to Mashobra

I told Mr Sharma, a bit awkwardly, that I was a student from Delhi, had spent two summers in Mussoorie and was now looking for a place in the mountains where I could read and write for a few years.

Mr Sharma gazed uncertainly at me for a moment, and then said that he would show me a cottage he had just built. We walked through an orchard—I didn't know then that these were apple and cherry and peach trees—and came to a narrow spur at the corner of the hill. It was here that a small cottage stood, directly above a cow shed and what looked like storage rooms for fodder.

It was just about functional: there were altogether three rooms, built in no particular order or design, but plonked next to each other; a bathroom and kitchen had been tacked on to them almost as an afterthought. The rooms were still full of the aroma of wood shavings—it stayed for many months until pushed out in October that year by the fragrance of freshly plucked apples stored underneath.

It was the balcony, however, that held me. It had the same view I had seen as I came out of the bus—the valley and the sky locked in a trance so private that you could only watch and be still yourself. In my mind's eye, I could already see myself sitting there on long evenings and gazing at the darkening world.

To my surprise, Mr Sharma asked for only Rs 1000 per month. He said that he too had come to Mashobra many years ago, wanting to read and write. His father had set up the first Sanskrit college in Shimla; he himself published a magazine in Sanskrit. He said he hadn't built the cottage to make money; it was meant to host needy scholars like myself.

I felt uncomfortable with being called a 'scholar': I had two mediocre degrees in Commerce and English; I hadn't written anything more than a few ill-considered reviews; I had barely any idea of what I could write about. But I didn't correct Mr Sharma; I did not wish to disappoint him. I had lived far more precariously in Mussoorie, at boarding houses run by Christians missionaries who saw me as a potential convert, who accosted me on my evening walks and wished to know the state of my soul. As I saw it, I was closer to being a scholar than a Christian.

And then it didn't really matter after I moved to Mashobra—just a few days after my first visit—and began to look like, with all my books and my steady absorption in them, a scholar of sorts.

I was awakened very early in the morning, the sun bullying its way even through the thick coarse-textured blue curtains of my window. The day stretched long and somewhat emptily, even though I went to bed babyishly early, at around 9pm, by which time the whole village was already asleep. I read all morning and then walked up the hill for lunch at a dhaba called 'Montu'. It was run by a hospitable Punjabi couple from the Kangra valley who lived in two low-roofed rooms at the back, curtained off from the dhaba with a torn cotton sari. I seemed to be their only customer at lunch: I sat alone on the wooden bench, under the outdated calendar with pictures of Shiva's exploits, and read the censorious articles in *Punjab Kesari* about masturbation (bad for eyesight) and blue jeans (bad for blood circulation), while Neeraj, the couple's young son, kept bringing in warm chapatis on a small aluminium plate.

Under the Greenwood Tree: trekking through the valley

The food was unremarkable, the menu, unchanging. There was frequently a lot of something called 'mixed dal,' which was all people could afford by way of dal in those days of post-liberalisation inflation. But Neeraj asked hopefully each time if I had found the food satisfactory, and I had to lie.

On the way back I stopped at the post office, a large dusty room with a disused telephone booth and an old damaged clock. There usually wasn't much mail for me; but the ageing postman was always grateful to give some for my landlords and save himself the steep walk to and from the house. I, in turn, would hand it to Mr Sharma's mother who sat knitting at the open second floor window.

She would sit there from late morning, all through the long drowsy afternoons until the sun disappeared behind the hills to the west, when the shadows glided swiftly across the orchard and the valley, and the soft golden peaks in the distance seemed to hold, briefly, all the light in the world.

The days acquired a rhythm; began to pass. The Sharmas sensed my mood and left me undisturbed, except on early mornings when Mr Sharma's mother would send around a plate of aloo parathas and a steel tumbler with steaming chai.

The Sharmas themselves lived quiet if disciplined lives, except when a special occasion—a festival, a *shradh*, or a yagna—brought the scattered family together in a happy whirl of silk chunnis, crying babies, and sizzling puris (some of which came my way). Much of their time went into tending the fruit trees and the cows. Mr Sharma's father, Panditji, a sprightly octagenerian, was also known as an astrologer; people from places as far off as Chandigarh came to consult him. And each month, Mr Sharma brought out a Sanskrit magazine, *Divyajyoti*, from an antique printing press kept in one of the dark rooms just below my cottage.

Mr Sharma told me that it had a circulation of 500 copies, and it went out to Sanskrit colleges and institutions. He wrote most of the magazine himself during the first half of the month—articles on social and political issues—and brought the loose pages to the press, smiling awkwardly when I passed him on the narrow path through the orchard. For the second half of the month, Daulatram, the big round-faced jovial printer and handyman, would laboriously hand-typeset the longhand version, a lonely figure in a corner of the dark room messy with wooden galley trays and metal sticks: the tips of his finger were stained black when he came up to my cottage to replace a fuse, or to offer some peaches. A week before the fifteenth of each month, the issue would be printed. The press would begin to loudly hum as Daulatram turned on the power, and then after an uncertain staccato start, ease into a regular beat, its rhythms as peculiarly soothing as that of a train at night. Then, on the morning of the fifteenth, Daulatram would jauntily walk up the hill to the post office, holding the finished copies in a small bundle under his giant arm.

My association with the Sharmas gave me a certain status in the village. Strangers said *namaste* as they passed me on the road; the *dukaandaars*, idle behind open sackfuls of *rajma* and *chana* and rice, were attentive, eager to talk, and offer me gossip about panchayat politics. But I was shy with them. I did not want to get too involved in the life of the village, or with anything that took me away for too long from reading and writing and the silence of the valley.

A Room of One's Own: Mishra's cottage

I was grateful for the lack of middle-class people in the village; it would have been more difficult to avoid them. The owner of the small fruit juice factory, a certain Mrs Jain, rarely left Delhi, and left most of the management to an old Gurkha. I did see once or twice the retired colonel who lived in a strange looking house which I subsequently realised had been modelled on the semi-detached houses of England. He made mushroom pickles, and sold them in jars of Kisan jam that were placed in neat rows on a rickety table underneath a fading beach umbrella in his front lawn.

There were other old houses, built during British times, and never properly possessed by their later owners. One of these, I heard, belonged to Waheeda Rahman, although I never saw her in Mashobra, never saw the chains taken off the iron gates to her house. One summer, the gates were painted over with black. I thought then that she might be on her way. But weeks went past; the monsoons came; the paint began to peel off and reveal the rust underneath; and the tufts of wild grass covered the cobbled driveway to the house.

The bells on the old church that loomed over the village were silent on Sunday mornings, until the time the local diocese set up a drug-rehabilitation programme there, when trendy-looking young men from Assam and Meghalaya appeared in the *kiraana dukaan* with unusual demands for Maggi soup; and you heard, passing below the church, the soft guitar chords of songs by John Denver, and Simon and Garfunkel.

The summer months saw a few bored-looking tourists in the village. They didn't stay for more than an hour or two; there was little to hold them: most people, I had heard, came to Shimla for the promenades on the Mall, idlis and softies at Baljis, and the video games parlours.

When I came to live in Mashobra, its first big hotel called The Gables had just come up. I went there occasionally, when wearied by Montu's unchanging fare. The vast panelled lobby and giant-sized paintings of durbars and banquets could be unsettling after the dusty shabbiness of the village. The menial staff consisted of villagers who were always embarrassed to be found out in their Raj-style cummerbunds and tunics. Conversation with them was always strained in that setting, the stylish young manager from Sector 17, Chandigarh watching us warily from behind the reception counter. I was always relieved when the time came to pay the bill and get out of there.

Another tourism venture began to come up towards the east of the village, in a hamlet called Daojidhar, where fluorescent-bright tents appeared one day on a grassy spur. I often went walking there; the views of the snows and the valleys were more extensive from that side of the hill, beyond which lay Kufri and Wildflower Hall, the house Kitchener, the commander-in-chief of the British Indian army, had lived in. One evening, I met the entrepreneur. He was from Shimla, and restless with plans. Shimla was dead, he declared; it had been killed by tourism. Mashobra could be a wonderful alternative to those who loved quiet places in the hills.

He had some partial success, I think, with backpacking students. On cool summer nights, I saw bonfires on his property, and heard sounds of singing: once again, college-festival favourites. But the summer remained serene for the rest of the village. The afternoons were particularly still, for the inhabitants found the thirty degree

Celsius heat excessive. Maruti vans loaded with tourists and blaring Hindi songs would arrive at the spot where I had my first glimpse of the valley and then hurtle off to Craignano, two miles north, where an Italian adventurer had built a house in the mid-nineteenth century. Meanwhile, the kiraana dukaans remained closed, the men retired for siestas behind wooden multi-hinged shutters covered over with faded photos of Hema Malini endorsing Lux beauty soap, and Dara Singh weighing in for Milkfood ghee.

This Too Shall Pass: the valley is changing as time goes by

The village looked even more withdrawn during the monsoons, when some shops didn't open at all for days on end, the empty road offered a hundred small and big muddy mirrors, and the damp drew the map of the former Soviet Union on the white walls of The Gables. It rained heavily and almost constantly, but you got used to it quite fast—so much so that on nights when the drumming on the tin roof finally ceased and the thousand nameless creatures in the forest took up an eerie chant, I would wake up, feeling a bit desolate, and only renewed rain could then send me back to sleep.

The day was a grey blur; stray clouds kept sneaking into the house; you couldn't see more than a feet or two ahead. The sun would timidly break through occasionally, and then the rain-battered roof hurriedly tried to dry itself and cracked its joints in short sharp impatient bursts.

The rain abruptly ceased in mid-September. It was rarely overcast again before the first snow of the winter; and it was the best time of the year, the present, as well as the future, brimful of bright clear days. The apples were lazily picked; the corn cobs laid out on the roofs; and the long grass cut and patiently stacked into little igloos which were sunburnt blonde in a few weeks.

On autumn afternoons, it was chilly inside the house, and I lay on the grassy platform above my cottage. I smelt the dew-damp earth, gazed into the deep blue endless sky, which faded just above the snow-capped peaks, and felt the blankness that I was beginning to recognise as part of being happy and content.

Such luck! I felt blessed, but also anxious. I hadn't signed a lease with the Sharmas. I depended on their goodwill, but it could run out any moment. Even after many years in Mashobra I couldn't quite believe in my good fortune; never ceased feeling the fragility of my claim upon the place; and I returned to Mashobra at the end of each winter burdened with a grim sense of foreboding, my imagination hectic with scenarios of rejection and disappointment.

There were other, related insecurities. Mr Sharma had seen in me a needy scholar; he wasn't entirely wrong. I wasn't really a scholar but I was certainly needy—not so much for money, whose lack didn't preoccupy me as much as my desire to write, a desire that I felt I had no choice but to fulfil, but which seemed impossible to realise until I knew what writing was all about.

I thought I would find out by reading more books in Mashobra; but it didn't work that way. I felt dwarfed by many of the books I read; whatever skill and intelligence I managed to see in them seemed beyond my capabilities; and it didn't help that I was trying to assess them in print. Reviewing is, and should feel like, a fraudulent activity until you have done at least some good writing of your own; and I was troubled by the ease with which my callow glib judgements travelled into the world. I felt I could go on churning out these 800-word reviews and remain as clueless as before. I tried my hand at a couple of novels; but I quickly lost momentum after the energetic starts.

Then, one afternoon, when I hadn't gone out for lunch, the postman brought a letter from a publisher in Delhi. He had seen my reviews and he now wanted to know if I was interested in writing a travel book. I wrote back, proposing a book on small towns—somewhat rashly, since I disliked even the trip I had to make to Shimla once a month.

But the book was an opportunity to redeem at least partially all the promises I had made to myself; and for five months I travelled across small-town India. During that long absence, I never really stopped missing my life in Mashobra, never stopped wishing that I was in my cottage instead of the grim dhaba-hotel full of echoing television noises where I usually found myself at the end of a day's journey.

It accounted for the impatient, frequently intolerant tone of the book I wrote, working flat out in Mashobra for three months. I barely looked at it again after I sent it off to the publishers. I went out of my way to avoid reading the reviews.

As it turned out, the book was noticed. The postman suddenly had more mail for me. One of the letters asked me if I was interested in a job in publishing. I should have said no. I had spent too much time by myself; I could no longer work in an office. But I was seduced by publishing's glamorous image.

And the decision exposed me to many more worlds and people than I had known in Mashobra. I travelled to England and America. My desires began to change, became more complicated, until the point where I couldn't quite recognise them as mine. They involved me with more and more people; kept me out of Mashobra for long stretches, and took me back there only for very brief periods.

On one of these short trips I learnt that Mr Sharma's mother had died the previous week. Mr Sharma and his father had just returned from immersing her ashes in the Ganges at Hardwar. The next issue of *Divyajyoti* was dedicated to her memory. The cover had a photograph of her, taken one bright summer afternoon from my camera. Inside, there were tributes from her son, daughters, sons-in-law and other people whose lives she had touched, even altered, in small but significant ways. It made you see how much solid endeavour and achievement even a restricted life as hers could contain.

There were other losses. The entrepreneur at Daojidhar abruptly died. The brightly-hued tents disappeared; tall wild grass grew in their place; no excited singing voices drifted in from the east anymore. Wildflower Hall was burned down in one of the mysterious fires that had claimed many old buildings in Shimla. I went to see the charred ruins. The flowerbeds still bloomed in the blackened lawns and tourists in Himachali folk-dress posed for pictures amidst them.

The Sharmas' big house now felt oddly empty. The second floor window, where Mr Sharma's mother had sat on sunny afternoons, lay open as before, but the new void there came as a pang each time I walked past it. I noticed grief beginning to work upon Mr Sharma's face, deepening the melancholy in his eyes, lining his mouth.

It was a difficult time for me. The publishing job had ended badly; and I hadn't known what to do for some time. I saw myself drifting, and felt powerless before the fact. It was really out of boredom and confusion that one day a stray memory of an earlier time in Benares came to me.

I started to write about it. The piece went through a couple of drafts before being published. It found appreciative readers; and then grew, in my mind, into a novel. I went back one summer to Mashobra to write it, and had new reasons to feel grateful for the silence and the solitude that I had come almost to take for granted.

It has been two-and-a-half years since then. My life has changed even more. I feel much less insecure as a writer. I travel a lot, mostly for work. It has become harder to spend time in Mashobra. I once thought of it as home; I am no longer so sure what or where home is. The cottage is still there, with my books and music. But I really can't go back for too long, and I can't be too sentimental about it. The longings and aspirations that gave point and urgency to my time in Mashobra have been partly realised; they now take me further away from it, and into the larger world.

In any case, time hasn't quite stood still for Mashobra. Places as much as people can be unfaithful. My slow betrayal of Mashobra has been accompanied by its own keen embrace of the modern world. You can buy Maggi soup as well as Tropicana Orange juice in the jazzed-up kiraana dukaans. The Gables has a new wing. New buildings, some of them hotels, have come up in the vicinity of my cottage; the seclusion I so cherished, that made possible all my reading and writing, is gone.

This at least is what I tell myself—if not always convincingly. On days when I am far away from Mashobra, in very different landscapes, I only have to see a patch of mellow light on a lawn, only have to feel a fresh bracing quality in the air, or hear the rain being fierce with a roof, to know that I want to be back, and never leave; and it's no use reminding myself then that the senses—those semi-magical faculties of sight, smell, hearing—hold not only your most truthful memories but also your most hopeless desires.

A View From the Raj Bhawan

V.S. RAMADEVI

I have had the good fortune of being the governor of Himachal Pradesh for almost two and a half years. Within a few days of my taking over the charge, the then Chief Minister Virbhadra Singh informed me of his cabinet decision to convert Barnes Court into Raj Bhawan permanently. He further mentioned that when Smt Indira Gandhi was the prime minister, she suggested that Barnes Court may be declared as Raj Bhawan so that it would be maintained properly and would not collapse being an old building.

Once the decision was taken, the cleaning and renovation work started immediately as the backyard and a side of the building was sinking. The restoration was done keeping in view the heritage of the building; we took care to preserve the old wooden furniture brought from Sialkot long ago. So, Barnes Court became the official residence of the governor of Himachal, the Raj Bhawan permanently when I was the governor.

When K.R. Narayanan, the then president of India, visited Raj Bhawan he was surprised to know that the Shimla Agreement was signed here in Barnes Court. He saw the table and chairs in the main drawing room on which Shimla Agreement was signed by Indira Gandhi and Zulfikar Ali Bhutto. Narayanan said that he did not know about this but had heard only about the place and the table at which the decision of the partition had taken place in the Viceregal Lodge.

Former Prime Minister of Pakistan late Benazir Bhutto had accompanied her father Z.A. Bhutto during the peace talks between India and Pakistan. Bhutto and his young daughter had stayed in Barnes Court as state guests. Indira Gandhi, the then prime minister of India, personally supervised the re-decoration of their suits. She had arrived in Shimla two days before the talks were to be held. She had disliked their interiors and she changed them overnight to match the highly polished teak wood panelling. She did Benazir's suit in pastel pink and green feminine shades suitable for a young girl. She also thoughtfully ensured that Z.A. Bhutto's favourite brand of cigars was placed in his bedroom. Even Piloo Modi, Bhutto's old friend was asked to be in Shimla where he disclosed that soon he would pen his book, *My Friend Zulfi*. Meena Kumari's evergreen *Pakeezah* was screened for the visiting Pakistanis their choice being unofficially asked beforehand.

The story of the Barnes Court goes much back in time and the building is steeped in history. The name comes from General Sir Edward Barnes, who was the adjutant general at the famous battle of Waterloo in 1815. He occupied the place in 1832. It is recorded that the news of the start of the First War of Independence triggered by the uprising at Barrackpore led by Mangal Pandey was given to General Anson, the British commander-in-chief at Barnes Court on 12 May 1857. The place is witness to momentous historical events of post-Independence India also such as the Shimla Agreement.

Before 1981 the Raj Bhawan was in the Peterhof, but when Peterhof was gutted in fire the residence of the Governor was shifted to Barnes Court which was the State Guest House till then. Later when the Peterhof was re-constructed the Raj Bhawan was again shifted to Peterhof in 1993. But as the re-constructed Peterhof was thought to be too big, the Raj Bhawan returned to Barnes Court.

Barnes Court had remained the Summer Raj Bhawan of Punjab government up to 1966. But after the reorganisation of states, when Shimla was allotted to Himachal Pradesh, Barnes Court was converted into a State Guest House and in the late 1970s it was made into a state guest house-cum-tourist bungalow.

Barnes Court not only has history but also the architecturally beautiful complex is located in idyllic surroundings. A unique feature of the building is that wherever one sits in the building, the tall beautiful trees and the sky with its changing colours and patterns would provide feast to the eyes.

Located on the southern-most point of the heritage zone of Shimla, Barnes Court is on a commanding site overlooking the green blue hills and thick forest towards south. On the east is the thick forest and secretariat complex is on the west. The grounds and gardens are charming and beautiful and it has a look of an old English country house but, of course, a very big one.

The Tudor-style Barnes Court complex consists of the main two-storied buildings housing office and residence. The main entrance to the building is facing the south, courtyard and terrace gardens are also located in the south; lawn, fish pool, band stand (gazebo for sitting purpose like rain shelter) and glass house are located towards the east. A herbal garden is situated towards the north. The ground and the first floor are well connected with internal staircase. There is a central heating system. There is also a lift inside which can be used in case of fire. The walls have been plastered in mud-mortar and painted in white. The Summit Hall, Conference Hall, Darbar Hall, Billiards Room, Dining Room for VVIPs and sitting room for VVIPs like the President and the Prime Minister are located on the ground floor. Recently the library and the guest room have been established on the first floor. The rooms have been tastefully named: Mahapushp, Monal, Kinner Kailash, Tushar, Anamika, Shyamla, Kamna, Annapurna and Tara. The sitting room (named as Antara), the dining room, kitchen and pantry for the personal use of the Governor are located on the first floor. The office is made of brick masonry with wooden flooring supported by steel joists. There is a false wooden ceiling which is carved beautifully.

For me it was a privilege and honour to have occupied the Barnes Court, a heritage building, for two and a half years and I have sweet memories of the place and the affection showered on me by the staff and people.

The very mention of the names of Shimla and Kinnaur brings back the sweet memories of juicy apples and of course no need to mention the beautiful and warm shawls, caps, scarves, jawahar jackets and wooden artifacts.

Hill people, whether they live in shacks or good houses, take life as it manifests with courage and enrich their lives with dance and music. As far as women are concerned they are not only beautiful, picturesquely dressed, but also hard-working. No doubt they are empowered, but overburdened with work as menfolk are normally easy going and do not share the burden of work.

Certain places in Himachal take us to bygone era of Puranas and Ramayana, certain other places take us to Mahabharat era and yet certain other places to Gautama Buddha's times. While travelling by helicopter through Rohtang Pass no one can forget the experience of seeing the green carpet, studded with diamonds, rubies and emeralds, spread below.

The Himachalis rejoice in song and dance and several festivals which are held throughout the year give them ample opportunity to do so.

The gods and goddesses who assemble during the Dussehra and Shivratri celebrations, do very much care for befitting places as per their protocol. The protocol battles are very funny and foreigners capture them in their camera with great delight.

Two aspects that attracted me most were the determination of the people to get their children educated and keenness to have planned families.

The percentage of education is very high and compares well with Kerala state. The Horticulture University is perhaps the first of its kind in the country. Further, the Agriculture University at Palampur is well equipped with bio-technology laboratory. Educational institutions run by various Christian Missionaries and Arya Samaj are very famous. Moreover I did not see any child labour in Himachal.

No child is left uncared as there are many orphanages to take care of them. The value of family planning and the need to have fewer children has been internalised by the people here. That is why the population of Himachal has remained steady for decades.

Unfortunately, the enchanting nature is not only beautiful but cruel too. However, Himachalis take it in their stride, making friends with nature and as if no untoward incident has happened. They are god-fearing and well-disciplined. Here I would like to narrate one incident. There was a cloud burst in one village of Rampur near Shimla causing great damage not only to the village but also to the power house that was coming up near about. On behalf of the Red Cross, we went there to distribute food stuff and other necessities. We saw an aged woman standing aside. We called her and tried to give a tin of oil and a small sack of wheat etc. But she politely refused to take stating that she had already taken her share and she was only standing aside to ensure others also have their share. There was no stampede as we see in other so-called bigger and developed states. I was greatly impressed by their honesty and discipline.

When I was transferred to Karnataka I organised the State Red Cross Diwali Mela in Barnes Court and have fond memories of it. People from all over the state came and various stalls from all the twelve districts showcased their respective culture. In addition, the army arranged bunkers and tried to recreate the life in the battlefield of Kargil.

It may not be out of place to mention that I was so inspired by the places and the people of Himachal Pradesh that I wrote a book in Telugu with Himachal as its background. A few of my readers informed me that after reading the book they could not help but make a trip to Himachal.

Landscapes of the Mind

PUNAM GUPTA

'The artist does not see things as they are but as he is'.

—Alfred Tonelle

To create with your mind, something where nothing existed before is perhaps the most exhilarating yet also, the most terrifying act. To face a blank canvas and to know that once you have applied that first daub of paint, nothing will be quite the same is a feeling that can have the power to either create or annihilate you. George Bernard Shaw once said, a true artist will let his wife starve, his children go barefoot, his mother drudge for his living at seventy sooner than work at anything but his art.

What Shaw said then may be just a bit exaggerated, all things considered today, but the point is that the creative force within an artist is so awesome yet so magnetic that he soon learns to become a master of evasion and excuses. His instinct, therefore, is to run a mile from the prospect of actually putting brush to canvas.

Why then do so many artists seem to conquer that overwhelming dread and manage to produce such significant works of art in a fairly small hill station such as Shimla? Why does this township and the areas around it spawn and nurture so much artistic talent? In fact it may come as a surprise to many that even today, Shimla hosts and boasts of an array of painters—contemporary and traditional—some well known and some not quite, who have some sort of connection with this town. These are multifaceted creative artists with styles and techniques as distinct as their personalities.

◆

Among the best known, and perhaps most controversial, of Shimla's painters is, of course, Amrita Sher-Gil. In 1921, Amrita came with her parents and sister Indira to live at their family home in Summerhill. Amrita was inspired not just by the Indian Pahari traditions of painting but also by the grand Himalayan vistas which surrounded her. Her highly romanticised depictions of the simple hill folk she saw continue to win her worldwide accolades, imbued as they are with a technical finesse, depth and maturity far beyond the brief years of her life.

Amrita was born in Budapest in 1913, the elder of two daughters. Her father was a Sikh aristocrat Umrao Singh Sher-Gil Majitha, a Sanskrit and Persian scholar. Her mother, Marie Antoinette Gottesmann, who came from an affluent bourgeoise family of Hungary, was a pianist and opera singer. Both parents were artistically and intellectually inclined, a factor which helped shape Amrita's early aesthetic sensibilities and empathy towards the arts, both eastern and western. In fact, in later years as well Amrita's personality was to reflect an attractive though enigmatic fusion of her European and jat sikh heritage.

In 1921, when Amrita was eight years old, her family decided to move to their family home in Shimla since they felt their girls needed exposure to their Indian roots. En route, they stopped at Paris where Amrita was exposed to the treasures of the Louvre for the first time. It is said the young girl was so mesmerised by Da Vinci's *Mona Lisa*, she gazed at the masterpiece for a long time. That experience, perhaps, was to decide the course of her life as a painter.

After settling in Shimla the Sher-Gils became actively involved in the elite social and cultural activities scenario prevalent in the

The Mall in the winter

town at that time. By the age of nine, Amrita and her sister Indira were giving piano and violin recitals, acting in plays staged at the famous Gaiety Theatre and participating in other cultural activities in town. A local newspaper reported in September 1924 that 'The Sher-Gil sisters performed creditably in two different dances, one a Hungarian dance and in the other as 'god pan and the girl who lost her way in the woods'.

Personal accounts of the years of her life between 1921 and 1929 reveal glimpses of her strong character and rebellious nature. While studying in a Roman Catholic convent, she rebelled against the school's compulsory mass attendance and wrote a letter to her parents denouncing Catholic rituals, which she considered bigoted and narrow-minded. The letter was intercepted by Mother Superior who immediately expelled the girl from school. This embarrassing episode signaled the end of Amrita's formal education after which she spent her days sketching and playing the piano under her mother's tutelage.

Amrita was also known to have been influenced by an Italian sculptor who lived near their residence in Shimla. It was with his inspiration that her interest in painting began to take shape. In 1927, she returned to India and began taking lessons under her uncle Erwin Backlay, a painter also well known as a scholar of Indian Art. Backlay introduced Amrita to the principles of Nagybanya, a school of traditional Indian painting. Later, when Amrita became popular she told him, 'It is to you I owe my skill in drawing.' However, his insistence that Amrita should paint real models exactly as she saw them irked her spirit and she soon became impatient to break the fetters of conventional rules and discover her unique identity.

The Sher-Gils soon realised that Amrita was an exceptionally gifted girl who needed a far more stimulating milieu to help her talents blossom. In 1929, Amrita went to Paris to take her study of art to higher levels. Here she took a degree from the famous Ecole de Beaux school of Arts, successfully completing works of art such as *The Torso* and *Young Girls*, which besides impressing critics and art enthusiasts, earned her awards and accolades never before received by one so young.

In 1935, the artist came back to Shimla. By then she had evolved her own distinct style, which, according to her, was fundamentally Indian in subject, spirit and expression. She began painting poor hill folk who to her romantic and naïve mind embodied the spirit of India. Her studio was in the annexe of her parent's house 'The Holme' at Summerhill and her living quarters were above it. Her first few paintings in Shimla included *Mother India*, *The Beggars* and *Woman with Sunflower*.

She sent some of her paintings to the annual exhibition of the Shimla Fine Arts Society in which many important artists participated. Though she was given an award for one of her paintings, she was displeased and returned it in indignation since in her opinion, her best work had been rejected, while an inferior and undeserving painting was chosen.

In the winter of 1935 she painted *Hill Men* and *Hill Women*, her signature works that mirror 'romantic visions of poverty'. Her main artistic mission became to paint the silent images of infinite submission and patience. She now sought to depict the angular brown bodies and reproduce on canvas the impression of their sad eyes. The contrast between the simple peasant folk she found on her family estate and the sophisticated traditions of Pahari miniatures she had studied earlier fired her with a desire to reinterpret her country as she perceived it. However, she now carried a deep sense of existential pain which she transferred to her canvasses.

After a trip to South India and Bombay in 1936, Amrita returned to Shimla, to begin a fresh phase in her painting. She had been deeply touched by her experience of the lyricism and sensuality of paintings and frescoes at Ajanta and Ellora caves. Her paintings therafter, such as *Girl with a pitcher*, reflected her need to explore traditional Indian art once again. She had written to her parents: 'Ajanta was wonderful. I have for the first time since my return to India learnt something, from somebody else's work'.

The *South Indian Trilogy*, her most memorable work, was painted at her studio in Shimla between the summer and autumn of 1937. This was followed by *Bride's Toilet* and *Brahmcharis*. In October 1937 she painted *Story Teller* and *Siesta*. After her exhibition at Lahore in November 1937, she came back to Shimla and began work on *Hill Scene*.

In 1938, Amrita went back to Hungary where she decided to get married to her cousin Victor Egan. A year later, the couple came back to Shimla with the plan of living with Amrita's parents. They had planned that Amrita would now paint and Victor would practise medicine. Her mother, who was known for her hard-headed and eccentric behaviour was hostile towards Victor and made it difficult for the young couple to settle down. Despite domestic tensions, Amrita managed to paint *Resting*, a beautiful painting of four women and a young girl with the basket of flowers, surrounded by foliage. This was probably her last painting in Shimla.

At the invitation of Kirpal Singh her cousin, Amrita and Victor left for Saraya, a village in Uttar Pradesh where the family owned a sugar factory. However, Saraya was hardly a place that was aesthetically inspiring. Soon the young couple began to explore the possibility of settling in Lahore. All the same, Amrita continued to be drawn to Shimla her hometown, where she had spent some of her happiest, most fruitful years. She visited it several times while Victor explored Lahore.

In August 1941, Amrita Sher-Gil, also known as the Frida Kahlon of India bade her final farewell to Shimla and moved to Lahore where she died on December 6 of the same year, at the age of twenty-eight.

◆

Apart from Amrita Sher-Gill, there have been several other highly reputed artists with roots in Shimla. Ram Kumar, one of India's most feted artists, was born in Shimla in 1924, and spent his childhood here. His sublime landscapes in oils and acrylics with their sweeping strokes of colour even today carry that aura and freshness of the mountains only achieved by someone who has a special connection with them.

Krishen Khanna, another of India's foremost contemporary artists and the recipient of so many international and national awards spends long summers here at his family home in Chota Shimla, getting away from it all while creating most of his spectacular works of art.

Vivan Sundaram, Amrita Sher-Gil's nephew and an artist of international acclaim was born here, as was J. Swaminathan who also belonged to the Progressive School of Artists in the country, with India's top few painters amongst its members

Sanat Kumar Chatterjee is an accomplished and highly revered artist belonging to the Bengal school of art, who also lives and works in Shimla. 'Guruji', as he is respectfully known to his many disciples has to his credit over 10,000 paintings and 1100 sculptures. Over the years, Sanat Chatterjee has evolved a distinct style of painting on silk scrolls. His son Him Chatterjee is also an accomplished and versatile painter in his own right.

Like Shri Chatterjee, H.C. Rai was one of the pioneers of the fine arts movement in Shimla. A prolific painter of portraits and landscapes typifying and glorifying Shimla's natural beauty, Prof Rai was the first principal of the Arts College in the town and a well-reputed and popular artist like several of his contemporaries in Shimla such as M.C. Saxena, K.K. Kidwai and Jawaharlal Sharma.

Bani Prasanno is a Bengali artist who has lived and worked here for decades. His powerful and sensual acrylics, which reflect his vibrant personality, have won him huge appreciation in India and abroad. Billy Malhans is another of Shimla's well-known environmentalists and artists. His detailed pen drawings have immortalised some of Shimla's most awesome architecture.

During the pre-camera era of the nineteenth and early twentieth century as well, there were several painters of repute such as Emily Eden and Captain G.P. Thomas. Their meticulous brushwork and etchings record and portray the virginal, pristine hillscapes of Shimla at that time. Apart from being displayed and sold at periodical fairs organised at Annandale, their works of art, like those of some Indian painters at the time, were publicised by the Fine Arts Society formed in 1865. Arranged at the Bishop Cotton School as well as Auckland House and the Town Hall beside other venues, art exhibitions became a regular annual feature at that time.

Apart from professional artists of wide national and international acclaim who have chosen to make Shimla a temporary or permanent home, there is a range of talented amateur painters who live here, working quietly and unobtrusively, content to paint more as a hobby.

◆

So what is it about Shimla that converts latent ideas into full-bodied expression?

Could it be that Shimla provides that obscure nook; that all-important privacy where you can forget and be forgotten? You can safely crawl back into a warm and welcoming womb and be happy to just be, with only the benign gaze of the mountains to judge you. Living in a buzzing metropolis or larger city easily provides that escape from the responsibility of creating. Ideas just taking shape can easily die a premature death or get smothered under the clutter of chaotic routine.

Despite the modern-day façade of wine and cheese parties and apparent bonhomie, creative artists, by and large, are not exactly known for their sunny dispositions or bubbly temperaments. Although not all are Van Gogh, they do feel deeply and hurt longer. They are quick to anger, and as quick to rejoice. Their sensitivities are more acute, their sensibilities finer and less resilient to setback. Amrita Sher-Gil's wide-eyed portrayals speak volumes of her tendencies toward melancholia.

To such tortured souls, being in the hills can be just the balm needed to ease away the weight of their feelings. A place of solitude provides the silence and comfort so crucial to articulating and setting the artistic spirit free. Where the dirt of all those chaotic thoughts can just settle down and let the purity of dreams surface instead. Shimla may be just the place to relax a mind sore with too much interaction; like an emotional massage. With its laid-back soporific lifestyle, it seems to be just outside the realm of time, unjudgemental, unhurried. Here you need have no pretensions and you need fear no mistakes. Your art can then be as natural as you.

On the other hand, making something with your hands could also cushion the free-fall of utter boredom that can take over life here after a point. The absolute certainty of knowing no one will come, no one will go and nothing is likely to happen... unless you make it, can drive anyone to the edge of insanity. To a dynamic and creative mind, boredom can spur a restlessness that can be unbearable unless pegged down by tangible ideas. For a mind churning with such ideas, it could be just the barrenness so necessary to sow the seeds of creativity. That is why Shimla seems to be not so much for the debutante as for the virtuoso...for a person already brimming over with a rich and ready fund of imagination on which to feed.

On a clear day, the air in Shimla is translucent, actually providing an almost hallucinogenic and heightened quality to everything around. The blues are bluer, and the browns, browner. Like snow melting on grass or rising mist, your mind clears too, helping to make ideas more visible. Your imagination can take wing... swooping and soaring like mountain eagles, teasing and mercurial like the clouds, blowing your mind like gusts of icy winds.

It is equally true, however, that many artists see more with their eyes closed and their minds open. They prefer to paint not what they see but what they are. The landscapes of the mind reveal peaks and troughs, shadows and highlights, reflections and textures far richer and deeper than any field of vision.

An artist usually has a hundred reasons not to do what she can do when all she needs is one reason to do what she can. Shimla, perhaps, provides just that one reason.

Eulogy to the Green Hills

PANKAJ KHULLAR

The year is 1956. I am eight years old and the summer vacations are fast approaching. Kanpur is sweltering hot and dusty to boot. The smoke from the hundreds of chimneys dotting the skyline of this 'Glasgow of India' covers the sky like a dark pall. My sister and I are anxiously waiting for the day that we will begin the journey that will take us to Kandaghat, that little village nestled in the hills just beyond Solan. This is an annual feature, almost a ritual, though I will be joining for the first time!

Aunts and cousins gather at the railway station (fathers will join later) and soon we are aboard the Kalka Mail for the first leg of our journey. From Kalka we board the bus for our final destination, Kandaghat. As the bus literally moaned and groaned its way up the slope from Kalka towards Shimla (or Simla as it was then spelt), one could not help but recall the lines recorded by Sir Edward Buck in his paper presented before the Simla Natural History Society in 1855:

> Let us hasten up from Kalka, then, as quickly as we can, and pass by that noble mango tree which, spreading over the road a few miles from the foot of the hill, always seems to me like a huge boundary mark erected by nature for the purpose of noting the division between the flora of the plains and the flora of the hills.

The huge mango tree on the outskirts of what is now Parwanoo might well be the same tree as alluded to by Buck. Interestingly, there was hardly any tree vegetation up till Dharampur, from where the road branched to the left towards Kasauli, except for a few scattered mango, amaltas and semal. This I came to realise only after I joined the Forest Service in 1971 and got allocated to Himachal Pradesh. In 1956, however, the only indication one had of entering the coniferous tree zone, and thus really and truly the hills of Himachal Pradesh, was the cool, pine-oil-laden, breeze from Koti onwards. It is claimed that, while other trees during respiration take in carbon-dioxide and give out oxygen, the pine tree gives out enriched oxygen, or ozone. It was perhaps for this reason that TB sanitaria were set up in the hills, whether at Murree, Kasauli or Dharampur.

It was also at Koti, coincidentally, that the engine of the bus would get heated up. The bus drivers had it down to a T—either they knew the exact distance the buses would go before heating up, or they had conditioned their buses to heat up only at the locations where water springs were available—but the fact remained that whenever the engine heated up, and before the radiator cap blew off, the bus would stop at a natural spring. The conductor would extract an empty oil can from beneath the driver's seat, jump off the bus, rush to the water trough and start splashing water on to the radiator, with the driver gunning the engine all this while. Interestingly these water troughs were also the 'stages' where the ponies and horses taking the sahibs and tongas from Kalka to Simla prior to 1903 paused to refresh themselves.

As a matter of fact, soon after British officers started frequenting and spending summers at Shimla from 1820 onwards, the Kalka-Shimla Cart Road *via* Kasauli/Subathu was laid. There were seventeen stages of four miles each to cover the sixty-odd miles (ninety-six kilometres) from Kalka to Shimla. Since every 'stage' had to have facilities for food and water, for animals as well as humans, it is fairly safe to presume that there were at least seventeen 'baolies' or natural springs fairly well distributed along the entire route. I distinctly remember at least four natural springs in and around Kandaghat—one at 'Ded Ghraat', another two between that place and Kandaghat Bazaar, and another at Srinagar, just opposite the SDM residence. It is reputed that water from this last was transported to Patiala on a regular basis for use by the Maharaja there. About forty-odd springs and 'baolies' existed between Kalka and Shimla about twenty-five years ago; today there are just nine!

When we finally got to Kandaghat, our mothers and aunts got busy in gossiping, cooking and cards, and we children were more or less on our own, free to explore the bazaar, the railway tracks, and the hills and dales. Many were the forays we made down to the Ashwini Khud and up to the Karol Tibba and many were the scrapes and scratches we suffered from the falls we took and the thorny bushes we forced our way through. By the time our summer vacations were over, our arms and legs were covered with scabs and coloured red or blue, depending upon whether mercurochrome or gentian violet had been applied to the wounds.

I distinctly remember that the barberry (*Berberis aristata*) and the wild raspberry (*Rubus ellipticus*) used to be in fruit at that time and, as we wandered along the village paths and trails, we, along with the other village children, would gorge ourselves on the succulent berries. I am told that the number of such bushes has vastly reduced now partly because the barberry bushes have been overexploited for their medicinal roots, and also due to the construction of roads where the village paths used to be. Down by the Ashwini river (more of a rivulet really) one would be able to catch fish with a hook and line. On every trip we were able to hook a couple of fish, which we proudly carried home to be cooked. Now, I am told, the Ashwini has become so polluted that there are no longer any fish surviving in its waters!

The Karol Tibba, as I have already mentioned, was another favourite haunt. We would ascend to the railway line, walk along it for about a kilometre and then take the footpath leading to the small village of Mai, where dwelt a retired forest ranger, one Shri

Man Singh. His grand-daughter was my cousin Veena's class fellow; hence Veena was ever forcing us to accompany her there. Now that I think of it, it was perhaps Man Singh's stories that sowed the seed of desire in my mind to become a forester. Over some 'Makki' rotis and spinach, Man Singh used to narrate his experiences as a forester, sometimes thrilling us with his encounters with wild bears and leopards, and sometimes making our skins crawl when he talked about ghosts and 'churails' that abounded near the abandoned 'baolies' or village wells. The path to Mai was through dense forest of oak, beneath which hardly any sunlight penetrated. In fact it was quite moist and clammy underfoot, with rotting oak leaves strewn everywhere. At one point, just above Mai village, on the way to Karol temple, I was able to collect some calcium deposits with oak leaf impressions in the form of fossils, a treasure that I still retain. I am sorry to report, though, that the oak forests spreading all the way from Salogra to Kandaghat are today severely depleted partly due to the ever-increasing demand for fuel wood and green fodder, and partly due to the lack of regeneration, that is trampled over or grazed by the innumerable cattle that roam the hillsides. A good thing, however, is that the treeless hills facing the south are today covered with thick patches of chir pine plantations.

Kandaghat was a small village in those days. For that matter, it is still a small hamlet, located about thirty kilometres short of Shimla on the Kalka-Shimla highway. It had gained importance as the summer retreat of the Maharajas of Patiala, who built a palace (Chail View) and located some courts there. That is how a small community of lawyers and advocates (including my grandfather) set up base in this small village. Later the summer capital was shifted to Chail, when the erstwhile Maharaja was banned from entering Shimla due to some misdemeanour that annoyed the governor-general. Incidentally, it was from the Maharaja of Patiala, as well as the Rana of Keonthal, that the British had obtained in 1830, through exchange, part of the area in which Shimla was later located. Till the early 1970s the only lights in the village were at the railway station and in the bazaar. Our house, in the outskirts was lighted only by hurricane lanterns. As we sat in the open in the late evenings, under the canopy of stars, which appeared much closer to earth here than at Kanpur or Delhi, stories would start about shikar—tall stories obviously. What true shikari can avoid boasting? Talk would soon turn to the increasing number of leopards and hyenas in the hills. Sure enough, whenever a torch beam was directed towards the edges of the small clearing we sat in, we could see eyes shining like small lamps. 'There,' said an uncle, 'now do you believe me?' I never came to know whether the eyes belonged to leopards, hyenas or just jackals, but the sight was enough to chill us. It is no coincidence that every summer we would lose one or two pet dogs, obviously carried away by leopards.

The high point of our summer vacations used to be visits to Chail and to Shimla. I remember boarding the bus to Shimla with assorted cousins and aunts immediately after breakfast and, after an arduous but exciting journey of two hours, disembarking at the old bus stand near Thakur Hotel. From there we would slowly work our way through the crowded Ram Bazaar and Lower Bazaar towards the Mall. Once there, we children were shepherded to the Ladies Park (now Rani Jhansi Park), handed our lunch packets and severely warned not to move from the park while the adults took off for Jakhoo temple. Children were never taken along to Jakhoo on the excuse that the monkeys there were reported to often carry away little ones. I know now for sure that this was untrue, but who were we to question adults in those days? Regarding staying in the park—that was a rule made to be broken. Soon we were wandering along the Ridge, the Lakkar Bazaar and the Mall. A favourite spot was the wooden bridge spanning the 'nullah', at the point where the lift from the cart road today disgorges tourists, and where that hideous monstrosity—the Indoor Sports Stadium—has recently been built. What lay beyond the 'Combermere Bridge', as it was then called, I did not know, but no visit to Shimla was considered complete till one had walked on the bridge, and posted a letter at the quaint post office that bordered it. The bridge was dismantled and replaced with a concrete structure in

Jakhu Temple (in AD 1850)

1973, but the Post Office still stands, lost below the towering sports complex and the Bridge View Hotel.

The annual visit to Chail was much more interesting. The summer capital of the Maharajas of Patiala, the small village's claim to fame was the world's highest cricket ground, created by levelling the tallest peak of the place. Though it is reputed that the MCC once played a match here against a Patiala eleven, the ground is now part of the Military School. The chief attraction for us children was the bench of planks placed half way up a huge, gnarled oak tree bordering the ground. Many decades later I got a chance to go there again and, I am happy to say, the bench was still there and the school children were still clambering over it. As a forester, I also got a chance to carry out inspections in the forests around Chail. The dense oak forests spreading from Janedghat, a few kilometres from Chail, down to Junga and to Koti, on the Chail-Kufri Road, were a special attraction. One could spot red jungle fowl and sometimes kalij pheasants along the paths.

As a matter of record, even a hundred years ago, Simla was infamous for, and still is, for its omnipresent monkeys. As far back as 1862 a subaltern, who came up to Shimla just before Christmas, wrote:

> The monkeys and such leopards and other wild beasts as were gradually being driven in by all the encroaching snows made such a noise that a decent night's rest became out of the question. It was a wonderful sight, the spectacle of monkeys in their thousands careering about the Mall, or seated on the rails or the rocks, in the early morning.

Edward J Buck, in his book *Simla Past and Present*, first published in 1904 says:

> Of recent years, the monkeys have become a decided nuisance in Simla, as they are terribly destructive pests in station gardens and do not improve our houses by frolicking on their roofs.

The native population of the station, however, accepts the position with that quiet resignation for which the inhabitant of Hindustan is so famous, and in the Lakkar Bazaar, the 'bundars' are particularly numerous and mischievous.

Nowhere were the monkeys more numerous than on 'Jakko', as Jakhoo Hill was then called. It must have been on 'Jakko' that Rudyard Kipling penned his verses to the omnipresent rhesus macaque thus:

His hide was very mangy, and his face was very red, And ever and anon he scratched with energy his head. His manners were not always nice, but how my spirit cried. To be an artless *Bandar* loose upon the mountain side!

So I answered: 'Gentle *Bandar*, an inscrutable Decree Makes thee a gleesome fleasome Thou, and me a wretched Me. Go! Depart in peace, my brother, to thy home amid the pine; Yet forget not once a mortal wished to change his lot for thine.

What never ceased to excite me about Shimla was the huge swathe of greenery here. Having worked and lived in Himachal Pradesh for almost four decades, I now realise what drew the British to Shimla. It was not just a chance to escape the heat and dust of the plains, but also the opportunity to stay amidst the lush forests and partake of the fresh air, so to recuperate and refresh themselves for at least some part of the year. In fact, Shimla was initially seen as a sanatorium for rest and recuperation of the soldiers and officers suffering from the cholera epidemic then besieging Calcutta, and prevalent even up to Subathoo. Captain Mundy, *aide-de-camp* to Lord Combermere in 1828, recorded in his journal that 'The temperature of Simla seems peculiarly adapted to the European constitution. "The scorching ray Here pierceth not, impregnate with disease".' He went on to record that Simla offered a better alternative to South Africa, where the invalids and wounded had earlier made their way to recuperate, with little hope of returning.

While it is a fact that the ridges and slopes of Shimla were densely wooded and covered with huge trees of all descriptions when the station was first settled in 1816, it is also a fact that the forests were soon cleared and gaps created for construction of cottages and government buildings. Sir Edward Buck, in 1885, gave an excellent account of the 'twenty six commoner trees of the neighbourhood'. 'The twenty to which I draw attention are', he wrote, 'seven conifers, three oaks, the rhododendron and its congenor the andromeda, four maples, two species of cornus, and two laurels'. Sir Edward also gave a comprehensive account of the altitudinal zonation of the trees right from Kalka to Simla, and even beyond, up to 'Huttoo' (Hatu peak) overlooking Narkanda. While the lower slopes above Kalka abound with bamboo (*Dendrocalamus strictus*) and scattered broad- leafed trees, it is only from Jabli onwards that one sees the first pines. This is the Chir pine (*Pinus roxburghii*) that extends almost all the way up to Shimla. As one enters Shimla, the Chil first gives way to the dense oak (*Quercus leucotrichophora*) forests between Shoghi and Shimla, and then to the magnificient deodar (*Cedrus deodara*) forests for which Shimla is so justly famous. As one goes beyond Shimla to Kufri and Narkanda, one sees a lessening of deodar and a greater preponderance of fir (*Abies pindrow*) and spruce (*Picea smithiana*), with their accompanying broad leafed cousins, the oaks, maples and walnuts (to name a few).

Talking about the trees in and around Shimla, one must give credit to the British for attempting to restore what damage they had done. Realizing, perhaps, that the beauty of Shimla lay in its greenery and its woods, and also the fact that forests played a major role in the maintenance of the many natural springs on which the inhabitants of the station depended, the foresters of that time decided to carry out large-scale plantations in the area. As a result, not only were plantations of the local species, chiefly deodar, established, but a large number of exotics also introduced. Chief among the exotics were the wattles (*Acacias*) and chestnuts (*Castanea*). The acacias are to be seen today along the bridle path in the Catchment area, but the chestnuts seem to have vanished over time. Only the horse-chestnut (*Aesculus indica*) abounds in the shady and sheltered localities, but it is not really a chestnut at all. Altogether about fifteen exotic species of conifers and twenty-five species of broad-leafed trees were introduced within the Shimla municipal limits, but only a few survive today—a few larches, cypresses and podocarps can be seen near the District Courts and several Himalayan holly (*Ilex dipyrena*) trees can be seen along the road leading from Snowdon hospital (IGMC) to Jakhoo. Though these last look like the high level oak (*Quercus dilatata*), the two can be distinguished not just by the venation of the leaves, but also the fact that while the oaks bear acorns, the holly bears berries, the bright red of which stands out against the snow in winter. The colour red also brings me to the rhododendron (*Rhododendron arboretum*)—how could I have forgotten to mention it? These remarkable middles sized trese lie scattered amidst the oak forests of Shimla as also as an understorey in the shaded localities. Near St. Bedes College, the crimson rhododendron flowers vie for attention along with the rosy-cheeked students, and so is the case along the road leading from Chaura Maidan to Summerhill (HP University).

Any account of Shimla would be incomplete without mentioning the beautiful birds that frequent its woodlands. Apart from the hill crows, that are much larger and darker of plumage than their plains cousins, we have a bluish black bird that may resemble a crow from a distance but the semblance is soon forgotten when this bird, the Himalayan Whistling Thrush breaks into song. Its melodious flute-like warble fills the hills in summer and the lower valleys in winter. Come summer and flocks of minivets and sunbirds dart through the trees in clouds of yellow and red. The white-cheeked tits, the yellow vented bulbuls and the warblers are fairly common, but among the summer visitors the most exciting are the barbets, the copperheads and the red-billed blue magpies. Many a time, on my morning walk, I have seen Kalij pheasants crossing the road near Bishop Cotton School, or being deterred from doing so by the chain link fence so thoughtlessly put up by the Forest Department. The ever increasing motor traffic is no help either. If one gets up early enough, one may hear the crowing of the red jungle fowl, or even see one. Then, again, there are birds of a different kind—the kind one sees only from March to December. Some of these are the Pink-cheeked First Grader, the Yellow-shirted Collegian, and the Blue-blazered Cottonian. The brown-coated Aucklandian and the Red-Blazered Chelsean are also quite common. It is these birds, flowers and trees that lend colour to this hill station, and not just Shimla, but also the visitors to this Queen of the Hills will be poorer if these were to vanish.

Samuel Evans Stokes and the Apple Revolution

Vidya Stokes

When I hear someone suggest a trip to the mountains to convalesce, a smile comes to my lips and I wonder at the ways of destiny. As a young girl of seventeen, I had reached Kotgarh to recuperate where I met my future husband who was nursing his injured thumb in the mountains. Much stranger is the fact that my future father-in-law had also reached the beautiful Kotgarh village to rest and recover from an illness decades ago. No ordinary man, he had come there all the way from the New World! Had he known that his journey would change the course of not only his life but the life of the hill people forever, would it have made a difference? I can't say but I feel very strongly that our paths were fated to cross and we were destined to share each other's lives.

And this all started when Samuel Evans Stokes, twenty-one, son of a wealthy Philadelphia engineer-businessman, expressed his desire not to join the family business but to sail to India to serve at a lepers' home in a quaint little village located in the Shivalik Himalaya. Passionate to serve mankind and to 'spread the Gospel among those who have not heard of it' he left America on 9 January 1904. But his was a journey of no return. He reached India as a devout Christian to serve at a home run by the Leprosy Mission in India at Subathu in Shimla Hills.

Was it premonition which made him say, 'I shall as far as in me lies become an Indian, marry an Indian girl and, if God gives me sons and daughters, bring them up absolutely as Indians in the matter of life, language, dress and education. I shall try to make my home life, in all aspects a gospel of what Indian home life should be.' No one knows but it turned out that way only!

Samuel settled in Kotgarh to recuperate after a prolonged illness and then stayed on. He married Agnes, a first-generation Rajput Christian *pahari* girl; converted to Hinduism and became Satyanand Stokes and went on to change the lives of hill people forever.

I am filled with awe and wonder at the twists and turns that his life took after he set foot on Indian soil. He was the only non-Indian to sign the Congress manifesto in 1921 calling upon Indians to quit government service. He was the only American to serve on the All India Congress Committee and the only American to be jailed for actively participating in India's freedom struggle. He was disliked by the British for his articles in the newspapers and charged with sedition.

When Stokes was arrested, Mahatma Gandhi wrote in *Young India*:

> This is a unique move on the part of the government. Mr. Stokes is an American who has naturalized himself as a British subject who has made India his home in a manner in which perhaps no American or Englishman has…. But that he should feel with and like an Indian, share his sorrows and throw himself into the struggle, has proved too much for the government. To leave him free to criticize the government was intolerable, so his white skin has proved no protection for him.

Gandhiji also said, 'As long as we have an Andrews, a Stokes, a Perason in our midst, so long will it be ungentlemanly on our part to wish every gentleman out of India'. 'Non-cooperators worship

Andrews, honour stokes,' he said on another occasion. For Stokes, Gandhi was 'the part of my life of which I am most proud.'

Not only his own life was shaped by the hand of destiny in the most unexpected manner, he was the man who himself, almost single-handedly, changed the destiny of the people of Shimla Hills. Life of the poor hill folk living in the remote villages of Shimla hills would be changed beyond imagination because of him. He wrote the script which turned Himachal into the apple state of the country.

When he reached Subathu, he devoted himself to work for lepers under the guidance of Dr Marcus Carleton. His young sensitivities got a shock at the sight of the disfiguring disease but he felt 'no repugnance, only an intense feeling of sympathy for the affected.'

In May 1904, Dr Carleton sent Samuel to Kotgarh, the beautiful little hamlet fifty miles beyond Shimla, to escape the hot summer months. He walked the fifty-mile stretch in stages to reach the captivating and charming Kotgarh described as the 'mistress of northern hills' by Nobel laureate Rudyard Kipling.

After a few months in India, young Samuel Stokes felt the urge to do more. He did not wish to remain confined to the leper home in Subathu. So, he travelled to different missions in Punjab, understanding the work, helping out in whatever way he could. He also went to Kangra after the devastating earthquake of 1905 to help the victims. As a result of exhausting travels in an alien land with a hostile climate, he fell ill.

After remaining sick for months, during which his father sent him money to return to America, Samuel started for Kotgarh again in March 1906. This journey was to change the course of his life and the lives of the people in Shimla hills forever. Still unwell, he travelled on foot from Subathu to Shimla and then to Kotgarh in short stages. This long and lonely walk was taxing but made him introspect and reflect a great deal. The fresh cool air of the hills did a lot of good to his mind and body. While recuperating under the care of Emma Matilda Bates, who was a zealous supporter of missionaries, he decided to start a small orphanage-cum-school in the mountains and chose a small hamlet situated in an interior valley for the purpose. It was a remote place with no proper roads. He wanted to create a healthy, happy and carefree place for children.

I came to know later that his earlier plan to open the school in the remote valley was changed when Mrs. Bates offered to sell a part of her large estate at Kofni to him.

Years later when I reached Kotgarh I also had the aim of starting an orphanage. I had come there to nurse my right eye which I had got hurt after falling from a horse. During those days I loved riding. The doctor had advised me to go to the mountains. Though my family belonged to Kotgarh, we were staying out of Himachal as my father was in service. As destiny would have it, Lal, Samuel Stokes' youngest son, also used to come to the hospital at Kotgarh as he had hurt his thumb. He and my brother developed friendship and he got interested in me. I was tomboyish and marriage was the last thing on my mind. More of a sports person, I was interested in painting, writing short stories, hiking and riding.

My dream was not marriage but the home for orphans and a school where everyone would wear white, clean clothes and I would be a nun. My elder brother to whom I was very close at that time was working in Calcutta, I was so adamant and focused on opening an orphanage that I wrote a letter to my brother asking him to give me money for my dream as he was the son and would get all the property but he had to promise me that from that property he would give me money to open the orphanage and the school. At that time I could never imagine that I would get married in the next six–seven months.

This was the time when Mr Lal told my *mamu* that he wanted to marry me who then told my mother who agreed immediately as I would stay near them in Kotgarh.

Though I had met Samuel Stokes many times before my marriage as he was my father's friend and used to come over to our house, it was only after I got married that I got to know the real Mr Stokes, his life, mission and his views.

He was a very simple, jovial man with a good sense of humour. Once he caught an old servant stealing *bathu laddus* from the kitchen red-handed. Instead of yelling and shouting at him or removing him from the job he said to him, '*thoda thoda khao; hamare liye bhi chod do*' (eat little, leave something for us also). On another occasion, he told another servant who was stealing *lassi* (butter milk), '*thoda mere liye bhi chod dena*' (leave a little for me also).

At the time of my marriage, *ghagras* were in fashion in the plains and I had got many *ghagras* stitched for my trousseau not knowing that no one wore them in the village. One day wearing one such *ghaghra* I was going down to my mother's house when my father-in-law asked his companion, 'Who? What is this balloon?' The man replied sheepishly, 'She is your *bahu*'. The next day he said to me, 'Yesterday I saw a parachute going down the hill.'

This simple man was not only full of wit; he was repository of will, determination and perseverance. He wrote the script of economic revolution of the Shimla Hills on his seven and a half acre plot. The Delicious variety of American apples which he planted here transformed the economy of the region. Kotgarh appeared on world horticulture map of the country from nowhere and Himachal Pradesh came to be known as the 'Apple State of India.'

True, some varieties of apple were being grown in the region before him also but he pioneered systematic, scientific and commercial cultivation of apples and brought the American Delicious Apple to India. The first apple orchard in Punjab hills was planted in Kullu valley in 1870 by Captain R.C. Lee followed by English settlers like Colonel Rennick, Captain A.T. Bannon and C.R. Johnson who established orchards at Manali, Raison and Naggar in Kullu valley. Near Shimla, Alexander Coutt's orchard, 'Hillock's Head', was at Mashobra that was planted in 1887.

Even at Kotgarh there was a small Mission Orchard raised by a group of missionaries. In fact my great grandfather late Gudrumal, who was also the Tehsildar of the area, had planted a small orchard of about hundred trees in 1881. However, the main varieties at that time like the Newton Pippin, King of Pippin and Cox's Orange Pippin did not yield much. Total production was about hundred mounds (one mound or 40 seers (one seer=0.9331 kg) was equal to 0.37 quintals). Moreover, these strains of apples were sour in taste and not very popular.

Samuel Stokes transformed everything right from the new varieties, to cultivation methods to marketing strategies. His road was full of hurdles though. It was a difficult and costly proposition and the local farmers were poor and ignorant of better cultivation methods. The fear of change from conventional crops to the unknown fruit was on their minds. They refused to listen to him in the beginning and he decided to go for it alone.

In 1914, he took soil samples from Kotgarh to America for testing. He continued to experiment and imported and tested more than thirty-three strains of apples to select the most viable varieties for the soil and climate of Kotgarh. Finally, he chose the Red Delicious and its sub-varieties and the Golden Delicious. In the winter of 1916 Stokes planted a few saplings of apple, pear and plum trees in his orchard that he had brought with him from America and by 1918 he was already contemplating commercial cultivation of apples in the region.

The role of Florence Spencer Stokes, Samuel's mother deserves special mention here who painstakingly followed the American apple industry, the latest technological advances in apple cultivation, got in touch with different agencies to order and dispatch apple saplings to Kotgarh. Juicy Golden Delicious apple, popular for its crunchiness and shelf life today, arrived in India as a mother's gift to her son in 1921. She wrote to Samuel, 'My Christmas gift to you must be the Stark's Golden Delicious. For the other apple trees I have ordered for you, you shall pay, but these, which they seem to consider so wonderful, must be your mother's contribution to your orchard.'

The first consignment of Golden Delicious from Washington reached Kotgarh at a time when Samuel Stokes was in jail. Agnes Stokes, his wife, planted and nursed this gift of love. These trees bore fruit four years later. Samuel was overjoyed to see the look and taste of the fruit and vowed to make Kotgarh, the headquarters of the Golden Delicious apples for India. How prophetic!

Apples from Kotgarh edged out the imported Japanese apples from the market in 1926 and soon the import stopped altogether! In 1927 when the tasty apples from Samuel's orchard appeared in Shimla wrapped in green printed paper, other varieties selling for years had no takers. In the next season the boxes and the apple wrappings bore the trademark an encircled 'H.H.' (for Harmony Hall, his orchard). He was very particular about the grading and packaging and said, 'We shall make every effort to see that nothing short of first-class fruit goes under that mark. I intend, if I live, to make the name of this orchard so that when its boxes come on the market no one will dream of the necessity of examining their contents before buying them.' All his boxes also had the words 'Kotgarh Apples' as Samuel wanted the best apples in the town by the name of the place where they were grown.

Stokes kept the price of his apples to the minimum and said, 'After all, when you have good stuff you can afford to tell the public about it, confident that they will like it and ask for more'. By 1928 there were about a thousand apple trees in Stokes' orchard, the main strains being Red and Golden Delicious, Rich-a-red, McIntosh and King of Pippin.

By now Samuel was confident that the apple was the answer to the poverty of the people. He implored, goaded and coaxed them but initially they were reluctant as they feared that they will lose whatever little they had if they cultivated apple trees in the fields. Samuel distributed free saplings and kept on cajoling them to plant these on the divider between two fields saying (*Dhari mein lagaao, dhari mein lagaao*).

His task was not easy; the elderly locals made fun of him while the young were least interested in what he was doing. The gestation period of six years seemed too distant to them but Samuel was persistent. Slowly he was able to change the attitude of the people and the terraced fields were interspersed with apple trees. This revolutionised the economy of the region within a few years' time.

Samuel Stokes' concern about the people went beyond their economic interests. He was a deeply humane and sensitive person and was distressed and disturbed when he saw human suffering. He always helped in whatever way he could to reduce the pain and suffering of people especially children. His love was for humanity as a whole without any distinction or discrimination. Once we had gone to our summer retreat near Satluj river. I was reading the book *Dracula* and it was past midnight when I finished reading it. I was so engrossed in the book that I did not hear someone pacing outside my room. After finishing the book when I noticed the sounds I became very scared. A little later I realised that it was coming from the adjoining room where my father-in-law was staying. Worried I knocked at his door, thinking that he must not be well. He said, '*Kaun hai?*' I said, '*Papa main hun, aapki tabiyat theek nahin hai kya?*' he opened the door and said, 'I am worried, very worried. I can't sleep, there are thousands of children dying because of hunger in India. There is nobody to look after them.' I was surprised; how did he know about this? He said that he got letters and newspapers by post. He was very sensitive and he sent a cheque of rupees 10,000 for their relief.

Samuel Stokes had fatherly love for the people of Kotgarh. He was so protective of Kotgarh area that he refused to supply saplings to highly placed friends in Shimla and people of other areas. His protectionism gave farmers of Kotgarh farmers an edge over others.

His Hindi was not very good and he did not speak much Pahari but he could connect with people easily. He smoked a *hukka* which he learnt to smoke in the jail. He used to say that it was the cleanest way to inhale tobacco and also the surest way to bond with the local people as every hill man smoked it. Everyone called him sahib ji.

After gaining the confidence of the locals, Samuel focused his attention on the road to Kotgarh. Prevalent mode of transport on mule back was not at all suited for a perishable crop like apple. He urged British authorities at Shimla to improve the condition of the existing road.

A powerful lobby in the government was in favour of extending a railway line from Shimla up to Narkanda. Stokes opposed the idea saying that was sheer wastage of funds and there was no point to extend the line given the fact that there was a road in existence which needed improvement. He was of the opinion that the cost of the survey of railway line would be sufficient to widen and metal the existing road.

Success of Kotgarh apples and their impact on the market led the Punjab Agricultural Department to launch a massive campaign to popularise its cultivation in the entire hill territories under its control.

Within fifteen years time (1921–1936) farmers of Kotgarh progressed from ridicule to solidarity. The Kotgarh Fruit Growers' Association was established in 1936 with Satyanand (Samuel) Stokes as Secretary. He continued the good work of educating, training and organising the new orchard owners. And he spent from his own pocket. Area under apple continued to grow and in 1946, when Satyanand Stokes died, apple production in the province was 15,000 boxes per year with Harmony Hall orchards contributing nearly one-third share.

Kotgarh is unique in the sense that while in all other parts of the country, education led to a change in the standard and outlook of the people, here 'transformation in the economy and way of life of a people, the primary cause (if any single factor can ever bring about a socio-economic revolution of any substance) was not education—but apples. Education has followed the apples. It did not precede them.' This study by anthropologist Kusum Nair highlights the contribution of the American who donned Khadi and lived like a pahari.

The state has the highest per capita production of apples in the country and also the highest percentage of cultivable area under apples. It is true that Himachal is now emerging as the fruit bowl of the country with production of peaches, plums, apricot, pears as well as citrus and other sub-tropical fruits but apple takes the crown.

When Samuel first introduced the Delicious variety in Kotgarh, the total area under apple cultivation was only twenty-five acres. It gradually extended to 150 acres in 1930, to 250 acres in 1940 and 1,500 acres in 1950. Today with 92,000 hectare area under apple cultivation, almost one-eighth of the total cultivated area in Himachal Pradesh, total Apple production in the state is 268,402 Metric Ton. In 2007, nearly 1.7 crore apple boxes were transported to various parts of the country from Shimla district alone. Ninety per cent of the present plantation of apples in Himachal Pradesh constitutes the Delicious variety introduced by Stokes. The fact that more than eighty per cent of orchardists are marginal farmers with the average size of an orchard being less than one hectare speaks volumes about Stokes' success in making the common man realise the importance of apple as the economic liberator.

Before marriage I was not interested in religion but after marriage when I came in contact with my father-in-law I became aware of the philosophy of Hinduism. In fact for my wedding gift he translated the *Gita* into English. Samuel Stokes was a spiritual and religious person. Every day he used to go to the temple to meditate and pray in the mornings and evenings. I used to accompany him. The temple he built at Kotgarh was influenced by the Arya Samaj so there was no idol there but many paintings adorned the walls.

Once when I was going to the temple with him, I asked him why people were afraid of the body or the spirit when a person, even if that person is your own family member, dies. He said it depends on the person, if he was a good human being with a good *atma*, then there was no need to be scared.

He was frail in health and on a number of occasions he could not go to the temple, so I used to go on his behalf. One day as I sat there meditating I saw his dead body. I got very scared that something might have happened to him. An old servant who was waiting outside said, 'Did you see sahib's *parchain?*' I retorted, 'It must be him, not the *parchain*, he must have come out of the house.' But I was worried and ran back to the house. He was very ill and was taken to Shimla that day where he died.

He was disciplined and used to remain busy at his typewriter, writing books as well as letters to his mother and the leaders involved in the freedom struggle. He wrote a number of books, the most prominent being *Awakening India* and *Satyakam*.

I was inspired by his zeal and spirit for social work. He was always thinking how to help everyone, especially the poor and the disadvantaged.

From Shimla

MAHARAJKUMAR RAGHUVIR SINGH

There are very few accounts by Indians of Shimla during the British period. This account of a visit to Shimla in 1927 by Raghuvir Singh (1908–1991), the ruler of the small state of Sitamau in Malwa, now part of district Mandsor in Madhya Pradesh, would, we hope interest our readers. The Maharajkumar was a man of many personalities: prince and politician, historian and a creative writer. He wrote this article *(Shimla Se)* when he was in his teens and had not even taken his BA degree. It was first published in the *Saraswati* of Allahabad and later reprinted in the volume of collected essays titled *Sapta-Dip* (Hindi Grantha Ratnakar, Bombay) and published in 1938. The Maharajkumar then considered it to be his best essay. It tells us much about Shimla as about the author himself, his love for of nature, his concern for the poor, his fine sensibilities, and his patriotic sentiments.

We owe this article to Prof S.R. Mehrotra, who discovered it in the famous library of the Natnagar Shodh Samsthan, Sitamau and translated it fom Hindi. We are grateful to the authorities of the Natnagar Shodh Samsthan for allowing us to include the article in our present collection.

Dear...,

It seems that I have come far away from your earth, into some realm of the demigods. This place is situated in the lap of mighty mountains that kiss the sky. This is the abode of the affluent. Though it cannot be said that the people living here do not fear old age, sickness and death, yet there can be no doubt that people tend to forget their worries and anxieties on reaching here, and they seem to think that life is only a play, a joyous dream. It is not that everyone here is affluent. If everyone here were affluent, who would have served them? The poor are needed only where there are the affluent. They highlight the prosperity of the prosperous. If misery and poverty were not there, who would notice the significance of the pleasure-seekers and the prosperous? Where there are masters, there would be servants; where there are rulers, there would be subjects; where there is luxury there would be deprivation.

There are several hill stations in India which are the summer seats of our rulers, but the most charming of them are located in the Himalayas, which is India's crown jewel. Of these the most prominent are Shimla, Mussoorie, Nainital and Darjeeling. Shimla is, from the political point of view, the most important of them all, because the viceroy of India resides here in the summer. In a sense, Shimla becomes the capital of India for six months, from April to September.

Describing Shimla, a writer says: 'This small town of Shimla is the capital of the Indian empire. Many Rajas, Maharajas and high officials of India, and even distinguished travellers from abroad, are seen wandering about in its bazaars. For six months long rows of bullocks and camels are seen engaged in continuously carrying the luxury goods available in India to this town. Hundreds of small and beautiful bungalows have been built on the hills up and down. During summer months, every evening, its clean streets present almost an exhibition of the latest fashions and beauties.'

In order to reach Shimla we have to go to Kalka, which is a station of the N.W. Railway. From here there are two routes to Shimla: one by motorcar and the other by the railway train. Work on the motorway began in 1850 before the coming of the railway (1903), all used the motorway. Even now so many go by the motorcar. The motorway is fifty-eight miles long. The engineers seem to have exhausted their entire skill in constructing it. It is so laid on the hillside that one does not feel the ascent. About fourteen miles from Kalka lies Dharampur. There is a sanitarium for TB patients here. The road to Kasauli branches away from here. It has a Dak Bungalow. One can get eatables at the railway station. There is also a road from here to Subathu, where leprosy patents are treated. As we go ahead, the road to Shimla passes below the Dagshai hill. The army is stationed on this hill. There is a dense forest here, but we can see the barracks at a distance. Then we come to the small village of Kumarhatti from where the ascent to Baroghat starts. After about two and a half miles we reach the top of the hill and get a good view of Solan valley. From here the descent starts again. For some distance there are dense bushes. The road here is very dangerous. On the one side there are high hills, and on the other side, the deep valley. After about a mile we reach Solan. The Dak Bungalow here is very good and usually every traveller has some snacks or meals here before starting the ascent. After some distance, the descent starts again which stops at Kandaghat. From Kandaghat there is a road to Chail, the summer seat of the Maharaja of Patiala. Here one can also see the Ashwani river down below.

There is an ascent of about five miles from Kandaghat up to Kiarighat, where there is a Dak Bungalow. The road from Kiarighat to Kaithlighat is straight and smooth, but from Kaithlighat the ascent starts again. We reach Shoghi and then Taradevi. There is a branch of the Aligarh Dairy Farm at Taradevi. Three miles ahead of Taradevi and we are within the limits of Shimla Municipality.

Having told you the journey by road, let me now tell you about travel to Shimla from Kalka by rail. The railway track from Kalka to Shimla is two feet and six inches wide (Narrow Gauge). From Kalka itself the railway line starts going up the innumerable hills of the Himalayas. One marvels at the skill of the engineers who laid down these continuous ascent. At a short distance from Kumarhatti the train enters the tunnel of Barog. This tunnel is 3,700 feet long. As soon as the tunnel ends we are at the station of Barog. Here elaborate arrangements have been made for food and beverages for the passengers, and the train stops here for half an hour for their convenience. At Barog the travellers experience for the first time the peace and coolness of the hills; they forget about the hot winds blowing on the plains. From here to Kandaghat the train goes down. From Kandaghat the train starts going up again until we reach Shimla. As the track goes up, the travellers have a wonderful view. On the one side there are the mountain ranges almost touching the sky, and on the other side, only a few feet away from the railway track the frightful valley about a thousand feet deep, as if reminding the high and mighty pleasure seekers that death would devour them all before long.

There are 103 tunnels on the railway track, whose total length is more than five miles. This track was constructed at a cost of rupees 1,80,00,000. We soon get a glimpse of Shimla in the distance (Taradevi), and the hearts of the first-time visitors are filled with a curious delight. At long last Shimla is reached.

(II)

Now, let me take you round Shimla. One only gets the rickshaw here to roam on the hills. Yes, if we try we may hire horses.

The Ridge is the most open space here. The Christ Church is located on its eastern side. Here you see the ayahs sitting with English children in the evening. The annual parade on the occasion of the birthday of the emperor of India is held here. The British lion unfurls his victory banner on the Himalayan summit. On the western side is the Band Stand built by Kunwar Jeewandas of Jabalpur. Here the band is played every Monday evening. The Jako (Jakhu) hill is seen in the east, and in the north there are the snow-capped mountain ranges. You would be amazed to note that every passerby bustles along as if he is going on some important errand and that for him nothing else matters. At a short distance there is the beautiful view of the hills and the valleys. This view reaches its pinnacle of beauty when the snow-capped mountain ranges become visible behind the hills covered with trees. On the other side, beyond the open space, one can see the Satluj like a silver streak in the distance. This beauty can be discerned and enjoyed only by the lovers of nature. When one thinks of those who hustle by and fail to appreciate the purity and beauty of this splendid scene of nature, one realises how man has made his life so artificial. He finds no peace and bliss in these pure and beautiful scenes of nature. His eyes seek satisfaction in watching man-made buildings and objects. The bazaar has a greater attraction for him than the peace of the high hills, the deep valleys and the far-away open spaces.

Where shall I take you now? Let us take the path to the left of the Church. This goes to Lakkar Bazaar. Here one can look at the beautiful handicrafts of woodcarving and the artful brass and ivory decorations on wood. Most of these shops are owned by the Sikhs. A little ahead we can see 'Snowdon', the residence of the commander-in-chief of India. At one time this house was owned by Lord Roberts, but the commander-in-chief of India has been staying here since Lord Kitchner's time (1902–1907)[1]. As we go ahead we see the Mashobra hill and behind it the 8,500 feet high Shali peak. At some distance from here we see the Mayo School and Orphanage. Then we reach the village of Sanjauli. Because of its location this village looks very beautiful from a distance. From here we have two roads: one goes forward through the Sanjauli bazaar, while the other goes towards what is called the 'Ladies Mall' (*Ladies Mile?*). This road is to the right and was constructed during the time of Lord Lytton (1876–1880). This is a broad and level road, whose beauty is enhanced by the dense foliage by the roadside. The road follows the natural curve of

---

[1] The author was obviously misinformed on the subject. 'Snowdon' remained the residence of the commander-in-chief of India continuously from the time of Lord Roberts in the 1870s.

the hill. About half way through we can see the rocks on which the minerals coming out with the water of the mountains have frozen. These rocks also have distinct marks of the flowing water. They are called 'Devil's Paint Box'. From the Ladies Mall *(Ladies Mile?)* a road branches out which is named 'Lover's Walk'. What a strange name! On this road we shall meet the lovers and people fond of walking. The road is shaded in the mornings and there is peace and quiet all around which is seldom disturbed except by the sound of the hooves of the horses used by someone fond of horse riding or by English maidens. This place overwhelms with happiness the hearts of those who love peace and solitude. This is a very level walk and it braches off to the residence of the Governor of Punjab, called Barnes Court. The house has been named after Sir Edwards Barnes who was the associate of the Duke of Willington at Waterloo, where the hitherto ever victorious Napoleon, by quirk of fate, suffered defeat. Sir Edwards Barnes came as Commander-in-Chief to India in 1832 and stayed in this house for some time. After this we have the Punjab Secretariat. Not far from here, a narrow road enters the bazaar of Chotta Shimla and through Kasumpti bazaar goes to the distant hills. Kasumpti is situated on the borders of the Shimla Municipality and those of the small states of Junga and Kothi. If we walk beyond Kasumpti we see desolate hills and valleys, here and there dotted by small villages. There are a few level patches also which have been converted into fields for agriculture.

Now, I take you back towards Shimla. We take the road to the right of the Punjab Secretariat. Here we find the post and telegraph office of Chotta Shimla. After a short ascent the road levels up once again. While there is a right about-turn to the Barnes Court, our road pierces through the hill at a spot which was earlier called the Khyber Pass. Look, here we have the houses of the Maharaja of Patiala. Oakover is to the left, while the other houses are on the right side.

While walking on this road we shall come across Kashmiri Muslims and other hill people carrying wooden sleepers and other heavy loads on their shoulders. These are the sons of the Himalayas. They have shoulder-length hair and wear dirty, tattered woollen clothes, with sheepskin slung on their shoulders. Their pale faces, small and flat noses and upturned eyes suggest that they are not the inhabitants of the Punjab. They are smoking a wooden *hookah* all the time and their faces are always lit with a joyous smile. They are always ready to talk and eat. These hill-men of the Punjab (sic) are very sociable. They also have other qualities. They are reliable, honest, pure, satisfied and happy with little. Rows of them can often be seen carrying huge wooden sleepers from the Pachhu mountain. They tie these sleepers with a thick rope made of old and torn clothes to their shoulders, and though they are bent with heavy load and their broad foreheads are due to hard labour covered with sweat, which they keep on wiping, they carry on. When they get too tired, they rest for a while using the hill slope or some other thing as a support for their load, but as soon as they recover a little, they start immediately again. Sometimes one sees even young women carrying such heavy loads. They spend most of their lives like this. Though they are bent under the weight of the heavy loads they carry, they seem to be happy and contented with their lot. Sometimes one encounters a whole family—mother, father, brothers and sisters—in a row, each carrying a heavy load according to one's capacity. They go smoking a *hookah* and talking merrily. The wooden sleepers are normally long enough to cover the width of the road, sometimes they are longer. These poor coolies have to bring these sleepers from Pachhu, which is some ten miles away from Shimla. Whenever someone riding a horse or a rickshaw is approaching, they turn the longer sleeper to align with the length of the road by turning their bodies in an amazingly swift action which is worth watching. Just ponder for a moment over the plight of these poor coolies. There is neither joy nor sorrow in their lives; they work so hard to earn their livelihood and whatever is left after filling their bellies they spend on tobacco and other vices. They are not bothered about the future. The adversities of life have so hardened them that they fear them no more. When adversity comes they bend to bear its burden, but as soon as it disappears, even the thought of it disappears from their hearts. This is a living example of how a man's life depends upon his circumstances. If you wish to see what becomes of a man who has to bear sorrow and adversity continuously, how they shape his thoughts, look at these people who, though living, are almost like corpses.

(III)

Now I move forward. Look, here on the left there is a path which leads to where Lord Reading hospital stands. Women and children are cared for in this hospital. A little further ahead, a path branches forth to go to the Central Hotel, later meeting the Cart Road. But we are going straight along what is known as the Mall. In front of us there is an old bandstand where maidservants and wet nurses sit with children. In front of us, to the left is the Clarkes Hotel. After a short distance from here rows of shops on both sides of the road start. This road is always a scene of hustle and bustle. Mostly European men and women are seen here. Look, how rickshaws are passing by us, and there in front of us is an English couple on their horses. This hustle and bustle is from sunrise to sunset. The streets of Shimla are not deserted until after 9 p.m. in the evening. Here someone is entering a restaurant, while another person is going out of a hotel. One is going to this shop for purchase, while someone else is going to another shop for the same purpose. One wonders from where this crowd comes and where it goes. One also wonders whether these pleasure-seekers have anything else to do except making purchases, and where from they get the money to do so.

As pointed out earlier, mostly European men and women are to be seen on the Mall. If you wish to see different specimens of their fashion, just stop here on this road for a moment. You will see everything in front of you. Even the few Indians here are imbued with Western culture. You see here two contrasting scenes. On the one hand, there are people whose all wants have been satisfied and who have all sorts of luxuries to make them happy, but even then they are not satisfied with their situation. On the other hand, are those poor who hardly get two meals a day, but they are happy and satisfied with their lot. What a great difference! On the one side, are those who are soaked in luxury but still want more. On the other side, are people who have to thank God each day that they are not starving. Some come to Shimla seeking pleasure. Others come here to earn their daily bread by the sweat of their brows. If the pleasure-seekers ever look worried it is because of their jealousy of those who are more affluent than they are. Others there are whose bodies are covered with wrinkles in young age and whose backs are bent because of hard labour, but their faces exude contentment. At every step of their lives they have to struggle for their livelihood, and each wrinkle of their forehead and face is a sort of reward for their bravery. Who can fathom the hearts of these moving lumps of clay? Though outwardly they are mere lumps of clay, their hearts have become purified like gold in the fire of adversity. Those who battle against adversity rank higher than the soldiers who fight on the battlefield. Our hearts are filled with admiration and our heads bow down in reverence to those victorious heroes who had to struggle against heavy odds at every step, but who emerged victorious in the battle of life. Such contrast, especially in this land of luxury, is worth seeing. The sight fills one's heart with strange thoughts. One realises the futility of power and pelf and begins to hate them. He unconsciously begins to sympathize with the poor coolies.

(IV)

Come, let us go forward. Look, here to the left of the shop of Cotton Morris is a street which leads to the lower Bazaar. The municipal market is here. We shall wander here for a while. It is full of small shops where Indians, Afghans and Tibetans sell their wares squatting. You can get everything here; the only difference being that these shops are not as spic and span as those of the Europeans (on the

Mall). That is why you get things cheaper here than on the Mall. It is a very busy shopping area. Even English men and women are sometimes seen shopping here. Describing this market an English writer has remarked: 'Everywhere in this bazaar is loud noise, quarrels, eating and drinking, haggling over prices. In this crowd you find men and women of every nationality, religion, caste and age. It is difficult to meet such a crowd anywhere else. This is the place where the politician and the conspirator meet. Students of Psychology can find much material here for their work and speculation.'

Let us go back to the Mall. On the left side there is a long row of shops. In front of us there is a large house. This was earlier the Town Hall. Now it is the Gaiety Theatre. It is used in the summer season by the Amateur Dramatic Club for its performances. Next to the Gaiety Theatre there is a big building which houses the Station Library. It was established in 1844. It is considered to be one of the good libraries of the India.

As we move forward we come to the General Post Office of Shimla. Further ahead there are houses on both sides of the road. Some belong to various institutions; others are the offices of government departments. At some distance we notice the Grand Hotel of (Chevalier) Peliti. It has a long history, for it has been the headquarters of many institutions and several important and famous men have lived here. At some distance from here a road branches off to the beautiful valley of Annandale, where there is a Club, a race course and a ground for playing Polo.

As we move forward we reach a junction of many roads, one of which leads to the Indian Legislative Assembly building. From here we get a good view of the race course in the valley below and of the charming snow-covered mountain peaks in the far distance. We then come to the Cecil Hotel. It is a very large hotel. Only Englishmen and highly placed Indians stay here. This road leads us straight to the Viceregal Lodge, which is built on the Observatory Hill. It has been tastefully decorated. There are beautiful lawns around it. Its garden is also very good. Near the Lodge is a church and three houses for the Viceroy's ADC and others.

We go to Summer Hill from here. This road from the Viceregal Lodge to Summer Hill passes through a dense forest until we reach the Summer Hill railway station. The population of this locality has been steadily growing for some time past, and now looks almost like a small town. For their convenience a special train runs between Shimla and Summer Hill.

There are two roads going from Summer Hill to Boileauganj, both passing through beautiful landscapes. From Boileauganj a road goes to Jutogh. We turn back from here and take the road which goes from below the Viceregal Lodge and Peterhoff. The latter building was used as the residence of the viceroys for about twenty-six years (1862–1888), and is now occupied by the member of Viceroy's Executive Council in charge of the education, health and land department. Going past the Foreign Department of the Government of India (now the site of the All India Radio), we come to Chaura Maidan. We follow the same road by which we had come, but at the next crossing we turn right and going past the office of the Imperial Bank (now the State Bank of India) and the huge building of the (Central) Telegraph Office, arrive at the Mall. After a short distance we take the left-side path and return to the Ridge, from where we had started.

I have taken you around Shimla.

But where is that *yaksha-lok* (land of demigods) of ours (of which we have a description in Kalidas's *Meghdoot*)? The Himalayas still stands there.

> *The mount with its high lily-white*
> *Peaks pervades the sky and stands*
> *As the condensed loud laughter*
> *Of the three-eyed Siva*

But where is that land where there is no old age, no suffering, no death? The cloud still comes to the Himalaya season, but does it bring any message to it now? Tormented by the fire of pain and poverty, annoyed at her subjugation and humiliation, does India not send any message to the Himalaya now?

Maharajkumar Raghuvir Singh of Sitamau (Malwa)
(May 1927)

Beyond the Veil

Minakshi Chaudhry

Do ghosts exist? I can't say. But ghost stories do.

A few years back at British Library in Chandigarh during a discussion on my book *Ghost Stories of Shimla Hills* I was asked by a doctor, 'Do you believe in ghosts? And if you do, what is the proof that they exist? They cannot be proved by science, they have no form and are not visible.'

As I was raking my brain for an ingenious retort another participant, a lady doctor said, 'Doctor *sahib*, do you believe in God?' I got my cue as he replied, 'Yes'.

'But God has no form, can not be seen and science doesn't accept him!' I stated cheekily.

Ghost or no ghosts, proof or no proof—in the end it all boils down to personal belief. Interestingly Shimla hills resound and echo with as many ghost stories as there are other folktales. And many generations have been brought up on tales of the supernatural. These stories are now a part of folklore and have a special place in literature. Haunted houses and roads, wandering spirits, dark moonless nights with brooding trees, grotesque gothic structures built by the British in the dim street lights—all these have a long association with Shimla and me.

A decade back I had wandered around the town and other small towns of Shimla hills investigating and collecting stories of the supernatural. During this endeavour I was questioned by the

Army about my credentials and attacked by a priestess who, after our discussion, suspected me to be an incarnation of a *churail*. Once I had to take shelter in one of the Shimla jails to escape the wrath of two lathi-wielding men who found my inquiries about the ghost of a *pahari* girl blasphemous. A school principal threatened to sue me if I wrote about the two popular ghosts of the school as this would 'bring bad name to the institution'. The owner of a rumoured haunted garden sent me packing with his two dogs chasing me out of the gate. A lawyer in a written complaint to a daily newspaper accused me of trying to come into limelight to become another Arundhati Roy by writing on such controversial and bizarre subjects.

On top of it all—I was subjected to ridicule while gathering the material—'What! Ghosts! *Bhoot! Aaj ki dunia mein? Kahan se aayee ho?*' I would be interviewed by one and all.

But as the saying goes 'all is well that ends well', it did. I collected about fifty stories and brought out the book. Surprisingly a number of people called me up to reveal many more unusual tales and personal encounters with the supernatural. Some were disappointed that I hadn't covered the 'popular ghosts' of their areas.

◆

Shimla hills have a perfect setting for these spirits—an ideal home to live in this world: creaking floor boards and panelling; pattering raindrops on tinned roofs and bleak and cold mist covering every possible space. The snaky narrow roads; cool breeze ruffling and disturbing the foliage and the trees; houses nestled against hill sides; the woods thick and dark with deodar trees interspersed with quiet dwellings—which other place than Shimla hills would these unearthly creatures dwell in! This is their home, the environment that they are comfortable in. As the lords of this world, we human beings should let them live in peace and harmony—that is, if they do exist!

For some, Shimla hills have more than their share of the supernatural, spectral sightings and unexplained phenomena. The ethereal denizens may follow you; rub shoulders with you; bump into you or for that matter ignore you—mainly during the night. Of course, sometimes you may also come across them in daytime. If you happen to meet a group of Englishmen and ladies dressed in attires of their times chatting animatedly near the five benches, or the *ghost* that gives you company on the Navbahar cemetery road, take care and just remember that it is said that they live here...

During the night, these *homo sapiens* wander on their favourite roads and in the houses of Shimla—Lord Dufferin's phantom walks leisurely in the gardens and lawns of Indian Institute of Advanced Study; founder of the Indian National Congress A.O. Hume's spirit wanders in the Rothney Castle popularly known as *sheeshey wali kothi*.

The night-rider lady on the rickshaw; the bride on Scandal Point; the Englishman wearing a bowler hat asking for a lighter and a cigarette on the Summerhill road and Ava, a forlorn British girl dressed in white, roaming near the Avalodge Boys Hostel in Summer Hill—all continue to *live* in Shimla, even after they *left* the place long, long ago!

Then are the *churails* with their signature-feet turned backwards! They seem to like water bodies the most, so we have the chakkar *churail* and the *churail* of churail bauri on the Chotta Shimla-St. Bedes Road.

Trot of horses, footfalls, loud piercing screams, howling dogs, long sighs, the tapping of a walking stick in the dead of night are the other paraphernalia lurking around that can leave anyone full of doubt and dread. To add colour to the picture, Shimla hills have so many haunted places—houses, infamous roads, popular spots like the Ridge, the Mall (Scandal Point), US Club road, Lover's Lane and Annadale Road where our unearthly friends roam; but the story is incomplete without the fruit-seller with hairy inward turned hands on the Lakkar bazaar-Sajauli road and the ghost on the railway line...

At times you may encounter the popular faceless ghosts. The one near the Indian Institute of Advanced Study roams the surroundings in the night; the other in a popular boy's school walks with the head on its palm and the one on the Sanjauli road prefers riding a bicycle.

◆

There are many stories relating to buildings that were built on old cemeteries and the spirits residing in them. A popular hotel near Lady Reading Hospital, (Kamla Nehru Hospital), is one such where the spirit of a woman is said to wander. Peterhof, the VIP guest house now, is said to have been built on an old cemetery. After Shimla (then Simla) was declared the summer capital of the British Raj, Peterhof became the first proper Viceregal Lodge. Lord Elgin, the first viceroy to occupy it, fell down while crossing a rope bridge on the river Chandra on a journey between Kullu and Lahaul; he later died of a heart attack in Dharamsala where he is buried. As every death or illness of an occupant of Peterhof was attributed to its cemetery connection, the death of the Lord added much fuel to the cemetery story.

Another story that does the rounds concerns a government building in Nigam Vihar. This building, said to have been built on a cemetery, rests on the grave of two drunkards, amongst others. The funny anecdote attached is that at least two employees of the office are in an inebriated condition, always. The spirits of the drunkards enter two chosen employees daily coaxing them to drink and be merry. 'It is not the fault of the poor fellows that they are high on liquor, they are helpless; it is the work of the spirits,' said an office-goer. 'Thank God they don't enter women's soul,' said a lady employee jokingly.

Shimla hills have their share of haunted houses; claims and counter-claims apart, these stories are not only part of Shimla folklore but also keep on appearing in print and electronic media. The ghosts too crave for publicity, it seems!

Among these, the Sanjauli *bhoot bangla* remains the most popular even though it has now been dismantled and a government colony stands on it. It was said to be haunted by the spirit of a mad woman who was kept under lock and key and whose screams were heard in the night. Anees Villa, Salman Rushdie's never-lived home, is the popular *bhoot bangla* of Solan town, located on Tank Road. Now surrounded by concrete houses on both sides, it had thick woods around it. I have been to the house many times and the big red villa encircled with flowers (asphodels and hyacinth) looked far from sinister, but every time an eerie feeling started to creep in whenever I stepped down the fleet of steps leading to it. The story goes that the villa located on the periphery of a cemetery is witness to a number of strange events—hair-raising screams, howling voices and falling stones on tin roofs—the story gets queerer...

Salogra House now known as Amrit Bangla is also the popular *bhoot bangla* on Kalka-Shimla highway. The chowkidar, an old man belonging to UP, claimed that many years back he was attacked by a ghost. According to the story, in the 1970s its upper portion housed a *theka* (tavern) and a drunkard fell down the ravine and died. Later his son met with an accident at the same spot and got killed. Spirits of both father and son roam inside the house and on the nearby curve of the highway where several spectral sightings have been noticed. Foot-falls in the night are still heard in the house.

◆

Rudyard Kipling based his popular ghost story Phantom Rickshaw in Shimla. According to *Plain Tales from the Raj* edited by Charles Allen, Shimla was one of those places in India where there was 'a tremendous feeling of the supernatural'. In Shimla and elsewhere 'many people felt they had experiences at houses reputed to be haunted and there were many stories about the hauntings. All around us there was death and that led naturally to a feeling of ghosts.'

Stories of the inexplicable and the unknown arouse two emotions contradicting each other—fear and fascination. This fear of supernatural and the unknown is as old as mankind itself.

The Ridge during the winter

A new fiction trend 'the Gothic' appeared in the English literary traditions around AD 1720. It talks of horror and mystery, grim atmosphere which is hair-rising at its climax coupled with the baggage of ghostly apparitions coming alive. This type of writing brought about a new spark in literature. The unknown spiced with haunted castles, eerie graveyards, decaying corpses, creaking doors, bloodshot eyes, and blood-stained daggers had the ingredients of a mouth-watering recipe in the stories. Thereafter, the perpetual recurrence of the supernatural and the unexplainable in literature throughout reflects one of the most fundamental emotions of mankind—fear—and there is no fear greater than the fear of that which cannot be understood and explained. The demand for such stories became strong and insatiable. Science and education have not been able to erase the deep-rooted superstitions and thus supernatural powers appeal to this basic hereditary emotion.

As we read stories of werewolves, draculas and vampires, we are not scared thinking that it happened in the past. However, when mysteries are left unanswered, they become more 'real' and the inconclusive endings leave us with a nagging fear. This ominous warning of something lurking around the corner coupled with our helplessness fuels our imagination. To know but also not to know is the 'poetry of life'.

Readers, do not fear as in Shimla Hills I have not come across stories of 'scary and dangerous ghosts'; most of them are harmless, a few funny and naughty, some helpful, others want to be left alone believing in the philosophy of live and let live. But who knows 'what kind' you may come across. *Bon Voyage…*

Seasons of a Kind

Vepa Rao

On the slow fire of snows
on hill-tops
is life un-cooked
towards the true, first, instinct
frozen
before the way was lost
in becoming.

During my travels, I receive special attention when I tell people that I live in Shimla. It's the same whether in trains, planes or gatherings in big cities. First a curious glance, then questions about snow and ice. Hindi movies have obviously contributed a lot to people's image of Shimla.

A touch of envy in their eyes tells you that they are probably thinking of Shimla as a heavenly centre for romance round the clock. A place meant only for couples jumping around bushes, making funny faces to filmy tunes!

At a wedding in Hyderabad recently, my long kurta, pyjama and whitish beard were at once linked to my life in Shimla. 'I believe most sadhus, and sanyasis live there. Do you do yoga and meditation?' Another gentleman said he had heard it was 'somewhere in the Himalaya mountains of the Shiv-Parvathi fame'. Arunachal,

Uttaranchal, Meghalaya, and Himachal meant the same thing to most of them.

This was followed by an old man's eager inquiry whether I had 'visited the Kailash Parvat', and how far it was from my place.

An ancient aunt I had never met before, summoned me. After a brief prologue, she mentioned the sanjivani-type magical herbs famed to be available in the Himalayas. 'I suffer from these terrible pains in the joints,' she wailed, 'can you help me with some *moolika* (medicinal herbs) or *mantra*?'

My feeble protests that I was just an ordinary fellow were at once dismissed. No one there would believe that I had found the rat-race revolting and decided to run away from the big city life and active journalism into the docile existence in the hills. And, that I enjoy feeling life's hazy past as I walk the tracks on Summerhill.

As human as nodding grass
above rain-stream sculpted
rock figures
wet, wet earth
the unlabelled articulations
behind cob-webbed cave faces.
This curve on Summerhill
…even the rare ray of sun,
an interference here.

As human as
the roots hanging out
(on dark wayward mounds)
co-existing
with creepers twining up deodars
And the norm-filled presence
of fungus, moss, fern and creature
around the hospitable trunk
of silver oak.

Human, then, as
this slope of Summerhill
...yes, a garden rose too
is an interference
here.

◆

Himachal's beauty is linked mostly to its scenic splendour at every step—the rolling hills, snow-covered mountains, undulating valleys, gurgling streams, and fabulous sunsets. These elements overshadow a deeper beauty—the peoples' nature, their culture, the basic *sanskaar*. Writers have tried a range of words to describe them: simple, honest, gentle, god-fearing, peace-loving and hospitable. All very inadequate.

Here, honesty has been an ordinary part of life, it touches you somewhere.

Seeing far, and farther
I have touched
the eye
of the child
in me.

◆

When was the last time you watched quietly, say for thirty minutes, the glorious sight of the evening sun melting away behind a wavy hill-range? Those changing hues, the twittering birds? A serenity, a sublime feeling all of its own? Probably not in recent times—unless your balcony is so positioned, or you were so situated at that time purely by chance.

Living in this beautiful state, we tend to take its bounty for granted. We tend to care less for things available in plenty.

Ugly high-rise constructions have begun to hide the slanting sun and the full face of the rising moon. Nervous birds twittering in fear are replacing the playful sort, where the forest cover is depleting. If the trend continues, and the hill slopes get relentlessly flattened, what will be the difference between this and the plains?

Light brown stone crags
hanging
from the blasted hillside
were carved out of the
smoked flesh
of unknown beings

They glisten painfully
in moon's angled rays
as the metalled road
runs below—like a sinister thought.

Tourists come from thousands of miles away, stay for a few days, and talk about their visit to Himachal for years. They mention the inadequacies here—but still crow about the same sunsets, the colourful play of clouds with their lower layers slowly submerging the tree-tops, buildings, pedestrians.

Those mist-covered mountains moan,
Hush.
Shafts smile through sky doors
layers light and dense
and some through wide open
mountain lips.
They linger before the lamps take over—
and who lingers better than a lover on a threshold.

In Shimla's peaking coolness
Love, Beauty, God—all,
all, chiches this evening.

Watch the mist-covered mountains
moan.
Hush.

But we, blessed with residence here, are losing our love for nature's bounty. We want to protect the environment—merely for the sake of our physical survival. Such a limited view, devoid of love for the dynamic canvas and dimensions of nature, cannot take us far. A good environment is not merely one without air and other pollutions—it should inspire, touch the strings of our heart like a rainbow in the sky does.

Even if we love nature as much as we love this land of gods and goddesses, doing nothing for its upkeep is sinful.

◆

The first rain of the monsoon in the hills had a ring of romance fifteen years ago. First, the colourful clouds would waft around, like gentle smiles in a celebrating home. Thick, dark ones that followed bellowed like wild buffaloes on the loose. Lightning streaked across the black sky ferociously, like many flashing steel blades coming down to behead.

Then followed both straight and slanting torrents, the refreshing aroma of rain digging into the earth, and the great gurgling sounds that could silence a thousand pot-bellied bursts of laughter. Against the backdrop of a relentless pitter-patter, families huddled together, reviving human warmth and adding an extra coziness at home.

Blue black clouds, moist,
surf down the lush green cover.

Eyeing the bed between
the two big hills,
feel the tune
of the loan star (through ajar clouds)

...in the lamps that glow little, little
along the rim of this valley spared
by mountain streams flowing
in rare disunity.
Man's roofs are safe
here.

Alas! The monsoon is more of a scattered rainfall—weak downpours, a mere relief from heat and dust. Romance is bowing out, nature yielding way to machine-driven pleasures.

Even so, a bit of it is still there, but we have to look around.

Toothless smile
on an ageless face
               – the stream keeps

hurrying down
the mountain slope
(like a white patch
on the hump of a black bull).

Its youth
flows in its gurgle
we hear among homing children.

The green, hooded, cobra-like plants (arisaema) still crop up on the hillsides (though scantily), confirming the monsoon's arrival, irrespective of the weatherman's utterings. This plant is part of the visual feast, like the green ferns swaying in rain-streams, the lush lively creepers shielding bird-nests, the layers of moss on tree trunks which you feel like peeling with your nails.

Leech (*jonk*), an inspiration for many ignoble expressions and proverbs, is slowly becoming less visible in Himachal's big towns. There was an interesting case of a veterinary attendant. Like many of our rural folk, he used to drink from natural streams with cupped palms. He developed violent headaches. After several tests and doctors' failure to diagnose, it was a vet who suspected that a leech might have got in through the nasal passage. There is a standard line of treatment for this common occurrence among cattle. The creature was evicted from the human host.

What a natural herbarium Himachal has always been! Rain-streams feed the flora with mixed nutrients from varied terrains, making them especially rich. But with pills and tubes over the counter for every ailment, very few use the home remedies these days.

For years I had watched with fascination a gentleman obsessed with drying clothes in the wet season. Whenever the sun sneaked through cloud-cover even briefly, he would rush out to turn over the wet clothes on the railings outside his flat. To ensure that the wetter side of garments got the heat and breeze for drying uniformly, he would keep shifting and turning their sides, every few minutes.

God, it was some sight, some obsession! And that pleased look on his face when he held aloft a dried shirt or whatever and carried it away from the railing! His wife, obviously tired of his restlessness, has bought a washing machine limiting the scope of his peculiar skills. I am told many people share this anxiety (about drying washed clothes) during the monsoon phase. That too will be a thing of the past!

◆

One day, I saw a goat and a lamb being dragged into a famous temple for sacrifice. What a relationship, between man and animal, between life and death!

Shiver came upon the skin and stayed,
coats shook.
Goats and lambs stood
defying stairs to the shrine.

The cherubic child in glee,
(whose welfare is the issue)
yelled and passed
to mother's fold, an indulgent frown

freeing paternal hands…
free to hold ropes
around the tender necks
of goat and lamb yelping
in the pain of a one-sided battle.

Drums, conch and big bells
prop the fading bleats to eternity
as lamb and goat are dragged—
the path is famed for fragrance
webbed by priests of Mother deity.
The temple doors are shut.

See the speeding sparks of life
in the stillness of eyes—
of goat and lamb
the lamb and goat—
Still beats of grounded hearts,
of a death that came before the sword
—life had flowed back to source
in anticipation.

Little, little lumps of shit
shed in scare by all goats and all lambs
line the track that awaits us all.
Nature knows one-way
as no way…

◆

Slowly, the big winds of change sweeping the plains are rising to the hills too. Himachal is at the crossroads of transition, with all its complexities.

Look at the ancient 'wish-fulfillment tree' at the entrance to the famous Kamna Devi temple above Boileauganj. Anxieties and worldly burdens of people must be weighing heavy on the brittle, rapidly withering walnut tree carrying all signs of an approaching end. Devotees tie threads, cloth etc, to its branches with frantic wishes in their hearts—they return to untie them on fulfillment. In between, hordes of monkeys ravage the tree daily for its fruit and tender leaves. They tear up the threads and coloured cloth, and pluck out the bangles hung on the tree by young brides. Already a *kainth* tree on the other side of the entrance (equally famed for fulfilling wishes) fell a few years ago during a snowstorm—it was disposed of unceremoniously.

The deity, considered *kul devta* for several surrounding villages, attracts scores of pilgrims and tourists. Their wishes, revealed only after fulfillment, reportedly centre on daughters' marriage, money and service matters and, of course, chronic ailments. The Punditji, whose family has been in charge of the *mandir* for four generations, is also the region's much sought-after astrologer.

Giving insights into the problems that people bring to him, the tree and finally to the '*Maiyya's* durbar', he says: 'About twenty years ago, people used to ask whether those who tied threads etc would attain spiritual goals like *moksh*—our hill-folk had limited requirements, and were more at peace with themselves. Now, things are changing rapidly. People are tense, and come here seeking quick relief and easy remedies. What can the tree give that the Mother Goddess cannot?'

Interestingly, right behind the temple stand a few sky-scraping metal towers for mobile phones. We see hordes of visitors depositing their worries at the tree and the temple, and moving on quickly towards the awe-inspiring towers. Cell phones keep buzzing from their pockets even while receiving *prasaad* from the Punditji. Their sounds now compete with the temple bells.

The share of their time and attention is shifting from the traditional mechanism to the modern technology: fair indications of the way things are moving, changing. And who cares if the old walnut tree withers after satisfying its customers? *Uski kya zaroorat hai!*

Five Hundredth Storey

MAHATMA GANDHI

From collected works of Mahatma Gandhi, translated from
Gujarati published in *Navajivan*, 22 May 1951

I had heard of Simla. I had not seen the place. I often wished to
see it but was always afraid to go there. I felt that I would be lost
there, that I would be a barbarian among the others.

I have seen the place now. I have come here to see Bharatbhushan
Pandit Malaviya, who has taken me under his wing. The house is
named 'Shantkuti' and I am in the midst of co-workers here. The
climate is lovely. Nature has withheld nothing of her riches. These
hills are a part of the Himalayas, but I get no peace whatever from
outside of me. In fact, if my having peace depended entirely on
external surroundings, I would have to run away from this place or
else I would go mad.

Simla is named after Mother Simlala, as Mumbai [Bombay] is
named after Mumbadevi and Calcutta after Kali. All the three goddesses
have proved faithless or, maybe, the devotees have forgotten them.
The mere though of the Kali temple fills me with horror. How can the
place be called a temple at all? In literal truth, rivers of blood flow
there every day. Who knows what the thousands of goats slaughtered
there in the name of religion say in the court of God? How infinite
is Mother Kali's patience? Does she really demand cruel sacrifices?
People who offer them tarnish her sacred name.

They are guilty of no little wickedness in Bombay, but no daily evil is perpetrated there in the name of religion. The people who frequent share-markets or madly throw away money on horse-racing know evil and admit their weakness. Animals are killed in its slaughter-houses for the belly's sake, and not in the name of religion. The knowledge of this slaughter does not make it utterly impossible for one to live in Bombay.

But Simla? Delhi, most certainly, is not the symbol of India's slavery. The place which is the real headquarters of the rulers is Simla. The Simla Municipality told the viceroy that every year the officials formulated their policies in the quiet and coolness of the Simla hills. We had full experience, in the summer of 1919, of what these policies are. Even the hottest parts of the country cannot give an idea of the temperature of these policies.

After seeing Simla, my views have not changed. No end of money has been spent over the place. Even a proud man like me has had to eat humble pie. The only means of conveyance here is the horse or the rickshaw. I never used the latter while in South Africa, but here I did, thanks to my weakness. All, whether grown-ups or young, men or women, use it. The car is justifiably prohibited. The horse-drawn carriage can be used only by the viceroy and one or two other officials, and this also seems to be justified. The roads in this place are narrow; roads cut through steep hills cannot but be so. Naturally, the plying of horse-drawn vehicles on such roads must perforce be restricted.

What is strange, however, is that the rickshaw has become quite an ordinary conveyance, as if it was the most natural thing for any of us to be yoked to a vehicle! I asked the men who pulled the rickshaw which carried me why they had taken up this work. Did they not have a belly to fill? They queried in reply. I know this reply is not quite convincing; it cannot be said, though, that they take pleasure in becoming beasts of burden. On the contrary, my charge is that it is we who force men to become beasts. Why should it be surprising, then, that we have become the Empire's bullocks?

It is not the British alone who use the rickshaw. We use it as freely as they do. We who join them in turning people into bullocks have, therefore, become bullocks ourselves.

There are four men for every rickshaw. Three of them get rupees eighteen a month each and the fourth, their leader, gets rupees twenty. The slopes up and down along the roads are so steep that, even though there are four of them, the men get out of breath. The rickshaw is made to accommodate only one person at a time. Even this is something to be thankful for. Simla is at an altitude of 7,500 feet. If people understand the implications of the fact that the government is carried on from such a height, they will know what the Empire means. If in Bombay all the shopkeepers had their shops on the topmost floor in the chawls, what would be the customers' plight? The fourth floor probably goes up to a height of sixty feet. The thirty crore customers of this government, the country's shopkeeper, have to climb not 60 feet but 7,500 feet! Bombay, we know, cannot carry on its trade on the fourth floor. India's trade is carried on, actually, on the five hundredth floor! Is it any wonder that the country starves? It should no longer seem strange that, in the foothills of Simla, three crore innocent children famish for want of food.

So long as a distance equal to be height of five hundred floors separates the Empire from us, Dyerism must needs be used for maintaining the distance.

Swaraj, if run from this height, will be no swaraj.

But the comparison I have made is not just, a thoughtful person may protest. Maybe the master lives on a height of 7,500 feet, but he posts his employees, the *talati*, the *patel* and the *mamlatdar* on the ground floor! There would be some substance in this argument if it were true that the master lived on the five hundredth floor at his own expense. As a matter of fact, however, he lives there at the customers' expense. He recovers the expenses of living where he does and also charges his usual profit. What wonder that the customers of such a business man become bankrupt become paupers?

The arrangement is costlier than even the practice of carrying Ganga water on the *kavad*. It used to be carried to as far as Rameshwaram! Anyone who has paid for a small-sized pot of it knows whether Ganga water is costly or cheap.

Simla is all congestion. The houses are full, every one of them. Things are bound to be dear. Even water is brought up from 2,000 feet below. One feels embarrassed to use even so much as a jugful of water. In the building in which we stay, we do get water but it takes the carriers, fetching it over a long distance, a whole day to fill enough for our needs. There are no streams in the vicinity of Simla. To win swaraj means to oblige the government—whether it is British or Indian – to descend from the five hundredth floor to the ground floor and introduce naturalness in its relations with us. The discrimination is not as between white and coloured, but as between high and low. He is a true Brahmin who serves a *Bhangi*, and not the one who rides on the shoulders of one. He is no king who maintains a distance, the height of five hundred floors between him and the subjects. It is in virtue of one's deeds in the past life that one is born for happiness or suffering, as king or beggar. The happy man exerts himself to relieve the sufferings of others, and the king to raise the beggar to his level, which means that, though a king, he voluntarily becomes a beggar. God, the Ruler, earns his title to rule by the making Himself the slave of his slave, makes Himself worthy of worship by purifying the sinner. In Simla I saw the reverse of this and my heart bled.

Notes on Contributors

ASHOK DILWALI

Ashok Dilwali, a chartered accountant by qualification and a traveller and photographer by choice, manages his family Studio (Kinsey Bros.) at New Delhi. Nature photography remains his first love and he spends lot of time in the Himalayas photographing the myriad moods of nature in the mountains and hills. The travel bug that bit him at Shimla as a child, has taken him to all parts of world. He has travelled extensively in Asia, Europe and Africa besides exploring all nooks and corners of India. In his travels spanning over five decades he has not only captured the landscapes but has produced twenty books. He has published several picture books on Himachal (*Himachal, Himachal Pradesh, Pictorial Himachal*). Among his other books are *Ganga-Origin and Descent of River Eternal, Garhwal Himalaya, Kumaon Himalaya, Badri Kedar Yatra, Andaman and Nicobar–Islands in the Sun, Himalayas-Dawn to Dusk, Ganga, Bhagvad Geeta-An Essence* and *Vedas–An Essence*.

ASIF JALAL

Asif Jalal an Indian Police Service (IPS) officer of Himachal Pradesh cadre. He is an MA from School of Social Sciences, Jawaharlal Nehru University, Delhi. Presently posted as superintendent of police in Hamirpur district he was superintendent of police in the tribal and remote district of the state, Lahaul and Spiti. He was also posted at Shimla, the state capital, as assistant superintendent of police. He frequently contributes articles on socio-political issues in various national newspapers and magazines. His book *Stir in the Waves* is under publication with a Delhi based publisher. Besides writing he is interested in reading and traveling.

DEEPAK GUPTA

Deepak Gupta completed his schooling from St. Edwards School Shimla. He studied law at the Campus Law Centre, Delhi University and started legal practice at Shimla in 1978. Zealous about protecting the environment and ecology of Shimla and Himachal Pradesh, he filed a number of Public Interest petitions in this regard. Deepak is a keen trekker and an avid photographer. He is fond of reading and has a large collection of antique books. He also possesses some rare photographs of Shimla. He is a lover of nature and spends his spare time looking after his apple orchard.

Deepak is presently a judge of the High Court of Himachal Pradesh.

DEEPAK SANAN

Deepak Sanan is an IAS officer of 1982 batch belonging to Himachal Pradesh cadre, who has trekked extensively in the state. He remained posted in the tribal areas of the state first as head of the local administration in remote Spiti valley from 1985 to 1987, and subsequently, from November 1990 till August 1993 headed the district administration of the tribal district, Kinnaur. He travelled extensively over the two regions covering all inhabited areas and most walking routes. His experiences there led to a book, *Exploring Kinnaur & Spiti in the Trans-Himalaya* which he co-authored with his wife Dhanu Swadi. He contributes articles on economic and development issues to various newspapers and journals. He has also worked as consultant with the World Bank and DFID.

DR. PANKAJ KHULLAR

Dr. Pankaj Khullar belongs to the Indian Forest Service and is presently posted as principal chief conservator of forests, Himachal Pradesh at Shimla. After completing his graduation from Jhansi (UP), he joined the service in 1971. His love for nature and wild fauna and flora has led him to travel extensively not only within Himachal Pradesh, but also throughout the country as well as the world. Dr. Khullar has been a teacher (Indian Forest College, Dehra Dun), a researcher (Forest Research Institute, Dehra Dun) and a forest administrator.

As a youngster, Dr. Khullar grew up in army cantonments across the country but spent almost all his summer vacations in the hills and forests around Shimla. His keen observation and his interest in nature have endured. Dr. Khullar has a son and a daughter, both of whom share his concern for the environment.

EMILY HANSEN

Emily Hansen spends her days between Istanbul, Taiwan and India, teaching English and writing. When she grows up she would like to be a Chinese calligrapher with red toenails. After earning her bachelor's degree in Women's Studies from UNBC in Prince George, BC, Canada, she left for Asia, never to return again. Her inspirations include Charles Bukowski, Michael Palin, and Madonna. She lives happily with her Himalayan man and finds Shimla to be her *home*.

H. KISHIE SINGH

Kishie Singh was born in Shimla and went to the Bishop Cotton School, Shimla. His work for Investors Overseas Services took him to Bangkok, Beirut, Geneva and finally to Montreal where he left the corporate world and graduated in Visual Communications from Dawson College, Montreal. He then worked for the National Film

Board of Canada and contributed to *The Montreal Gazette* and numerous magazines as a freelancer.

In 1975 he decided to move back to India. Being a motoring aficionado, he drove overland from London to New Delhi and traced Alexander the Great's journey from Macedonia to India.

A freelance photojournalist, he continues to travel extensively is active in motor sports activities. He writes a column 'Good Motoring' for *The Tribune*, Chandigarh. H. Kishie Singh currently lives in Chandigarh with his wife, daughter, and ninety-eight-year-old mother of the Clippity Clop story fame.

HARISH KAPADIA

Harish Kapadia has made a unique contribution to our knowledge of the Himalaya as the editor of the *Himalayan Journal*, one of the most authoritative and comprehensive records of exploratory activity in the Himalaya; through his numerous books and as a leader and organiser of countless expeditions over the last forty-five years. He has personally climbed more than thirty Himalayan peaks, many of them first ascents. He has crossed more than 130 Himalayan passes to explore different valleys.

He has received many awards including the Royal 'Patron's Medal', by the Royal Geographical Society, the first Indian to receive this highest adventure award after 125 years. The president of India honoured him with the prestigious 'Tensing Norgay National Adventure Award' (2003) for lifetime achievements, and he received the prestigious 'King Albert I Mountain Award' in Switzerland. He is married and lives in Mumbai.

HIS HOLINESS THE DALAI LAMA

His Holiness the 14th Dalai Lama, Tenzin Gyatso, is both the head of state and the spiritual leader of Tibet. He was born on 6 July 1935, to a farming family, in a small hamlet located in Taktser, Amdo, northeastern Tibet. At the age of two the child, who was named Lhamo Dhondup at that time was recognized as the reincarnation of the 13th Dalai Lama, Thubten Gyatso. The Dalai Lamas are believed to be manifestations of Avalokiteshvara or Chenrezig, the Bodhisattva of Compassion and patron saint of Tibet. Bodhisattvas are enlightened beings who have postponed their own nirvana and chosen to take rebirth in order to serve humanity. His Holiness began his monastic education at the age of six. At twenty-three he sat for his final examination in the Jokhang Temple, Lhasa, and was awarded the Geshe Lharampa degree, the highest-level degree equivalent to a doctorate of Buddhist philosophy.

In 1950 His Holiness was called upon to assume full political power after China's invasion of Tibet in 1949. In 1954, he went to Beijing for peace talks with Mao Zedong and other Chinese leaders, including Deng Xiaoping and Chou Enlai. But finally, in 1959, with the brutal suppression of the Tibetan national uprising in Lhasa by Chinese troops, His Holiness was forced to escape into exile. Since then he has been living in Dharamsala, northern India, the seat of the Tibetan political administration in exile.

His Holiness the Dalai Lama is a man of peace. In 1989 he was awarded the Nobel Peace Prize for his non-violent struggle for the liberation of Tibet. He has consistently advocated policies of non-violence, even in the face of extreme aggression. He also became the first Nobel Laureate to be recognised for his concern for global environmental problems. Since 1959 His Holiness has received over eighty-four awards, honorary doctorates, prizes, etc., in recognition of his message of peace, non-violence, inter-religious understanding, universal responsibility and compassion. His Holiness has also authored more than seventy-two books.

His Holiness describes himself as a simple Buddhist monk.

Three Main Commitments in Life

Firstly, on the level of a human being, His Holiness' first commitment is the promotion of human values such as compassion, forgiveness, tolerance, contentment and self-discipline. Secondly, on the level of a religious practitioner, His Holiness second commitment is the promotion of religious harmony and understanding among the world's major religious traditions. Thirdly, His Holiness is a Tibetan and carries the name of the Dalai Lama. Tibetans place their trust in him. Therefore, his third commitment is to the Tibetan issue.

KHUSHWANT SINGH

Author of over hundred books, best known for his work of fiction, *Train to Pakistan* and his *History of Sikhs* and his joke books Singh is one of the most widely read and recognised writers of India today. His weekly columns are reproduced by over fifty journals in all the regional languages in the country. He has done different things at different times: practiced law, diplomacy, politics and edited the *Illustrated Weekly of India* and the *Hindustan Times*. He has written regularly for several European and American journals including the *New York Times*.

MAHARAJKUMAR DR RAGHUVIR SINGH (1909-91)
(*Translation* by **Dr. S.R. Mehrotra**)

Maharajkumar Dr Raghuvir Singh (1909-1991) edited and wrote dozens of books in English and Hindi, including *Malwa in Transition or a Century of Anarchy* (Bombay, 1936); *Durgadas Rathor* (New Delhi 1938); *Studies on Maratha and Rajput History* (Jodhpur, 1989); *English Records of Maratha History: Poona Correspondence, Vols. 9 and 10* (Bombay, 1943,1951); *Bikhre Phool* (Banaras, 1933); *Saptdapi* (Bombay, 1938); *Shesh Smritiyan* (Kashi, 1939); *Jeewan Kan* (New Delhi, 1991); *Jeewan Dhuli* (New Delhi 1949).

Dr S.R. Mehrotra (b.1931) is former professor of history, Himachal Pradesh University, Shimla. He worked as a professor at Maharshi Dayanand University Rohtak and Jawaharlal Nehru University Delhi.

He has also taught at the Universities of Saugor, London, Wisconsin and Rabindra Bharti. He was a fellow of the Indian Institute of Advanced Study, Shimla and a visiting fellow of St John's College, Cambridge. He is the author of *India and Commonwealth 1885-1929 (1965); The Emergence of the Indian National Congress (1971); The Commonwealth and the Nation (1978); Towards India's Freedom and Partition (1979); A History of the Indian National Congress (1995)*

MEENAKSHI F. PAUL

Meenakshi Faith Paul is a translator, teacher and writer. She teaches English at Himachal Pradesh University Centre for Evening Studies, Shimla. She is presently engaged in research and translation of folk literature of Himachal. She has translated the images of Sita as found in *Pahari Ramayana*, select short stories by Krishna Sobti, a couple of stories by Munshi Premchand and is documenting and translating the temple narratives of Mandi and Kangra districts of Himachal Pradesh into English. She has published the translations of *Short Stories of Himachal Pradesh*.

MINAKSHI CHAUDHRY

Minakshi Chaudhry is an author based at Shimla. Her interest in studying nature and people's lifestyle grew in Nigeria, West Africa, where she spent her formative years. She has worked with *The Indian Express* as a reporter for over three years. She also worked with *Outlook Traveller* magazine. She has trekked extensively throughout Himachal and written various books including *Destination Himachal: Over 132 Offbeat and 12 Popular Getaways, Himachal: A Complete Guide to the Land of Gods, Ghost Stories of Shimla Hills; Guide to Trekking in Himachal: 65 Treks and over 100 Destinations; Exploring Pangi Himalaya: A World Beyond Civilisation*. Presently she is working on two books simultaneously one on mountain mysteries and the other is tentatively titled *Love in Shimla*.

MOHANDAS KARAMCHAND GANDHI

Mahatma Gandhi, 2 October 1869 – 30 January 1948, was a major political and spiritual leader of India and the Indian independence movement. He was the pioneer of *satyagraha*—resistance to tyranny through mass civil disobedience, firmly founded upon ahimsa or total non-violence—which led India to independence and inspired movements for civil rights and freedom across the world. He is commonly known around the world as Mahatma Gandhi (Sanskrit: mahātmā or 'Great Soul', an honorific first applied to him by Rabindranath Tagore) and in India also as Bapu (Gujarati: bāpu or 'Father'). He is officially honoured in India as the Father of the Nation. His birthday, 2 October, is commemorated there as Gandhi Jayanti, a national holiday, and worldwide as the International Day of Non-Violence.

Gandhiji first employed non-violent civil disobedience as an expatriate lawyer in South Africa, in the resident Indian community's struggle for civil rights. After his return to India in 1915, he set about organising peasants, farmers, and urban labourers in protesting excessive land-tax and discrimination. Assuming leadership of the Indian National Congress in 1921, Gandhiji led nationwide campaigns for easing poverty, for expanding women's rights, for building religious and ethnic amity, for ending untouchability, for increasing economic self-reliance, but above all for achieving Swaraj—the independence of India from foreign domination. Gandhiji famously led Indians in protesting the British-imposed salt tax with the 400 km (249 miles) Dandi Salt March in 1930, and later in calling for the British to Quit India in 1942. He was imprisoned for many years, on numerous occasions, in both South Africa and India.

Gandhiji was a practitioner of non-violence and truth, and advocated that others do the same. He lived modestly in a self-sufficient residential community and wore the traditional Indian dhoti and shawl, woven with yarn he had hand spun on a charkha. He ate simple vegetarian food, and also undertook long fasts as means of both self-purification and social protest.

PANKAJ MISHRA

In 1992, Pankaj Mishra moved to a village, fourteen kilometres north of Simla, and began to write. His first book, *Butter Chicken in Ludhiana* (1995), brought to life the small towns of India, describing them not in exotic terms, but rather in the complex context of modernisation and globalisation. His first novel, *The Romantics*, is an ironic tale of people longing for fulfillment in cultures other than their own. It won the Los Angeles Times' Art Seidenbaum award for first fiction. Mishra writes political and literary essays for the *New York Times*, the *New York Review of Books*, the *TLS*, amongst others. He also publishes in the *International Herald Tribune*, the *Washington Post*, *New York Times Magazine*, and *Granta*. His book about the Buddha, *An End to Suffering: the Buddha in the World*, was published in 2004. He divides his time between London, Delhi and Shimla, and is currently working on a novel.

PUNAM GUPTA

Punam Gupta worked in New Delhi as a copywriter and illustrator for over a decade before she married and moved to Shimla in 1991. Since then, she has been involved in a range of creative pursuits including stage acting, research and documentation of Shimla's folk theatre, freelance writing and more notably, painting. Punam is the daughter of Santosh Manchanda, an artist of national renown from whom she inherited the flair for creative expression. Although she studied art at New Delhi's Triveni Kala Sangam, the artist is largely self-taught and specialises in abstract oil landscapes and collages. She lives in Shimla with her husband Deepak and two daughters Diya and Damini. Shimla hills continue to inspire her to paint and write.

RAAJA BHASIN

Raaja Bhasin, author of *Simla-The Summer Capital of British India* lives in Shimla. He has published over a thousand articles, reviews and stories published in various leading publications in India and abroad. He has documented the traditional and colonial architecture of Himachal for the Department of Culture, Government of India and handled assignments for Department of Tourism and Civil Aviation, Himachal Pradesh, the UNDP, the BBC. He is on the Heritage Advisory Committee for Shimla town and is the managing editor of *Mional* Himachal Tourism's magazine. His other books and booklets include *Shimla on Foot, Himachal Pradesh: A Himalayan Experience, Viceregal Lodge and the Indian Institute of Advanced Study*, Shimla. He conducts heritage and nature walks in and around Shimla town which are described by Frommer's India as 'intelligent, entertaining and exclusive.'

RAKESH KANWAR

An officer of Himachal Administrative Services (HAS), he was born, brought-up and educated at Shimla. He has done his Masters in Journalism and Mass Communication and attained MBA (Personnel Management) from Himachal Pradesh University, Shimla and MBA (Public Policy) from ICPE Slovenia. He edited *Administrative Pulse*, the Quarterly Journal of HAS Officers Association. He has varied interests like trekking, travelling, reading and theatre.

RUSKIN BOND

Ruskin Bond, well-known as one of India's best loved and most prolific writers, has been writing novels, poetry, essays and short stories for almost half a century now. Apart from this, over the years he has expertly compiled and edited a number of anthologies. For his outstanding literary contribution, Ruskin Bond has been conferred with the John Llewellyn Rhys Memorial Prize in 1957, the Sahitya Akademi Award in 1992 (for English Writing in India), and the Padma Shree by the Government of India in 1999. His story *The Blue Umbrella* (Rupa) was recently filmed by Vishal Bhardwaj.

SATISH GUJRAL

Satish Gujral was born in Jhelum, West Punjab, in December 1925. At the age of eight an accident deprived him of his hearing. He studied at the Mayo School of Arts, Lahore and later at the JJ School of Arts, Bombay. Following partition the family moved to the Indian half of Punjab. Satish Gujral worked as a graphic artist with the Punjab government for two years. In 1952 he won a scholarship to study arts in Mexico, where he apprenticed himself to Diego Rivera. He has been in New Delhi since 1954.

Over the past five decades he has achieved world renown and critical acclaim for his work as a painter, sculptor, muralist, graphic designer and architect. He is married to Kiran Ram Nath, an artist in her own right. They have a son and two daughters.

Satish Gujral is an honorary fellow of the Indian Institute of Architecture. His portrait of Lala Lajpat Rai hangs in Parliament House; his depictions of Jawahar Lal Nehru and Indira Gandhi hang in Anand Bhawan, Nehru's ancestral home in Allahabad. Without holding any degree in architecture, he designed, among other structures, the Belgian Embassy in New Delhi, a building which has been hailed as the most authentic expression of the Indian psyche in this medium. He is the only non-Belgian architect upon whom the Belgian government has conferred the Order of the Crown, one of the nation's highest honour.

USHA BANDE

Dr Usha Bande taught English Literature for over thirty-five years to undergraduate, postgraduate and honours students. She has numerous research papers and more than a dozen books to her credit. She completed a major UGC project on Indian Short Stories in 1998, and has recently worked in the field of Women's Studies at the Indian Institute of Advanced Study, Shimla. She is a regular contributor to *The Tribune, Alive, Women's Era, Sarita, Griha Shobha* and many other newspapers and magazines. Dr Usha Bande is a visiting lecturer in several Indian Universities and a Counsellor for Creative Writing Course for IGNOU. She has authored several books including *Ecology and Folk Traditions in Himachal Pradesh*, and *Writing Resistance: A Comparative Study of Women Novelists*. Her forthcoming books are *Forts and Palaces of Himachal Pradesh* and *Himachal through the Eyes of Travelers*.

V.S. RAMADEVI

V.S. Ramadevi, former governor of Himachal Pradesh, from 26 July 1997 to 2 December 1999, fell in love with the beauty of the hills and the valleys. She was equally enchanted by the simple and hardworking hill women and men.

Born at Chebrolu in Andhra Pradesh she was educated at Eluru and Hyderabad. After her education she enrolled as advocate in the high court of Andhra Pradesh before joining the Central government service and after working in various capacities as a member of the Indian Legal Service in the Legislative Department, she served as special secretary in the Legislative Department. She remained the member-secretary of the Law Commission and secretary to the Government of India. She also served as honorary advisor to the National Commission for Women. She was appointed as secretary-general, Rajya Sabha from 1 July 1993 to 25 July 1997.

Her interests include spreading legal awareness, particularly among women and weaker sections of society and studying political developments, national and international. She writes regularly on legal topics like women and law, children and law, handicapped and law, anti-defection law and Constitutional issues.

V.S. Ramadevi has also authored novels, short stories, essays and plays in Telugu. She also writes middles in Telugu dailies.

VEPA RAO

Vepa Rao, who lives in Shimla, has worked as a senior journalist with *The Hindustan Times*, *The Tribune* and *The Statesman*. He was in Kolkata, Mumbai and Delhi for four decades and decided to move to the hills of Himachal Pradesh in 1987. He was a Fellow at the Indian Institute of Advanced Study and a professor of journalism at the Indian Institute of Mass Communication and Himachal Pradesh University.

Apart from newspaper articles, Vepa Rao has published numerous humour columns, short stories and poems. *Liquid Folds*, his first volume of 'multi-channeled' poems (his second is in the making) also shows his special interest in some aspects of evolution.

VIDYA STOKES

Vidya, daughter of late Rai Sahib Amin Chand was born at Kotgarh in Shimla district on 8 December 1927 studied at Delhi University. She was married to late Shri Lal Chand Stokes, son of Samuel Stokes. She joined active politics when she became member of the Indian National Congress in 1970. She held various positions in the Congress party both at state and national level.

She remained president of the Indian Women's Hockey Federation in 1984, 1988, 1994 and 2003; vice-president of Asian Hockey Federation (1986-90 and 1990-94); and has held other important positions.

A social worker of repute, she is honorary general secretary, Indian Council of Child Welfare for more than ten years. She has setup schools/homes for the visually impaired, hearing and speech impaired and physically challenged children and is running several training centres for girls.

She was elected to the State Assembly in 1974 (by-election), 1982, 1985, 1990 and 1998 from Theog and in 2003 from the adjoining Kumarsain constituency as Congress candidate. Remained minister of State for Rural Development (Independent Charge) 1984-85; Speaker, State Legislative Assembly, 1985-90; leader of the Congress Legislature Group, 1990-92; and minister for MPP & Power, from 2003 to 2007. She was elected to the Assembly for a seventh term in December 2007 (Kumarsain).

She has travelled extensively all over the world and loves gardening, reading and painting.

VIPIN PUBBY

With a career spanning about three decades in journalism, Vipin Pubby is now the resident editor of *The Indian Express* at Chandigarh.

Having joined *The Indian Express* as a trainee reporter in 1979, soon after completing his post-graduation in English Literature from Panjab University, Chandigarh, Pubby reported extensively from various parts of the country and abroad. He has the unique distinction of writing on all the major hot spots in the country—the North-East, Punjab, Gujarat and J&K. He has published hundreds of analytical and opinion articles.

He grew up in Himachal Pradesh, having studied in the Chail Military School, near Shimla, for about eight years. It was during his reporting stint in Himachal Pradesh from 1983 to 1987 that he travelled extensively in the state and wrote *Shimla—Then & Now* which provides an Indian's insight into the life and times of Shimla.